The Experience of Managing

658.4

D0268445

The Experience of Managing

A Skills Guide

Chris Clegg, Karen Legge and Sue Walsh

Editorial and selection © Chris Clegg, Karen Legge
and Sue Walsh 1999
Individual chapters © individual contributors 1999

First published 1999 by
MACMILLAN PRESS LTD
Houndmills, Basingstoke, Hampshire RG21 6XS
and London
Companies and representatives
throughout the world

ISBN 0–333–71415–6 hardcover
ISBN 0–333–71416–4 paperback

A catalogue record for this book is available
from the British Library.

This book is printed on paper suitable for recycling and
made from fully managed and sustained forest sources.

10 9 8   7 6 5   4 3   2 1
08 07 06 05 04 03 02 01 00 99

Editing and origination by
Aardvark Editorial, Mendham, Suffolk

Printed and Bound in Great Britain by
Creative Print & Design (Wales), Ebbw Vale

Contents

Introduction

This book comprises 31 contributions aimed at developing skills in managing. As such it is principally directed at postgraduate students (for example, those undertaking MBA courses) and participants on post-experience short courses. But, apart from this bald statement, a few words may be useful to clarify our thinking behind this volume.

Some of our readers may be familiar with earlier collections of case studies compiled by two of the editors. This is a rather different book, with a different purpose. The earlier collections were case studies in organisational behaviour, information technology and human resource management that aimed to give students practice in using concepts derived from organisational psychology, behaviour and theory as analytical tools to dissect, understand and prescribe for a range of real-life problems. All the case studies were based on empirical research in major UK organisations in public and private, manufacturing and service sectors. The focus of these case studies was largely the identification and analysis of problems and the proposal of strategies and the design of policies and procedures to overcome the problems. Hence the questions in the case studies were of a 'what' and 'why' variety: 'What is the problem?', 'Why has it occurred?', 'What should be done about it?'. What was not highlighted in these cases was the difficult question that bedevils management action: 'How do we implement the proposals in the most effective manner?'. In other words, the focus of analysis here is on managerial processes and style, and the development of skills in achieving effective action. It should be noted at this point that, except where clearly indicated to the contrary, most of the companies and individuals quoted in the case studies are purely fictitious. Any similarity to existing companies or individuals is completely unintentional.

This focus has arisen from the emerging demands of our students over the past 8–10 years. During that period, we have each been active teaching on postgraduate courses in Business Administration, Clinical and Community Psychology and Occupational and Organisation Psychology, as well as on a number of post-experience courses. Increasingly, our experience is that course participants have been seeking more than an understanding of the theories embraced by the various disciplines and their application. They have been asking for experience and practise in the skills that they need and use in their work and wanting to exercise them in well-prepared and 'richly textured' situations. We have chosen to call these 'managing' skills because they contribute to the process of managing, but these skills are not the sole province of managers. Skills in assertion, negotiation, listening and problem solving are just as relevant to people working in professional, specialist or supervisory roles.

We have given the authors of each 'chapter' a clear brief. They were asked to provide some practical exercises that would give the participants experience of developing and using skills in a particular area. The exercises might involve some combination of role plays, case studies, small group exercises, working in pairs, working alone or plenary group discussions. Where possible, all the material needed by the participants is present in the chapter, although some supportive reading may help in gaining further benefit from a particular session. The supporting Tutor's Notes are for use by the tutor and offer further detailed information, advice on how to set up the session (including timings) and what usually happens, along with some background theoretical information. The aim is to support the tutor with enough information to set up a lively and stimulating session.

The intention is very much to provide 'hands-on' sets of exercises to enhance an awareness of 'how to do it' issues, the theory behind alternative styles of practice and, most importantly, the experience of enacting simulated day-to-day management skills and activities. Hence we have not attempted to impose, as systematically as in the past, standard sets of headings and labels. Some authors refer to their contribution as a 'chapter', others as a 'case study', 'exercise' or 'role play'. We have decided to celebrate this diversity of language rather than impose editorial fascism! Furthermore, again in contrast to our earlier books of case studies, we have deliberately made no attempt to 'chunk' contributions according to either a model of organisation ('individual', 'group' or 'organisation') or a discipline ('OB', 'IR' or 'HRM') or theme ('Flexibility, quality and HRM in manufacturing' or 'Towards an enterprise culture'). We consider that many management skills, although analytically separable, are in action indivisible. For example, awareness of stakeholders goes hand in hand with negotiating, and negotiating is often part of the decision-making process, which can in turn involve communicating 'good' and 'bad' news. All of these skills are involved in project management – and in managing such apparently diverse activities as dealing with sexual harassment and appraisal. And so on. We consider that management skills should be seen holistically – as all combine elements of analysis, interpretation, reflection, empathy and presentation – so that attempts to slice up what is properly seen as a whole would be inappropriate. Thus contributions are presented in alphabetical order, by topic, and we invite readers to 'pick and mix' their own selection. We envisage that tutors will put together a selection of the material best suited to the needs of their students and the time available. We must confess, however, to some satisfaction that, as a result of our alphabetical ordering, 'appraisal' and 'assertion' skills that are necessary to most effective managerial action, kick off the book!

The people preparing the material have been carefully selected by the editors as experts in their fields. The authors are teachers, researchers, consultants and practitioners of various kinds, with backgrounds in HRM, organisation behaviour, theory and psychology, as well as in clinical and community psychology, reflecting both the backgrounds of the editors and what we see as the community of practice on which a collection such as this should draw and to which it should contribute. Most of the material presented has been used by the authors in 'live' sessions. We know that these sessions work.

One issue with a volume of this kind concerns the 'comprehensiveness' of coverage. We do not claim to have covered every conceivable skill. For example, we have no entries on 'how to manage difficult people', 'how to cope with being bullied', 'managing cross-company relations' (for example, as in outsourcing), or 'leading and being led'. As with all compilations, this selection reflects our own and our contributors' interests and commitment to write on some issues rather than others. In any case, comprehensive coverage would give rise to an unmanageable length. Perhaps a second volume may enable us to address further needs.

We should be clear what claims we are making for this book. The aim in each case is not to make its users experts in all the fields covered by the book. Instead, we are aiming to give participants the experience of using skills and some insights about their personal strengths and weaknesses, upon which they may then wish to act. Almost without exception, the objectives of each chapter are to:

◆ give an understanding of, and insight into, the skills involved in a particular area
◆ provide experience of practising those skills
◆ encourage a critical awareness of some of the complexities involved in the area.

In any case, we anticipate that users will typically have quite different and varied levels of expertise. Our experience is that some members of our groups have had extensive experience of managing meetings, interviewing candidates for jobs or negotiating, while others in the class may have had little or no direct experience in these areas. In practice, of course, the presence in a group of different patterns of expertise represents an important resource to be drawn upon in these sessions.

So here are the contributions. We hope you will enjoy working through them as much as we have enjoyed editing them.

KAREN LEGGE, CHRIS CLEGG AND SUE WALSH
May 1998

CHAPTER 1

Appraisal

Dot Griffiths

OBJECTIVES

The objectives of this chapter are to:

▶ explore some of the issues raised in the management of appraisal systems
▶ explore the differences between a traditional appraisal system and a performance management system
▶ explore the covert and overt objectives of appraisal systems
▶ review good practice in giving and receiving feedback.

INTRODUCTION

This case describes the different experiences of appraisal encountered by a manager in two different companies.

Following the case study, there are four exercises. Each is designed to be undertaken in small groups with a plenary review. Alternatively, they can be undertaken individually with a small group or plenary review.

Jack Moore's appraisals

The present

Jack Moore had an uncomfortable feeling in his stomach. Today he was due to meet his new manager, Steve George, to discuss his performance contract. Jack is the newly appointed training manager for the Garden business of Global Products plc. Global Products is a UK headquartered company involved in the supply of a range of agricultural and horticultural products. It consists of four businesses: Agro-Chemicals (responsible for the manufacture and supply of a range of agricultural chemicals: fertilisers, pesticides, herbicides and so on; Seeds (responsible for the production and supply of seeds and seedlings for a variety of agricultural crops); Horticulture (responsible for the supply of wholesale stock to garden centres); and Garden (a retail operation).

The Garden business is new. Global decided that it needed to think outside its traditional box if it were going to facilitate continued growth. Worldwide, the market for agrochemicals is very competitive. Demand, in terms of the number of purchasers, might continue to increase, but the use of more sophisticated delivery mechanisms and spraying strategies, together with the emergence of genetically engineered crops incorporating pest resistance and other properties, means that the market is ultimately limited and probably in decline in the medium to long term. The future of the Seeds business is genetic, both in terms of access to plant varieties and in terms of genetically engineered varieties. To this end, Global recently purchased a 'seed bank' and has increased its R&D spending on new products, so there is a 'valley of death' to be funded in Seeds in the short term. Horticulture has been the only division that has achieved organic growth. As the US and European populations have acquired more leisure to consume, so they have started to spend ever larger amounts on their gardens. The corporate sector has also grown over the past couple of decades. The fashion in corporate architecture for glass and atriums has favoured suppliers of plants. Horticulture has seen its Corporate Division, which supplies and maintains plants in corporate locations, quadruple its turnover in the UK and North America. It has recently moved into South and South-East Asia.

The move into garden centres seemed logical. Global has expertise in the production of the plants, the market is growing and becoming more sophisticated, and Global was looking for new areas. It took over a small, rather moribund chain of garden centres called Green Fingers. Green Fingers has 20 outlets, concentrated in the south-east of England. They had been poorly managed in terms of stock and inventory control, which meant they were often either poorly stocked or overstocked with half-dead plants. Staff morale was low and customer service fairly awful. The old chief executive, Albert Trudge, and most of the board went as part of the take-over deal. In Albert's place, Global put one of their rising stars from the horticultural division: Karen Deborah. Karen was full of ideas for the transformation of Green Fingers into Garden Concepts. Garden Concepts was to be much more than a garden centre. It would not only supply a wide stock of garden plants and accessories, but offer a number of additional services as well. These would include a well-informed staff, garden/landscape design, short- and long-term maintenance, a help desk and facility, and a bookshop. All Garden Concept centres would have a coffee shop (playing classical music), a supervised children's play area on Saturdays and Sundays, and a gardening club. In short, Karen planned a customer service revolution. If the UK operation took off, she planned to expand into Eastern Europe.

Global had long moved away from a traditional bureaucratic structure. Some 5 years earlier, it had introduced a culture change programme entitled 'People and Performance', which had been accompanied by a major reorganisation into the Agro-Chemical, Seeds and Horticulture businesses and a downsizing of the corporate HQ in London. The business chief executives could manage their businesses as they wanted. Their only constraints were that their operations had to be safe and legal, and to comply with the Global code of principles, which set out Global's environmental objectives, the terms of its human resources commitment to its staff and its ethical principles. The way in which the HQ controlled the individual businesses was through their performance. Each chief executive is set a number of performance objectives in the form of a performance contract. These are reviewed with the Global board on a quarterly basis. The substantial performance bonus available to the chief executives depends on the achievement of their performance contracts.

The past

Jack Moore's last job was as training manager at a large paint company called Slosh and Drip. The company was a major player in the UK DIY market and had also been developing its European markets. It was strongly hierarchical, with much upward management and 'turf protection'. The chief executive proclaimed himself a self-made man, having worked his way up through the Slosh and Drip ranks. His style would best be described as high control/low trust and it set the style for the organisation. Slosh and Drip, at the point at which Jack's appraisal took place, was operating in a very tight market. It had many competitors in the UK DIY market, and the move into Europe had been neither as easy nor as successful as Slosh and Drip had hoped it would be. Consequently, everyone felt under pressure to perform.

Not unexpectedly, it was managed along more traditional lines than Global. For example, the content of the training courses was decided by the senior trainers and enshrined into a Course Handbook that contained the course programme and a copy of all the handouts that were to be used. The theory was that any tutor could then run any programme. The director of training, Bill Kendrew, to whom Jack had reported, was a man of strong views, among which was the view that specially designed courses for particular groups were not a good idea and that the function of course feedback was to evaluate the performance of the tutors rather than the content of the course – so despite consistent feedback about the content of some of the courses, he refused to countenance changes in course design. However, he still made his tutors produce a formal report on each course.

Jack's last appraisal with Bill had been a disaster. Bill saw appraisal as an HR-imposed burden whose only possible role was to provide him with an opportunity to give one-way feedback to his staff about their performance. Like most of his colleagues, Jack had a difficult relationship with Bill. Jack felt that Bill never listened, that he was too quick to judge and to criticise, that he was inflexible and intimidating, and that he was not quite as clever as he thought he was.

Slosh and Drip had an appraisal form consisting of four sections. Section One was a record of the objectives that the appraisees had set for the previous year (in their appraisal interview with their managers). Section Two consisted of the employees' assessment of the extent to which they had achieved these objectives. Section Three was their manager's assessment, which was (in theory) completed following the appraisal interview. Section Four consisted of the objectives set by the appraisees for the forthcoming year (to be agreed at the appraisal interview).

Jack always dreaded appraisals with Bill. They were always uncomfortable and demotivating. No-one likes having their faults paraded in front of them by someone who clearly believes that they are themselves faultless! On the last occasion, Jack's appraisal had ended up being spread out over 3 days. The first sessions had lasted two and a half hours and had consisted of Jack and Bill arguing about whether Jack had achieved the objectives he had set himself for the previous year. Jack thought he had; Bill thought he hadn't. Bill's secretary had heard Jack shout '...but that's not fair. You didn't tell me that was what you wanted', and Bill shout back 'Tough. You're grown up now, stop whingeing!' Jack said afterwards that he and Bill hadn't agreed about measures of success so they had argued about them and that Bill had not accepted any of the reasons that Jack had given for being unable to complete some of his tasks. The session stopped because Bill had to go to another meeting. As Bill stormed out of his office to go to this meeting, he said to his secretary, in a loud voice that was overheard by others (but not Jack), 'Book that idiot Jack in for another session tomorrow morning. I don't know why we bother with appraisals. They serve no point with staff like him. I've got better things to worry about.' The 'appraisal from hell' continued the next day. It got no better. Bill attacked Jack for his 'attitude' the day before and said that his career would never progress until he could learn to accept feedback. Jack, incensed, attempted to give Bill some feedback on his management style, whereupon Bill terminated the discussion and told Jack he was wasting his time and to come back the next day when he was in a more receptive frame of mind. Jack is still wondering why he didn't walk out of Slosh and Drip there and then. He thinks he was simply too shocked.

Jack looked grey with fatigue and tension when he went back to Bill's office the next day. His appraisal had already been 4 hours long; for how much longer could it go on? When he got into Bill's office, Jack found that Bill was not alone. A young member of the HR staff called Hamish McLeod was sitting there looking hugely uncomfortable. 'I've just had a meeting with Hamish,' Bill explained, 'so I thought he might as well stay while I finish your appraisal so that he can see what you need.' Jack felt himself blush: it would be humiliating to have Hamish listen to Bill's verbal assault. Hamish, seeing Jack, a man considerably his senior blush, wanted to crawl under the desk in embarrassment. His presence was not required for long, however. Bill told Hamish to please note that Jack needed a course on interpersonal skills because he didn't have any and could Hamish please note that now so that Bill didn't have to have a development discussion with Jack in 6 months' time. After Hamish left, Bill systematically rubbished Jack's proposed objectives and said he should keep the ones he had had last year since he hadn't achieved them and that he hoped he'd be more successful with them in the forthcoming year than he'd been in the previous one.

Jack felt crushed, enraged and exhausted as he crawled out of Bill's office. Bill had told him not to expect a decent performance grade, which would mean no bonus. He cast his mind back over all his positive achievements over the past year and all the good course reviews. He reflected on his proposed objectives for the forthcoming year. He had wanted to design some new courses to meet the changing requirements of the DIY marketplace. And what had Bill said... something about running the existing courses properly first, not the time to start making changes, not a good moment to take risks or be too visible, protect our performance and so on.

That evening Jack decided that however much he enjoyed the work at Slosh and Drip (the staff on the courses and his other colleagues were great people), he did not have to accept Bill's bullying. So he decided to leave. He saw the ad for the Garden Concepts Training Manager post a few weeks later and, encouraged by the strength of his anger at Bill, applied. In the interview, Steve and Karen had made him feel really at ease; he had performed well and been offered the job.

New start

Steve had been away for Jack's first couple of weeks In the Job but he had arranged for Jack to attend a corporate induction course and had arranged a series of visits and meetings for him.

Jack had now been in the job for 5 weeks. When Steve had asked him to fix a meeting to discuss his performance contract, Jack's heart had sunk a little. He couldn't help but dread such discussions after his experience with Bill. The experience could not have been more different, however.

'Come in, sit down, get yourself a coffee,' said Steve. 'How are you getting on? Can you give me some feedback on how we've managed your induction and what we should do to improve it?' Jack nearly fell off his chair. Steve wanted feedback from him! After some discussion about Jack's induction, Steve moved the conversation to performance. In preparation, Jack had made a list of objectives for himself for his year, which he started to suggest to Steve. 'That's not the way we approach it at Global,' he said, smiling. 'Our system works from the top down. Global's chief executive, Rifat Türcel, is set a number of performance objectives by the chair of the board of directors. These are put into his performance contract. But for Rifat to achieve his objectives all of his direct reports will need to deliver certain things to him. So these are put into their performance contracts. Then they have to get things from their direct reports and so it goes on, cascading all the way down the organisation. We all have an individual performance contract that relates to those above and below us in the company. In this way, everyone works towards the same performance objectives. This means that this discussion is for me to show you my performance contract so that we can discuss the contribution that I need from you. You can then hold similar discussions with your staff about what you need from them. Global is driven by performance,' he continued, 'everything we do is driven by the bottom line. If there isn't a bottom line impact, we don't do it. So for training, you will need to devise a training strategy that is clearly focused on business needs.'

'My contract has two objectives related to you. One is the production of a business-led training strategy. The other is to deliver on our commitment to give all new employees 3 days' training in their first year in addition to their induction. And we're going to have a lot of new employees in Garden Concepts who will need to learn about our ways of doing things,' he added, beaming, 'so you're going to be busy, Jack.' 'Let's put some timings on these items. I need your outline training strategy by the end of the first quarter. I need the detailed implementation plans by the end of the second quarter, and I need it all to be operational by the end of the year. Karen thinks that it is crucial that we get the right attitudes and behaviours from the staff in Garden Concepts from the beginning. We're bringing in Competence Associates to work with us on the competences of staff at all levels. You'll be working with me on this. They will report in time for you to build the training strategy by the end of the first quarter. We need to recruit the right people, and we need appropriate training in place when they start to arrive.'

'I know you're new to your job and to Global, but Karen and I were really impressed with you at your interview. We wanted you to come to work with us because you shared our values and our 'can do' attitude. Garden Concepts is a risk for Global and we're going to make sure that we deliver the business. My job is to support you so that you can deliver the objectives I need from you. I don't mind how you do it; that's your choice, as long as you deliver. I want the performance and I want my bonus. We'll be seeing quite a bit of each other over the next few weeks with the Competence Associates work.'

Jack's head was reeling a bit. It was all so different from Slosh and Drip. He mused over a few of the differences: top-down, business-led, competences, a manager who was empowering him to manage his own work while making him accountable for delivery. Well, there certainly wouldn't be room for arguments, as at Slosh and Drip, about whether he had or hadn't delivered. You either did or you didn't, and Jack had a definite feeling that if he didn't deliver what Steve wanted, Steve would hold him responsible. He'd better get going discussing his performance contract with his staff.

Six months later

'Jack, come and see me when you have a moment. I want to talk to you about the second quarter performance review we've just had. I've been set some new objectives, which I need to discuss with you.'

Jack went to see Steve a couple of days later. 'We had a good second quarter performance review. They liked your plans for the training strategy, so you need to push on to get them up and running. Have you decided on how you're going to resource the training? Will you build a team of internal staff or use consultants or both, or do you plan to outsource the lot?' Jack replied that he was still thinking about this. While it would be nice to have his own team, he felt that it might be more flexible to buy in trainers for specific courses. This was the route that he, Kitty and Sandy (his assistant training managers) currently favoured. 'Your decision,' said Steve, 'but keep me informed because if you decide to outsource, we need to think about the contract. Talking of which,' he continued, 'there have been some changes in mine following the last quarterly performance review, which have implications for you. The directors have decided to move to a system of 360° feedback for all staff in the senior managerial grades. It's in my contract to set it up by the end of the quarter. I'm going to need some support from Training to do this.' Jack asked why the Global directors had decided to go for 360° feedback. Wasn't it rather radical? 'Sure is,' Steve replied, 'but if we're saying, first, that behaviour is important, and second, that there are appropriate and inappropriate ways to behave, we need to monitor and measure it. What is the point of having all that work done by Competence Associates on the behaviours, skills and knowledge needed for different positions, if we don't apply it? The plan is to introduce it to all the management grades next year. Part of every manager's performance contract will include the 360° feedback. We can't allow unhelpful behaviours to continue to be rewarded. In future, if you get lousy feedback, you won't get a bonus no matter what you have delivered. There's no place in Garden Concepts for "old-style" managers.'

the exercises

The case can be used in a number of ways.

- to compare and contrast the ways in which Slosh and Drip and Global Products manage appraisals and individual performance
- to compare and contrast the management styles of Bill Kendrew and Steve George
- to reflect on the covert and overt objectives of appraisal and performance review
- to explore some of the issues involved in the management of appraisals
- to review 'good practice' in giving and receiving feedback.

Each exercise can be undertaken individually or in a small group with discussion in a plenary session.

Students should undertake some of the reading in advance.

exercise
1

Slosh and Drip and Global Products

Compare and contrast the appraisal system in Slosh and Drip with the performance management system in Global.

Questions that might be helpful are:

- What objectives do the systems serve in each company?
- How, and how well, does each of the systems 'match' its respective company?
- How are the systems linked to other HR processes?

exercise
2

Bill Kendrew and Steve George

Compare and contrast the person management style of Bill Kendrew and Steve George.

Questions that might be helpful are:

- How well do their respective styles complement the culture of their respective companies?
- What different forms of power are they exercising?
- What aspects of 'good practice' in relation to performance management can you identify in Steve's behaviour? How could he have improved his discussions with Jack?

exercise
3

Managing appraisal

Appraisal is often – as at Slosh and Drip – a contested activity. Why is this?
Questions that might be helpful are:

- Is there a gap between the rhetoric and the reality of appraisal?

◆ Is there an inherent tension between the different objectives of appraisal?

Giving and receiving feedback

Appraisal involves the processes of giving and receiving feedback. Devise a set of guidelines for good practice in giving and in receiving feedback. As an optional extra, students can then role play giving/receiving feedback in a role play featuring Bill Kendrew. Bill is to receive feedback about the appraisal interview he conducted with Jack.

ESSENTIAL READING

Armstrong, M. (1995) *Personnel Management Practice*, 5th edn, Part VIA. Kogan Page, London.

or Torrington, D. and Hall, L. (1998) *Human Resource Management*, 4th edn, Chapter 4. Prentice-Hall, Hemel Hempstead.

Armstrong, M. and Baron, A. (1998) Out of the tick box, *People Management,* 23 July:38–41.

Fletcher, C. (1993) Appraisal: an idea whose time has gone?, *Personnel Management* September: 34–7.

Fowler, A. (1996) How to provide effective feedback, *People Management*, 11 July:44–5.

Hendry, C., Perkins, S. and Bradley, P. (1997) Missed a motivator?, *People Management* 15 May: 20–5.

Mabey, C. and Salaman, G. (1995) *Strategic Human Resource Management*, Chapter 4. Blackwell Business, Oxford.

Redman, T. and Mathews, B. (1996) Do corporate turkeys vote for Christmas?, *Personnel Review* **24**(7): 13–24.

CHAPTER 2

Assertion

Bryn Davies

OBJECTIVES

The objectives of this chapter are to:

▶ introduce the concept of assertiveness
▶ highlight the distinction between assertive, aggressive and non-assertive behaviour
▶ outline the benefits of acting assertively and the disadvantages of behaving non-assertively or aggressively
▶ explore the range of situations in which assertive behaviour can be useful
▶ identify ways of developing assertive behaviour
▶ promote the practice and development of assertiveness skills.

INTRODUCTION

This chapter is concerned with effective communication in the workplace. It focuses on the development of interpersonal skills that are useful for handling a range of awkward or tricky situations frequently faced by managers. These might include situations such as:

◆ dealing with poor performance by one of your staff
◆ handling conflict with a colleague
◆ refusing a request from your boss
◆ handling an angry customer
◆ being criticised by your colleague
◆ giving bad news to your boss
◆ handling grievances from one of your staff
◆ asking for an increase in salary.

Many people find this type of situation difficult, uncomfortable or anxiety provoking, either because they are concerned about upsetting others, because they are concerned about 'losing out' in some way or because they generally find it difficult to achieve a satisfactory outcome for all concerned. Indeed, they may not be clear about exactly why they find the situation 'difficult' or what they could do about it.

The concept of assertion provides a framework for thinking about, and under-standing, what is happening in these types of situation. It also offers some very concrete suggestions on how these interactions can be handled most effectively to optimise the chances of a satisfactory outcome for all those involved. Ultimately, because the effective handling of interactions with other people is such an important aspect of management, assertion is a vital skill for most managers.

The chapter starts by explaining the concept of assertion and then outlines the poten-tial benefits of assertive behaviour. The typical characteristics of assertive, aggressive and non-assertive behaviour are then described before the chapter turns to address the more practical issue of how to develop one's own assertiveness. Several exercises are provided, which can be tackled individually or in groups. Finally, the chapter concludes with some general tips on developing assertiveness.

What is assertion?

The basic concept of assertion revolves around three broadly defined styles of behaviour, termed assertive, aggressive and non-assertive. Essentially, the argument is that, across a variety of situations, acting assertively (as opposed to aggressively or non-assertively) is more likely to produce positive outcomes and results for all concerned. This argument is explained further below, but first let us look at assertive, aggressive and non-assertive behaviour in more detail.

Assertive behaviour involves directly expressing your needs, wants, views and feelings in such a way that you do not violate others' rights to do the same. For example, imagine that a colleague has requested your help but that you are extremely busy working on another urgent task. An assertive response might be as follows:

'I'd be happy to help Peter, but I need to finish this report first. Would 12 o'clock be OK for you?'

This response acknowledges the help-seeker's needs and their right to make the request, to have that request considered and to receive a courteous answer. Furthermore, it exercises your right to refuse.

Non-assertive behaviour involves an acknowledgement of *others'* rights to express their needs, wants, views and feelings, while failing to exercise your own right to do the same. Taking the same example as above (the request for help when you are extremely busy), a non-assertive response might be:

'Er... I'm a bit busy... but I guess... er... if you are in a hurry I should be able to manage it.'

In this example, aside from the initial tentative allusion to the inconvenience ('a bit busy'), you have entirely subjugated your needs while prioritising the help-seeker's needs (without even checking the urgency or importance of the request).

Aggressive behaviour involves expressing your needs, wants, views and feelings in ways that ignore or violate the right of others to do the same. Returning once again to the example of the request for help, an aggressive response might be:

'No way! I can't help you, can't you see I'm busy? Anyway, why can't you do it yourself? You should have asked me sooner if you're incapable of doing it.'

In this response, the help-seeker's needs have been ignored, and their right to make the request has been violated. Moreover, you have thrown in a personal attack for good measure.

These three different styles of behaviour are represented schematically in Table 2.1.

Table 2.1   Comparison of the three styles of behaviour

	Own wants/needs/views/feelings	*Others'/wants/needs/views/feelings*
Assertive	✓	✓
Non-assertive	✗	✓✓
Aggressive	✓✓	✗

Table 2.1 illustrates that while assertive behaviour represents a *balanced* approach, acknowledging both one's own *and* others' rights, aggressive behaviour prioritises one's own rights (at others' expense) and non-assertive behaviour prioritises others' rights (at one's own expense).

Benefits of assertive behaviour

As the previous section suggests, there are several advantages of behaving assertively in the workplace. These include:

◆ an increased chance of your *own* needs being met
◆ an increased likelihood of achieving a positive result, outcome or solution for *the organisation*
◆ feeling better about oneself (more confidence, or higher self-esteem)
◆ better working (and personal) relationships with others
◆ less time and energy being spent feeling resentful/irritated about what *did* happen
◆ less time and energy being spent in worrying about what *might* happen.

Characteristics of assertive, aggressive and non-assertive behaviour

In order to develop assertiveness, it is important to be able to recognise both your own and others' assertive, aggressive and non-assertive behaviour. The following section provides more detail about the verbal and non-verbal behaviours that tend to characterise the three styles of behaviour.

Assertiveness tends to be characterised by:

Verbal behaviour

◆ Statements that are clear, succinct and to the point
◆ The use of 'I' statements" 'I think...' 'I'd like...' 'I feel...'
◆ Distinctions between fact and opinion: 'My view is...' rather than 'Everyone knows that...'
◆ Questions to seek others' views/needs/wants: 'What's your view?', 'How does that affect you?'
◆ Avoidance of 'should' or 'ought': 'You could...' rather than 'You ought to...'
◆ The use of confident explanations rather than defensive justifications or threats.

Non-verbal behaviour

◆ Firm, steady, genuine voice
◆ Fluency in speech
◆ Regular eye contact (not staring or evasive)
◆ Open, interested facial expression.

Non-assertiveness tends to be characterised by:

Verbal behaviour

◆ Rambling, failing to get to the point
◆ Few 'I' statements: 'I think', 'I believe'
◆ An excessive use of qualifiers and permission seeking: 'It's just that...', 'It was only...' 'Would you mind if...?'
◆ Self put-downs and apologies: 'I hate to suggest this, but...', 'Sorry to bother you, only...'
◆ Fill in words: '... Er...', '... Um...'
◆ Being self-judgmental or blaming: 'I should have...', 'I ought to be...'
◆ Profuse apologising, an excessive use of 'Sorry,...' at the start of contributions
◆ Phrases that dismiss one's own needs.

Non-verbal behaviour

◆ Quiet voice
◆ Stilted, hesitant delivery
◆ Little eye contact
◆ Hunched body, arms crossed.

Aggression tends to be characterised by:

Verbal behaviour

◆ Opinions stated as facts: 'That's ridiculous', 'No-one wants that'
◆ The use of sarcasm
◆ Blaming or judging others: 'You should have...', 'You ought to...'
◆ Threatening questions: 'Why on earth didn't you?', 'Surely you don't believe that rubbish?'

- ◆ Requests in the form of instructions or threats: 'I need that done by this afternoon, or else!'
- ◆ An excessive use of 'I' statements.

Non-verbal behaviour

- ◆ Strident voice
- ◆ Sarcastic tone
- ◆ Rapid abrupt, clipped, delivery
- ◆ Stares
- ◆ Facial gestures to convey irritation, exasperation, disgust or 'pity' (shaking head, rolling eyes)
- ◆ Finger pointing, table thumping.

the exercises

Developing assertiveness

So far we have defined what is meant by assertion, and how it can be contrasted with aggressive or non-assertive behaviour. The argument has been put forward that an assertive style is, on the whole, more effective both personally and professionally, and the potential benefits of assertive behaviour have been described. Exercises 1–4 can all be done individually, but Exercise 5 can only be done in groups.

Identifying your style in difficult situations

Most people behave assertively for much of the time. They do not, for instance, respond aggressively to the question 'Would you like to pay by cash or credit card?'. Instead, it tends to be *only* in particularly 'difficult' situations that we lapse into aggressive or non-assertive styles. Commonly, people find that they have a *typical style*, either aggressive or non-assertive, that they adopt in the majority of difficult situations. The following exercise is designed to help you to identify your typical style.

Read through the descriptions of situations below, and try to identify how you tend to behave in such situations. In some cases, it may be difficult to choose. You may feel that none of the alternatives adequately describes your probable reaction. Nonetheless, try to pick the one that is closest to how you would be likely to react.

1.   When being unfairly criticised by a colleague, are you more likely to:

   (a) Fight back, dismiss the critic, point out *their* weaknesses, put them down, criticise them or make a sarcastic quip (Aggressive)
   (b) Feel upset, embarrassed, hurt or inadequate and stuck for words, and wish that the interaction would finish (Non-assertive)

(c) Seek more information about their concerns by asking questions; then respond to their criticism by firmly stating your alternative view (Assertive).

2. You feel you deserve an increase in salary or recognition. Are you more likely to:

(a) Go to your boss, tell them that your current remuneration is absurdly low and demand an increase, perhaps by using a veiled threat (Aggressive)

(b) Hope that your performance will be recognised, thereby avoiding the need to bother your boss with the issue (Non-assertive)

(c) Prepare your case, arrange to see your boss, explain your reasoning, while accepting that your boss has the right to say no (Assertive).

3. One of your staff has been performing poorly. Are you more likely to:

(a) Tell them straight that their performance is not good enough, that they have the wrong attitude, that they are lazy, or that they should 'pull their socks up' (Aggressive)

(b) Raise the issue tentatively, in order to avoid upsetting them, or delay tackling the issue, hoping that the situation will improve (Non-assertive)

(c) Ask specific questions to try to establish their awareness of, and reasons for, underperformance (not attacking them personally), listen to their response and move on to discuss suggestions for improvement (Assertive).

4. One of your staff comes to tell you that they have been severely overloaded with work over the past few months. Are you more likely to:

(a) Tell them to stop being selfish, you are all overworked and/or 'it's not that bad'. In any event, they're no worse off than the others (Aggressive)

(b) Try to placate them by taking on some of their workload yourself (Non-assertive)

(c) Listen to their concerns and form your own view about the situation. Ask them whether they have suggestions on how the situation could be tackled (Assertive).

5. You have missed a target or deadline on some important work for your boss. Are you more likely to:

(a) Speak to your boss, placing as much emphasis as possible on other people's or departments' contribution to the delay, while steering attention away from your own failings (Aggressive)

(b) Try to avoid your boss, and hope that they won't notice until you have had time to rectify the situation (Non-assertive)

(c) Take the initiative in contacting your boss; explain the position, the reasons (briefly), the consequences and your proposed action (Assertive).

Difficult situations

This exercise is designed to help you identify the *type of situation(s)* in which you are most likely to lapse into aggression or non-assertion. Read through the following list, thinking about examples from your own experiences at work (with colleagues, staff, senior management and customers/clients/suppliers). Which THREE do you find most difficult?

◆ Making requests of others
◆ Refusing requests from others
◆ Disagreeing with others and stating your view
◆ Giving praise to others
◆ Receiving praise from others
◆ Conveying bad news to others
◆ Giving criticism to others
◆ Receiving criticism from others
◆ Handling aggression from others
◆ Handling non-assertion from others
◆ Negotiating with others.

Try to think of a specific incident or example that illustrates each of the three. For each example, was your behaviour aggressive or non-assertive? How could you have dealt with the situation more assertively?

People at work

Think about the people with whom you have regular contact at work. These may be:

◆ your colleagues
◆ your manager
◆ your staff
◆ customers/clients
◆ suppliers.

Identify TWO people with whom you find it difficult to deal, or would like to deal with more effectively. For each person, think of an incident that illustrates this difficulty. Was your approach aggressive or non-assertive? What was the outcome? How did you feel afterwards? What could you have done to handle the situation more assertively?

'I wish I'd said...'

Think of a recent situation at work when you came away and said to yourself, 'I wish I'd handled that differently', 'I wish I'd said...' or 'I wish I *hadn't* said...'. What were your feelings as you reviewed the incident? What was the outcome? Was your approach aggressive or non-assertive? What could you have done to handle the situation more assertively?

Assertiveness role play

The best way to develop skills such as assertiveness is undoubtedly through continual practice. One way to start practising in a relatively safe environment is through role play exercises. The following role play exercise, which draws upon participants' own, very real experiences, is one that frequently produces powerful and rewarding results.

In essence, the exercise involves taking past incidents in which you behaved non-assertively or aggressively, and re-enacting those incidents in a more assertive style. It requires at least three people and ideally a tutor. A maximum group size of five people excluding the tutor is recommended, so larger groups should split into threes, fours or fives.

The exercise should be set up as follows:

1. Each person needs to think of an incident or situation in which they were non-assertive or aggressive. (Exercises 2–4 above should all be useful for generating material.) The incident should preferably be one that is likely to recur and one that they would like to approach differently next time.
2. Each person's incident should be taken in turn. Allow at least half an hour for preparation, role playing and discussion of each incident.
3. Two of the group will be directly involved in each role play, while the third person acts as an observer and advice giver.
4. Before starting, the person who generated the incident needs to explain to the other group members what actually occurred, who was involved, how they felt and what the outcome was. It is essential that all members of the group have a clear understanding of what happened.
5. Next, this person chooses the participants for the role play and assigns roles. This person can take *either* role: in other words, they may want to practise behaving assertively (that is, role playing him- or herself), *or they may want to take the role of the 'difficult person' in the incident* (while picking someone else to demonstrate 'behaving assertively').
6. Finally, the person who generated the incident should set up the room (chairs and so on) appropriately. You are now ready to start.

During the role play, the person in the 'behaving assertively' role is free to call 'time outs' (that is, temporarily pause the role play) at any stage to ask for advice from the observers and tutor about what they could say next. The role play then continues when they are ready.

Overall control of the role play belongs to the person who generated the incident. If at any stage during the role play, this person wishes to swap roles, they can do so. For example, the person who generated the incident may not want to start by playing him- or herself in the role play but may later want to have a go.

The observer should make notes on the performance of the person practising assertive behaviour so that they are in a position to lead the discussion and provide feedback at the end of the role play. It is likely that the observer's feedback will focus on what is said, but they should not forget that feedback on non-verbal behaviour is also useful.

Feedback to the 'behaving assertively' role player should include *at least two effective behaviours* (be specific) and *at least one concrete suggestion for improvement*. The 'behaving assertively' role player should start the process by giving feedback to him- or herself *in this format*.

After this (particularly if the person who generated the incident has *not* elected to take the assertive role), a more general discussion of learning points may be useful. You can then either re-run this same incident (perhaps with different role players) or move on to the next incident, repeating the process until all of the group members have had their incidents role played at least once.

TIPS FOR DEVELOPING ASSERTIVENESS

As mentioned above, developing assertion is best achieved by continual practice. This practice does not need to be restricted to work situations. Indeed, it is just as useful to practise in everyday situations such as returning faulty goods to a shop, dealing with 'pressure' salespersons or exchanging unsatisfactory food in a restaurant or hotel. This section provides some guidelines to help to maximise the likelihood of positive experiences, so your motivation to develop your assertiveness remains high.

◆ When starting, it is very important that you set yourself *relatively easy goals*, which you are likely to achieve. This means *not* picking the most tricky situations (or those in which you have a very strong investment in the outcome). Lack of success is likely to be discouraging and demotivating. In contrast, 'small wins' will build both your confidence and your motivation. Therefore pick situations in which you believe you have a good chance of maintaining your assertiveness.

◆ When you know that a situation is going to be tricky, *prepare carefully*.

   (a) Think about your objectives; be clear about what you want to achieve.
   (b) Consider what you are going to say (assertively).
   (c) Anticipate what the other person is likely to say.
   (d) Reflect on how you could respond (assertively).

◆ If you get stuck in preparing, discuss the situation with or *seek advice* from someone who understands the concept of assertion. This person may also be useful in discussing 'how it went' after the event.

◆ After a tricky situation, *review* your performance in a balanced way. If you were not entirely successful, do not punish yourself but focus on what you learned for the next time. If you learned from the experience, that *is* a positive outcome.

FURTHER READING

Alberti, R. and Emmons, M. (1970) *Your Perfect Right*. Ingram, Lavergne, Indiana.

Back, K. and Back, K. (1990) *Assertiveness at Work*. McGraw-Hill, Maidenhead.

Burley-Allen, M. (1995) *Managing Assertively*. Wiley, Rexdale, Ontario.

Cawood, D. (1993) *Assertiveness for Managers*. Self-Counsel Press, Vancouver.

Dickson, A. (1982) *A Woman in Your Own Right*. Quartet, London.

Fensterheim, H. (1975) *Don't Say Yes When You Want To Say No*. Futura Publications, London.

Rees, S. and Graham, R. (1991) *Assertion Training: How To Be Who You Really Are*. Routledge, London.

Smith, M. (1975) *When I Say No, I Feel Guilty*. Bannam, Toronto.

CHAPTER 3

Career Management

Sally Maitlis

OBJECTIVES

The objectives of this chapter are to:

▶ explain what is meant by 'career' and 'career management'
▶ identify the main steps of career management
▶ provide the opportunity to try out critical career management skills
▶ introduce some of the issues and techniques of organisational career management.

INTRODUCTION

This chapter begins with an illustrative case describing an individual's work history and highlights the issues facing her as she makes career decisions at different points in her life. By reading the case, and considering the case questions, a number of important points are raised concerning the meaning of careers and the nature of career management. The rest of the chapter describes five key steps of career management and offers a number of exercises that explore them.

The key career management steps are:

1. *Self-assessment* – identifying your values, skills, and interests
2. *Exploring career options* – identifying opportunities within and outside the organisation
3. *Matching yourself to opportunities* – determining the fit between yourself and different options
4. *Decision making and goal setting* – choosing a preferred route, setting realistic targets and action plans
5. *Follow-up* – ongoing monitoring and review.

The nine career management exercises in this chapter focus particularly upon the first three of these steps: self-assessment, exploring career options, and matching yourself to opportunities. These tasks are critical in starting the career management process successfully. The last two steps are also important and are discussed at the end of the chapter.

Introduction to the case

Take 20 minutes to read the case study below, and, individually, make notes on the questions given underneath. Then, working in small groups assigned by the tutor, spend 15 minutes discussing your answers. Rejoin the full group for a plenary session.

Juliet

Starting out

Juliet's first job, after graduating in Business Studies, was as a consultant with a small HR firm. She enjoyed working with people and had long been interested in personnel issues. This kind of opportunity seemed especially exciting since she believed that working as a consultant would give her a broad overview of HR as it was practised in a number of different organisations. Juliet enjoyed the role. She felt she was learning a lot about many kinds of companies, developing her general business awareness, while also strengthening her interpersonal and selling skills through her interactions with a great variety of clients. However, after 3 years, she thought it was time to seek a post that would allow her to develop her HR expertise in a more in-depth way, working full time within a corporate personnel function. While consultancy had provided the opportunity to see inside a great many UK organisations, Juliet was aware that she had never had responsibility for the full implementation and evaluation of a major project, nor had she dealt with the internal negotiations that she was sure this must entail. From her consulting experience, Juliet had come to believe that working for a major multinational company would be interesting since such organisations seemed to be at the forefront of HR practice. In addition, she wanted to be part of a larger organisation; for her first job, she had enjoyed the intimacy of a small firm, but she now sought a taste of what she believed would be proper corporate life.

After a few months of job-searching, Juliet took a position as an HR manager in a major retail store. A significant change was that she now had three members of staff working for her, and once she started to settle in, she found she was learning a great deal about staff management, as well as gaining a detailed knowledge of the retail sector. She also began to experience the internal politics that surrounded almost all of the HR department's activities. While she had to some extent expected this, what she had not anticipated was how much it would directly affect her in trying to carry out her work. Occasionally, Juliet looked back somewhat nostalgically to her previous job in the small consultancy.

By the time of her appraisal a year later, she felt she had learned to deal with the political tensions inherent in the role but was finding only certain parts of her job stimulating. She enjoyed staff management but did not feel that much of the project work she did was very different from that of her earlier consulting experience. When she expressed these frustrations to her manager, he suggested both broadening her role to include over-seeing certain training areas, as well as increasing her line management responsibilities. They also discussed the possibility of a secondment to an overseas branch, although such opportunities were quite rare. Although it turned out that Juliet stayed in the UK, she nevertheless found her new role more satisfying. She enjoyed the added responsibilities and being a member of a cross-functional working group set up to develop a company-wide training strategy. However, 18 months later, she again felt in need of a change. Unlike the previous occasion on which she had considered changing jobs, this time the decision seemed less clear to her. Evidently, since she was now part of a large company, there ought to be opportunities for growth within the organisation. However, she was not sure they existed within the HR function; although she was quite inter-ested in her manager's job, he showed no signs of leaving. She also felt that he had not done as much as he might have done to help her grow and develop her role. The organisation prided itself on its management training and development, yet she had received relatively little in her time there. Why hadn't she been put forward for a development centre? Or, she wondered, should she have pressed for more opportunities?

Juliet's thinking then turned to the specific content of her work. Could HR really offer her the challenges she needed? Although she had seen herself as an HR professional for almost 6 years, she now considered changing function – might she be more suited to marketing, for example? Then, suddenly, Juliet found herself questioning her desire not only for a career in HR, but also for a corporate career more generally – was she really happy in this kind of world? Her favourite part of her job was staff management, and most of all she enjoyed helping people who came to her with their problems. Maybe she should train as a counsellor? She had long wanted to do some work that felt really useful, something that seemed to make more of a direct contribution to society. But would she be any good at that? What skills did counsellors need to have? What skills did *she* have? But then, Juliet reflected, maybe all these thoughts were just a reaction to feeling bored and frustrated in her present role, and all she needed was a fresh challenge – perhaps she should join a large management consultancy and expand her experience that way. As she pondered these matters, she was also aware of her weariness with London life – the expense, the time spent travelling and, especially, being so far from her old friends and family in Scotland. Should she return to the north and try to find work there? Suddenly, Juliet felt quite unsure not only of the direction she wanted her career to take, but also of how much priority she should give it in her life. How could she be so confused, when, until now, she thought she had been managing her career so well?

Later years

Shortly after, Juliet was head-hunted by a large bank with headquarters in Glasgow. Attracted by the location, and curious to try working in a new sector, she accepted a job as Personnel and Training Manager. However, within 9 months, the bank undertook a major restructuring that left Juliet redundant. Once the initial shock had subsided, she sought to use this opportunity to take a serious look at her career. She decided to stay in Scotland but to apply to do a part-time course in counselling, earning a living by working independently as an HR consultant. After qualifying, she practised as a counsellor in the university counselling service for 18 months. However, over time, Juliet began to realise that she wanted to work with clients on a longer-term basis, so she decided to train as a psychotherapist. Five years later, she had established a small private practice just outside Glasgow.

CASE QUESTIONS

◆ What were the main issues Juliet considered when she sought to leave her first job in the HR consultancy?

◆ How well and in what ways was her career managed while she was in the retail organisation?

◆ What other approaches could have been used?

◆ Why did she find her subsequent career decision (while in the retail organisation) so much harder to make?

◆ How did Juliet attempt to make a decision at this time? What were the main issues that she considered?

◆ How did she make the decision to become a psychotherapist?

◆ How would you describe Juliet's career?

◆ Could Juliet's career have been managed in a better way? If so, how?

the exercises

Introduction to the steps

The nine exercises in this chapter are based around the main task steps identified as key to successful career management. This chapter concentrates on the first three steps, helping managers to assess their personal qualities and consider what motivates and satisfies them at work, giving them the opportunity to identify different career options and ways of developing their careers within an organisation, and allowing them to begin the process of matching themselves to possible career options.

The precise nature of career management will vary for different people, depending upon their current work situation and the extent to which, and the ways in which, they want it to develop. Thus individuals will find different exercises relevant at different times in their working lives. While the five self-assessment (Step 1) exercises can be thought-provoking for individuals at any stage in their careers, they will be most immediately helpful to those looking for at least a moderate degree of change. These people will particularly gain from spending time taking stock of their skills and work needs.

The second set of exercises is intended to facilitate the exploration of career options (Step 2). Here, Exercise 6 may be of greatest interest to those considering opportunities outside their current work boundaries, while Exercises 7 and 8 are concerned with organisational career management techniques and will be of most immediate relevance to someone looking to develop a career within his or her current organisation. Exercise 7 introduces the concept of individuals' career development stages and is discussed further below. Exercise 8 focuses upon one of the most popular organisational career management methods – mentoring.

The final exercise, Exercise 9, is concerned with matching an individual's personal qualities against different career opportunities (Step 3). Here, individuals evaluate various career options they have identified against the key factors that they have found bring them job satisfaction.

Step 1: Self-assessment

Establishing what you have to give to a job and what you want from work are important starting points in career management. Once you are clear about yourself and your needs, it becomes possible to start evaluating the suitability of different career options. The following exercises will be particularly useful for individuals considering taking a new direction in their careers or about to return to work after a break. They are concerned with answering the questions:

◆ Who am I?
◆ What do I want?

exercise

Lifeline – identifying motivators and satisfiers at work

When considering a new job or new organisation, it can be hard to know just what you are looking for and whether it will be as good as or better than your current one. Some clues to what motivates you at work can be found by reviewing past work experiences, identifying what it was that made them positive or negative. The first part of this exercise can be done prior to the workshop.

Take 10 minutes to reflect upon good and bad experiences you have had during your working life. If your work experience is limited, focus instead upon your educational experiences. Then take a blank sheet of paper and draw a 'graph' of your working life, which maps the good and bad experiences you have recalled. 'Time' should be represented on the horizontal axis, and 'feelings' on the vertical axis (Figure 3.1). Next to the peaks of good experiences and the troughs of bad experiences, write a note to yourself of what they were. Spend 10–15 minutes drawing the graph.

During the workshop, work with a partner taking turns to talk about the good and bad times you have identified in your working life. Consider the following questions:

◆ What was it that caused you to feel good on a particular occasion?
◆ What was it about the 'trough' experiences that made them so bad?
◆ What changed so that things became better?

Feelings

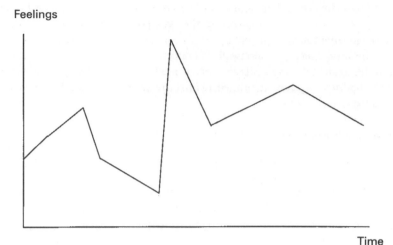

Time

Figure 3.1   Lifeline – identifying motivators and
satisfiers at work

Together with your partner, spend 5–10 minutes thinking across all
the good experiences and see if you can identify any pattern or themes
that have come up again and again over a number of work situations. Do
the same for the bad times, again looking for factors that may have
created negative feelings on more than one occasion. Make a note of these
themes or factors and, with your partner, consider what they tell you
about your needs at work.

Identifying personal skills and qualities

People considering future career options are often surprisingly unaware of
the skills and personal attributes they have to offer. Knowing these can
help you to identify jobs in which you are most likely to be successful, and
it can also assist you in getting them. Write down five things you have
accomplished, inside or outside work, and with which you feel satisfied.
Spend a few minutes identifying the skills and qualities you used to
achieve these things. Take a few more minutes to add to this list as many
of your other skills and qualities you can think of.

Identifying interests

While it is not always possible to fit a job directly to your interests, you
are more likely to enjoy and find satisfying work that to some extent
matches them. Write down up to six things that interest you. Spend a
few minutes considering how long you have had these interests and
how much time you currently devote to them. Think about what needs
they satisfy in you and write these needs down. Do any of them relate

to your current job or to previous ones? This exercise can be done on your own, or you can spend 10–15 minutes discussing with a partner how your different interests, needs and work experience are related to each other.

Career anchors – identifying work-related abilities, needs and values

Schein (1978) identified six career anchors, patterns of self-perceived abilities, needs and values that guide an individual's choice of career. While most people are motivated by a number of different things, Schein believed that, for each of us, one dominant career anchor plays a particularly significant role. Look at the career anchors listed below and give each one a rating from 1–5 depending upon how well it describes you (see below). It may be helpful to think back to some of the skills, interests and motivators you identified in earlier exercises. Look at the areas that you have rated most highly – these are your main areas of interest and those likely to motivate you in your career. Also note whether your abilities, needs and values are spread across a number of anchors (if you have given ratings of 4 or 5 for at least three anchors) or whether they are concentrated in just one or two areas.

Rating scale:
1 – not at all like me
2 – somewhat like me
3 – neither like me nor unlike me
4 – very like me
5 – exactly like me.

◆ *Technical/functional competence*
These individuals want to be challenged in their area of expertise. They are most interested by the intrinsic nature of the work they do, rather than external factors.
◆ *Managerial competence*
These individuals want to exercise responsibility and see their areas of competence as lying in broader management skills rather than technical excellence.
◆ *Security/stability*
These individuals place a high value on job security, a reasonable income and a stable future.
◆ *Creativity*
These individuals have a strong desire to create something, be it a product, a service or possibly their own organisation.
◆ *Autonomy/independence*
These individuals want the maximum freedom from organisational constraints in order to pursue and develop their own professional competence.

◆ *Social/moral*

These individuals are particularly motivated to do something which is valued by society, and want to avoid work which would compromise their personal code of ethics.

Identifying constraints

When thinking about career possibilities, it is good to try to think positively and to remain open-minded about the options. It is also important, however, to be realistic. Make a list of any really significant constraints that you know exist for you (for example, mobility, availability for full-time work and so on) and, alone or with a partner, reflect for 5–10 minutes on how such factors might affect your career choices. Even if you review these later, it is useful to have identified the constraints there appear to be at this time.

Step 2: Exploring career options

The requirements for this step of career management will vary quite considerably depending on your current circumstances. The first of the three exercises here (Exercise 6) is most relevant to people thinking of changing organisation or career direction, facilitating lateral thinking about a wide range of possible career options. It considers the question:

◆ What are the opportunities available?

There are also many other ways in which you can find out about career options, including reading up on different areas of interest, talking to people working in other occupations and visiting your local careers office.

If you are planning to stay in your current occupation and organisation, you may find the two exercises on techniques of organisational career management (Exercises 7 and 8) most helpful. These help to answer the question:

◆ What ways are there to develop my career in my current organisation?

All three exercises are concerned with identifying the career opportunities and choices available to you.

Generating career options

Work in groups of three (ideally with others of a similar work background). One person begins by briefly outlining his or her current work situation. The other two listen to find out more about the speaker's career-related thinking, and may ask questions such as:

◆ Which aspects of your current work situation would you most like to change?
◆ What possibilities have you considered so far, either staying in your current job or organisation, or doing something quite different?

◆ What is it about these options that makes them appealing to you?

◆ What makes them seem less realistic possibilities?

Working with this information, the group then identifies at least four or five career options. These may include ways in which the speaker could change his or her current job so that it is more suitable (for example, expanding the role to include a greater breadth of responsibility) and other jobs within the organisation (either within or outside the individual's current function), as well as offering completely new proposals. Suggestions should take into account the preceding discussion, but the group should try not to restrict itself only to ideas that the speaker has already considered. Each person is allowed 15–20 minutes to present his or her own career situation and discuss career options with the others.

Organisational career management techniques

Different career management approaches will be more or less appropriate for people at different stages of their working lives. This exercise is concerned with the kinds of career management techniques that are commonly found in organisations. Read the case study and suggest ways in which the careers of the groups identified at the end could best be managed within the company.

Foodco is a large multinational organisation employing 20,000 people in 17 countries around the world, producing and distributing a wide range of food products. In recent years, a large number of graduates have been recruited, selected for their senior management potential. However, many have found that the career opportunities within Foodco have not lived up to their expectations, and turnover at the junior management levels is high. Many of the older managers and technical staff have worked with the company for over 20 years. For a significant proportion, this has been their only place of work and it is where they intend to spend the rest of their careers. Not all of them are contributing to Foodco's success, and some are experiencing considerable difficulty adapting to the many changes that are taking place throughout the company.

Career management is currently done on a fairly *ad hoc* basis, with few formal structures or systems. A working party, of which you are a member, has been set up to consider ways in which Foodco can improve the career management of its managers at all levels. You have been asked to concentrate on four main groups:

◆ new graduates

◆ middle managers

◆ senior managers (those still experiencing continued growth and those starting to plateau)

◆ older senior managers, nearing retirement.

Working as a group, try to generate as many career management ideas as you can for the employee group assigned to you by your tutor. You have 30 minutes to prepare a presentation for the board, identifying different career management options and making recommendations for your particular employee group.

Mentoring

Mentoring is one of the most popular kinds of organisational career management technique. In groups of four, spend 15 minutes considering the following questions:

◆ What is a mentor?
◆ How can mentors help newer and younger managers?
◆ What are the problems that might be associated with mentoring?
◆ How would you go about developing a mentoring relationship in an organisation that does not have a formal scheme?

Return to the main group for a plenary discussion.

Step 3: Matching yourself to career opportunities

Once you have identified your skills and needs, and a number of career options, you may find it helpful to try systematically matching yourself against the various possibilities. This exercise is concerned with the question:

◆ Which career options will suit me best?

Evaluating the amount of satisfaction in different career options

This exercise allows you to estimate the amount of satisfaction you are likely to derive from a number of career options you have identified. It takes most people at least 40 minutes to complete and should be done individually, within or outside the workshop.

Draw up a list of 8–12 things that currently and historically have given you satisfaction in your work, such as autonomy, status, good colleagues and so on. You may find it helpful to refer to your findings from the earlier self-assessment exercises. Write these 'satisfiers' across the top of a blank sheet of paper. Then list up to 10 career possibilities (perhaps referring to the ideas generated in Exercise 6) down the left-hand side of the page. Include in these career possibilities your previous job, your current job and possibly your current occupation but in a different organisation, if this is an option you would consider. An example chart is shown in Table 3.1. Now rate, on a 1–10 scale, the extent to which you think you would find each job satisfier in each of the listed career options (that is, how much autonomy would you find in each job, how much intellectual stimulation and so on). When you have done this, add up the 'satisfaction' ratings for each career option and you will have an idea of how satisfying each kind of career choice might be. While the figures provide only a very rough estimate of relative job suitabilities, they may help you to identify the most realistic career options of all those you have considered.

Table 3.1   Evaluating the amount of satisfaction in different career options

	1	2	3	4	5	6	7	8	Total
Previous job	7	6	1	2	4	3	1	6	30
Current job	9	9	6	2	8	2	1	9	46
Same job, different organisation	9	10	6	2	8	2	1	9	47
Lecturer	7	8	8	7	7	6	4	7	54
Consultant	6	7	9	8	9	8	8	6	61
HRM manager	5	6	7	9	10	7	9	7	60
Trainer	4	2	7	6	8	9	9	4	49
Counsellor	6	9	4	6	8	5	5	4	47

Job satisfiers
1 – autonomy
2 – intellectual stimulation
3 – congenial work environment
4 – status
5 – working with senior people
6 – getting immediate feedback
7 – being part of a team
8 – using writing skills.

Final steps

These steps arc most usefully tackled after you have spent some time focusing upon the earlier ones. They can be addressed individually, or you may choose to discuss them with others. At the workshop, it may be useful to work with fellow participants to consider some of the issues that can often make decision making, goal setting and ongoing career monitoring so difficult.

Step 4: Decision making and goal setting

Once you have considered various career possibilities and identified a subset that seems most viable, you now have to make decisions about which ones to investigate further. Here you are concerned with the questions:

◆   Which options do I wish to pursue?
◆   How will I go about this, and by when?

Step 5: Follow-up

Working towards the targets you set yourself, this final, continuous step is about monitoring your progress. The key questions here are:

◆ How am I doing?
◆ Did I accomplish what I wanted?

REFERENCE

Schein, E.H. (1978) *Career Dynamics: Matching Individual and Organizational Needs*. Addison Wesley, Reading, MA.

CHAPTER 4

Communicating

Jean Hartley

OBJECTIVES

The objectives of this chapter are to:

▶ introduce the complexity of communications within organisations
▶ show how the experience of job insecurity may affect communication
▶ gain insights into how individuals in organisations interpret organisational information
▶ analyse some of the ways in which communications occur within organisations
▶ give some experience of developing and reflecting on communication skills.

INTRODUCTION

This chapter focuses on reflections about an everyday experience within organisations: listening to, reacting to and interpreting communications, both formal and informal, about matters that are affecting or might affect the organisation and its employees (or are believed might have this impact).

The particular setting for these reflections is the job insecurity that may occur in any organisation undergoing major change. Using this setting has two purposes. First, it enables the exploration of a fairly common feature of contemporary organisations – job insecurity and the management of uncertainty and ambiguity. Second, it explores the ways in which communications are 'sent' and interpreted. The exercises are both analytical and experiential. Three of the exercises involve analysing the sources of communication in the case and proposing the next steps. A fourth exercise is a role play. The role play provides an opportunity for class members to develop, and gain feedback on, their own presentation skills, based on communicating organisationally sensitive material, as well as to explore some of the ways in which the 'message sent' may vary from the 'message received'. The impact of the presentation on different employees can be explored. However, this exercise is more than interpersonal or intragroup communication: the focus is on communication in *organisational* settings. More information and advice on setting up the role play are contained in the Tutor's Notes.

The social services seminar

It was a grey April day, full of threatened rain and with a biting wind, as Iain Millett, Director of Social Services, walked across the car park at County Hall, the administrative base of Midshire County Council, to his car. It was only a 15-minute drive from his office out into the country to the national sports centre where the seminar had been booked, but he wanted to get there early to check on the final arrangements. As it was off-site, he wanted to see where he and others would be speaking and to speak to Alan Marris, who was responsible for organising the event. Alan Marris was one of his area managers, who had recently been seconded from his line management job in order to become New County Project Manager in social services, helping the department to develop plans for a major reorientation and reorganisation. This was to be the first of three seminars for social services managers across Midshire County Council to explain how the department would be restructured due to local government reorganisation, which was to take place a year hence.

The social services department, providing a range of services for vulnerable people in the county (elderly people, families and young people in stress, people in need of mental health support and people with disabilities) had just over 6,000 staff. It was the largest department in Midshire County Council in terms of staffing and the second largest in terms of annual budget. Services were delivered over the whole county – more than 216,000 hectares (675 square miles) – by a range of part-time and full-time staff working throughout the community out of area offices, in residential homes and hospitals and in support and administrative services at the corporate centre. Iain Millett reflected as he drove that it was important to get the communication right at this crucial time in the organisation's history. The seminar was for only 100 of the most senior managers. Even with three seminars, Iain knew he could only directly reach 300 in his department in this way. Would this be enough to maintain staff commitment and morale as the department went through turbulent change? There was a team briefing system in the organisation, but was this enough at this time of change? What else should he be doing to lead effective change management? Would his department be less effective in managing the change than other departments, and would this create a poor image within the wider County Council? He mused on his forthcoming talk and on the broader department strategy as he drove to the conference centre.

Alan Marris had already arrived at the conference centre and was surveying the main room where the initial presentations would be made at 2 pm. As New County Project Manager in the social services department, Alan had planned and organised the seminar with the department management team to try to ensure that the 'message' would be consistent with the corporate approach to reorganisation being adopted across the eight departments that made up Midshire County Council. Alan grimaced slightly when he saw the chairs set out in neat rows facing the long table and the overhead projector at the front of the room. If this was going to be two-way rather than merely one-way communication, the audience needed to be able to see and hear *each other* as well as the speakers at the front of the room. He worked with his administrator to rearrange the chairs into a horseshoe, which also gave the room a slightly more informal atmosphere. He placed an overhead slide on the projector and went to the back of the room to check that it could be seen and read clearly. On a table at the back of the room, he placed copies of the overheads showing the proposed new departmental structure for social services, which had been finalised for the top three tiers of the department at the management team meeting only the previous week. Alan placed chairs behind the table for the afternoon's speakers. The Director of Social Services would chair the meeting and open the proceedings. Alan placed his chair in the middle. Three other people were going to speak.

Uncertainty, turbulent change and restructuring

Midshire County Council was undergoing the largest and most far-reaching drastic change it had experienced in over 20 years. For more than 6 years, the County Council had been under the microscope held by the Local Government Commission, which was appointed by central government. The Commission had been reviewing the structure of two-tier local government in some parts of the UK. In Midshire, there were eight district councils providing a variety of local services, with the County Council providing another set of services, including social services, education, highways and transportation, and leisure across the whole of the area of the district councils. This had been a common structure of local government in the shire counties throughout England. However, the Local Government Commission had spent 3 years deliberating whether the major city in the county should become 'independent' from the county, responsible for the provision of all its own services, and leaving the County Council to provide services for the rural and market town areas. Six months ago, the Commission had finally decided that the city should gain unitary status. It had been, and still was, a great blow to the staff at Midshire County Council. It represented the breaking-up of an organisation that had been in existence for more than 100 years, and might involve some work teams, in some cases, being fractioned between the County and City Council. While the broad rules for staff transfer had been set at national level (those whose job was mainly in the city or mainly with city-based residents were likely to transfer), there was much room for local interpretation (and some negotiation between the two organisations involved). Initial calculations showed that about one-third of the staff would lose their jobs at Midshire – although the majority were likely to be transferred to the enlarging City Council. Not all though.

As if this wasn't enough uncertainty for staff, a further source of concern was the financial budget for the following year, which was yet again being cut. For the past 6 years, tightening public expenditure had led to a reduced annual budget for the County Council. Although it was still too early to say definitely, rumours were going around social services that the County Treasurer, responsible for the overall council budget, was going to be seeking cuts in social services of at least 7 per cent. In a department with a high level of expenditure on staff, this would mean job losses, whether through early retirements, a freeze on new posts or redundancies, as services were once more trimmed back. Staff were feeling nervous.

There had been some talk, on the TV and in the newspapers, about social services being taken out of local authority control and established as a separate body to run children's and adult services. This was also unsettling for staff and contributed to the general air of concern in the department.

Response to uncertainty: New County

With the prospect of a dramatically 'downsized' County Council and its potential for the plummeting of staff morale, both in the period until transfer and for the survivors, Iain Millett had worked, as a member of the chief officers' (that is, senior) management team in the County Council to address the key challenges facing the organisation. The elected politicians and the senior managers had developed a strategy for the future, which they called 'New County'. The aim was to use the unsought and unwanted imposed change to refocus the organisation on its key policy priorities and to counteract falling morale with a sense of new hope and new beginnings. The New County strategy aimed at reorganising the departments of the County Council so that they were better able to ensure that services were relevant to local communities and to target resources more closely on high-priority geographical areas. The organisation would also use the reorganisation to build stronger links with other organisations in the locality.

At the level of the Social Services Department, Iain Millett had worked with a small team of managers (including Alan Marris) to propose a new department structure, based on a reduced budget and workforce and with a new territory excluding the city, as part of the New County strategy. Although some smaller functions of the department were to be taken over by other departments (such as Leisure), the main functions of the department would remain largely intact overall. However, the organisational structure would be streamlined, with two out of the nine area offices being transferred wholesale to the City Council. It was not yet as clear what would happen to corporate and specialist services (for example, personnel and finance, and also adoption and fostering services across the county). In addition, although the new department structure had been revealed the previous week, following staff consultation, a number of questions remained, including *who* would fill the posts, *how many* posts would be available in particular areas, *which* posts would be 'ring-fenced' (not open to application except by the current job holder) and *when* the interviews for new positions would be held. Time and service pressures would also mean that some managers had not in any case had time to read or reflect on the proposals. Additionally, although County Council managers had worked closely with City Council managers about the transfer of staff, the City Council was not yet in a position to indicate what its own structures would be like following reorganisation: it was taking on social services and education services for the first time and had to design structures and integrate these two supertanker services into its own organisation without, initially, the expertise within the organisation.

The social services seminar was designed to address some of these uncertainties and to build enthusiasm for the New County strategy. Alan Marris had planned that it should have three speakers:

◆ Iain Millett, the Director of Social Services, spoke first, welcoming staff to the seminar and outlining what he saw as the positive new prospects for the New County and, in particular, for social services. Reorganisation was giving the department the opportunity to refocus its services around two main streams of delivery to young people and adult services, while retaining area-based organisation. Iain's delivery was upbeat and optimistic in tone, regretting the upheaval for staff but emphasising that it would not be long before the new department would be up and running.

◆ Helen Boyd, lead manager for the project team that had led the departmental consultation exercise with staff, spoke in more detail about the structure, based on functions rather than posts, for the new department. She sketched out the new management structure but said that it would still be several weeks before the details of posts and interviews would be known.

◆ Colin Robinson was from the personnel department of the County Council. He said that the city was looking forward to working with the staff who were transferring. Unfortunately, the planning for the new departmental structures for the city department was not so far advanced and he was unable to say in detail where staff would be located or when the interviews would be taking place for those staff who wished to transfer to the city.

Alan, through Iain, had tried to get the Chair of the Social Services Committee to speak as well but, as he had a full-time job as well as being involved as a councillor, this had not been possible, although he hoped to come to one of the later seminars. Alan had hoped that he would have been able to speak on the political priorities for the New County, especially as these would affect social services, setting the political context for the detailed management issues that were to be discussed in the seminar.

The initial session lasted an hour, and there was a little time for questions at the end of each 15-minute presentation, a few staff raising issues about the practicalities and procedures of the transfers. At the tea break, the room was buzzing with talk as staff compared their impressions and opinions about the presentations.

Mick Smith was a District Manager for the northern area of the county. His 'patch' would not be affected to any great extent by the reorganisation, although he was concerned about the effect of budget cuts on the number of home helps and other front-line staff he would be able to employ. He felt that Iain Millett had given a good account of the New County but that 'We know all about reorganisation, and it won't have a big impact on us – but why didn't he say anything about the finances of the New County. How can we be expected to run the same or an improved service with less money? My staff feel quite uncertain as a result of the lack of clarity about next year's budget.'

His colleague, Jenny Price, a social worker manager, had a different view point. She also worked from an area office that would be largely unaffected, but her own job felt very vulnerable. She had a county-wide responsibility for the fostering of teenagers, which was a complex and sensitive service for which the County Council had developed a national reputation. Jenny worked right across the 'old' county, managing social workers who were covering families in both the city and the county. But what was going to happen now that the county would have fewer cases to work with – approximately only two-thirds of the old caseload. Would she be out of a job? What would happen to her career prospects if the job was a smaller one – assuming that it still existed? There would still (presumably?) be a need for a county-wide service, but what form would it take, and who would she report to in the new structure? Would fostering teenagers still remain a policy priority in the new County Council? Jenny felt that the seminar had, so far, raised as many questions as it had answered. She had heard a rumour that her counterpart in the neighbouring Upshire County Council had taken early retirement in similar circumstances and that the specialist job had disappeared – might that happen to her? Jenny felt that it was difficult to talk to her colleagues about her uncertainties. However, she resolved to find out more and moved across the tea room to talk with Alan Marris.

Petra Burgess was the District Manager responsible for half of the city social services, which would be transferred with reorganisation. She was feeling angry at the presentations she had just heard. Colin Robinson was more junior than the other managers who had spoken from the platform. Why had the city not fielded a manager with as much seniority as the county? Was it symbolic that the City Council speaker had been seated at the far end of the table – almost into the corner of the room and half hidden by the projector screen? Colin had clearly tried to do his best, but his lack of detailed knowledge of the procedures of transfer, combined with the inability of the City Council, at this stage, to indicate the departmental structure that the city authority would be adopting, left Petra uncertain of how many staff, in the end, would be transferred. If the city had the budget problems it was rumoured to have, how many of her staff would transfer, and how many might be asked to look for jobs outside the authority? Might some of them experience redundancy rather than job transfer? It had happened in other councils undergoing reorganisation. How would she encourage front-line staff and back-office managers to maintain their commitment in the stressful conditions of working with deprived families in the city when it was evident that neither the City nor the County Council was showing much interest in them? She felt that all the attention in the New County strategy was addressed to the 'stayers' rather than the 'leavers', even though the transfers would not take place for nearly a year. How would she manage her staff in the meantime?

---

the exercises

Discussion exercises

The group is asked to identify all the sources of 'communication' that exist in this case study, covering not only verbal communication, but also other types of communication. What are the different messages that are being given in this seminar? Where is the 'good news', and where is the 'bad news'? Why might the three listeners in the case study have different emotional and cognitive responses to the communications given in the seminar?

Consider the next steps that Iain Millett might take following the presentations. The case has not revealed what happened in the one and a half hours after the tea break. If you were Iain Millett or Alan Marris, what communication would you want in that part of the seminar and why? What further actions would you take to communicate to the management group and the workforce in the months after the seminar in the lead-up to the transfer of staff?

How is job insecurity likely to affect the ways in which staff react to information and consultation? What practical steps might be taken to address the concerns of those who are likely to stay with the County Council while also meeting the concerns of those who are transferring to the City Council? How would you try to manage the staff's commitment to their work and the organisation in the period of uncertainty leading up to transfer?

Role play exercise

This concerns a role play of the presentation from the Director of Social Services to the seminar. Ask the person designated as the Director to prepare a 5–10-minute talk to the staff about the changes facing the County Council. The presentation should not avoid the difficult communications about reorganisation, the planned loss of one-third of the staff to the City Council and the probable job losses through financial cutbacks. Allocate three group members to listen and react to the talk in the roles of Mike Smith, Jenny Price and Petra Burgess. Allow 20 minutes for a role play question and answer session following the formal presentation.

If the group is sufficiently large, some class members may join the presentation as members of the three managers' work teams. However, some class members should be allocated to the role of non-participant observer, who can report back on what they have observed at the end of the role play.

What do the managers 'hear' in the talk? Why might their reactions be different? What might account for 'good news' for one manager being heard as 'bad news' by another manager? What else do the managers want to know about? What does this say about how communications are interpreted?

Note: For all these exercises, the impact of insecurity in the workplace on the perceptions by employees of information and communications should be introduced prior to the exercises by the teacher. Relevant reading is given below.

FURTHER READING

There are a number of texts that cover interpersonal and group-based communication skills, both verbal and non-verbal. These include:

Levens, J.-P. and Codol, J.-P. (1988) Social cognition. In Hewstone, M., Stroebe, W., Codol, J.-P. and Stephenson, G. (eds) *Introduction to Social Psychology*, Chapter 5. Blackwell, Oxford.

O'Reilly, P. (1993) *The Skills Development Handbook for Busy Managers*. McGraw-Hill, Maidenhead.

Weiman, J. and Giles, H. (1988) Interpersonal communication. In Hewstone, M., Stroebe, W., Codol, J.-P. and Stephenson, G. (eds) *Introduction to Social Psychology*, Chapter 9. Blackwell, Oxford.

Texts that set communications in an organisational framework include:

Morgan, G. (1986) *Images of Organization*, Chapter 4, Organizations as brains. Sage, London.

Weick, K.E. (1995) *Sense-making in Organizations*. Sage, Thousand Oaks, CA.

Wheatley, M. (1992) *Leadership and the New Sciences*, Chapter 6, The creative energy of the universe – information. Berrett-Koehler, San Francisco. This provides a quantum theory metaphor for organisational functioning.

A number of organisational behaviour textbooks have a chapter on the organisational context of communications. An example is:

Tosi, H., Rizzo, J. and Carrol, S. (1994) *Managing Organizational Behaviour*, 3rd edn. Blackwell, Oxford.

Readings on how job insecurity affects the search for and evaluation of information and how knowledge and understanding may have an impact on levels of insecurity can be found in:

Brockner, J. and Wiesenfeld, B. (1933) Living on the edge (of social and organization psychology): the effects of job layoffs on those who remain. In Murnighan, K. (ed.) *Social Psychology in Organizations*. Prentice Hall, Englewood Cliffs, NJ.

Hartley, J. (in press) Models of job insecurity and coping strategies by organisations. In Marmot, M., Ferrie, J. and Zigilio, E. (eds) *Labour Market Changes and Job Insecurity*. World Health Organisation, Copenhagen.

For those who wish to understand more about the particular organisational context of a politically managed organisation – the local authority, including social services – a good primer is:

Wilson, D. and Game, C. (1998) *Local Government in the United Kingdom*, 2nd edn. Macmillan, Basingstoke.

CHAPTER 5

Effective Confrontation

Chris Brotherton

OBJECTIVES

The objectives of this chapter are to:

▶ illustrate how problems may present themselves at work
▶ illustrate how problems become embedded one within another
▶ explore how problems may be denied and hidden
▶ explore how problems may be faced and dealt with.

INTRODUCTION

The chapter is designed so that it may be role played and then discussed. The case raises general issues about work performance and a problem with drink, and perhaps with the way in which drinking is seen both at work and in society in general.

This chapter presents a case that first appears to be one in which deadlines are not met and then becomes one of poor working practices and unreliability. Finally, the issue centres around an employee who has a severe alcohol problem. The chapter presents a case that could be role played. Alternatively, the scenarios could be read through and discussed. Finally, the chapter presents some literature on confrontation and on alcoholism.

International communications

A problem in the team

The roles:

Tom	A newly promoted manager. Mid-thirties and with a young family. Graduate
Brian	Project manager. Late thirties and a long-standing employee of International Communications
Phil	Graphics. Early twenties. Graduate
Sean	Software tools. Early twenties. Graduate

Claire   Programming. Early twenties
Michael Programming. Early twenties
David   Graphics. Early twenties
Derek   Education. Late thirties, divorced and overweight. He wears an open-necked shirt and has been very liberal with his after-shave, despite having a slightly unkempt appearance.

International Communications is an educational software company specialising in multimedia development. Multimedia software production is resource hungry. It is high cost and labour intensive. Companies operate in an increasingly competitive market. International Communications is seeking to establish a distinctive market niche for a range of high-quality products that take multimedia to the frontiers of its development. Its products add sound, video and art clips to text in systematic ways that are intended to enhance the instructional properties of the packages. Several international companies have recently established themselves in multimedia software. International Communications employs 120 people with a variety of discipline backgrounds. Educationalists and psychologists work with designers and software tool developers. The company employs computer graphics specialists and programmers. It organises a matrix management team-based system that draws specialists from each area, all of whom work with a project manager.

A new product has been ordered by a company that wishes to sell a point-of-sales training package to major banks. The product will provide computer-based prompts to bank employees as they make telephone contact with customers. The package will provide background details on customers' accounts, their family and personal history, and their other outgoings, and allow suggestions about new sales opportunities such as insurance, loans and holiday booking. The package offers some 250 possibilities for the point-of-sales conversation. This is a relatively complex product, but it is well within the capacity of International Communications to deliver a high-quality product on time. The development team has been working on the product order for 8 months and is coming close to the deadline for demonstrating its prototype to the customer's training staff.

Tom is the recently promoted Section Manager. He is a young graduate with a young family, and his new responsibilities weigh heavily on him.

Tom has become worried for some time that design deadlines have been slipping. He is also concerned that the team appears to have been working late into the night on several nights a week without apparent progress. Tom calls in Brian, the Project Manager.

Brian is older than Tom and worries little about matters in general. He has been with International Communications since it was founded but has not progressed beyond the level of project management.

Tom   I'm worried that the team seems to be working long hours but that the package is nowhere near completion. What do you think is happening?

Brian We're working hard – but we're not working well together. Every time we look at the package, those folk in education seem to offer a new solution. We need some consistency from them. We can't keep changing what we're doing simply because they are not able to formulate their own problems clearly. There's just too much coding to be done.

Tom   Why do you think that they are changing their minds so often?

Brian   They say that they are testing ideas experimentally. They want to be sure that the eventual design does not overload the point-of-sales team.

Tom   How much of a problem is that?

Brian   Well, the product is likely to be quite demanding when it's in use, but then banking is generating more and more opportunities for sales. The task is no more complex than many knowledge-engineering projects that we've been involved in. The demands can't be the entire reason for the uncertainty. We did some preliminary investigations as we began, and these issues were not raised at that stage. They were just not mentioned.

Tom   I'll call a meeting of the team and ask them to take me through progress to date. Tomorrow morning at 9 am looks good to me. How's your diary then, Brian? OK. I'll e-mail everyone to tell them to be in your office at that time.

Tuesday morning, 9 am. Tom's office.

Brian and Tom meet with Sean, David, Michael, Philip and Claire.

Tom   How's the bank project going, Sean?

Sean   It's OK. We'll have the prototype ready to run by the end of next week.

Michael   Oh, that's a bit optimistic. I have about 200 hours of work still to do.

Tom   Why so much at this late stage?

Michael   I've been waiting for Phil to produce the graphics for the icons – there are too many of them for comfort, and the guys from the education team say that there's no coherence in the presentational style.

Tom   Why don't we have anyone from education with us this morning? Not only are those guys holding you up, they can't come to meetings when I call them!

Brian   Derek's always a bit late in the mornings. He works on his own here through the weekends and quite late in the evenings, but we often don't see much of him during the day. He says that he's testing our material, and I know that he spends a lot of time in the library.

Claire   Derek is just not helping. Any work that he is responsible for is delayed, or it's incomplete, or it's badly done. It puts pressure on everyone else when one member of the team does not pull their weight.

David   He seems to be having a bit of trouble at home. The landlord knows my sister and he was saying that Derek seems distressed when he arrives back at his flat. He had a bit of a fall last week and got very angry with the landlord about a carpet that Derek claimed was not secured properly. When the landlord visited the flat, he could see nothing wrong. He did say to my sister that the flat looked as though it hadn't been cleaned for months. My sister doesn't know why Derek should be distressed but says that Derek's father had died a month or so ago and perhaps that was still affecting him.

Tom   What other points does the team want to make about the project? Are we all happy with Derek's contribution?

Sean, David, Michael and Philip agree that they have nothing to add. Claire is unhappy.

Claire   The men always stick together on these points. Shouldn't we face up to the fact that there is a problem here? I don't know what the problem is, but it seems to me to be more than just a personal problem.

Tom   We need to support him a bit, but we have to get the project completed. Our customer will be pressing us soon. We know that the work is important to their company survival. We have responsibility to them, and we are in danger of not meeting it. I want to see Derek when he comes in, and we should meet again on Friday to review our progress.

10.15 am. Derek knocks on Tom's door and enters.

Derek   You wanted to see me?

Tom   Yes, why were you not at the team meeting?

Derek   I didn't know about it.

Tom   Everyone was e-mailed – you were the only one who missed it. Where have you been until this time in the morning?

Derek   In the library. I'm doing a search for the literature on icons for the bank project.

Tom   I'm not happy with the progress that the project is making. How do you think the project is going?

Derek   Well enough. I'm not very happy with the team. They seem to be against me. Always watching me. I don't know why. I work harder than everyone else. I'm always here. They don't work at weekends but I do.

Tom   The team are fine but they are worried about you. Are you having problems at home?

Derek   What have they been saying about me? I don't have any problems!! Just let me get on with things and we will all be fine.

Tom   OK. Let's leave it for now. We are meeting again at 9 am on Friday. Just come in with the others.

Wednesday, 3 pm.

Phil finds Derek deeply asleep at his desk. He tries to rouse Derek but with no success. Phil leaves Derek asleep and goes off to the coffee bar, where he meets Claire and Sean.

Claire   Derek's asleep at his desk. He really is the limit. I hear that he has a problem, but he's holding up the project and it's unacceptable. We should ask Tom to take action and not just let the situation drag on.

Phil   Maybe Derek will just come round. We are trying to support him but it's difficult. No-one wants to hit the guy when he's down.

Claire   Aren't we just making matters worse by not getting our manager to do something?

Sean   Maybe.

Claire goes back to her workstation. Michael is deep in concentration, working on a difficult aspect of the programme.

Claire   Can't we do something about Derek before things get worse?

Michael   I am. I have to work harder because he hasn't produced anything since he has been here. I'm just very fed up.

Thursday afternoon.

Derek has not been seen that day by the project team. Brian asks Phil where he thinks Derek might be. Phil says that he must be in the library. Phil makes a quick check of the library but cannot see Derek. That evening, Phil is taking a walk through the town when he spots Derek in the square. Derek is looking very much the worse for wear. He tries to take Derek by the arm in an attempt to get him back to his flat. Derek protests that he is OK, and Phil walks on, leaving Derek to his own devices. One of Derek's neighbours, seeing Phil trying to help Derek, tells him that Derek has been making a tremendous amount of noise in the small hours. He says that Derek became aggressive when the neighbour knocked on the door to see what was wrong. The neighbour says that there has been a considerable amount of noise over the past few weeks. The neighbour cannot provide a reason for Derek's behaviour.

On his way home, Phil meets Sean.

Phil   That man Derek is in trouble. He is in the town square and could hardly stand up. I have tried to get him home, but he just stands there, not wanting to move. I guess he's had too much to drink. His neighbour says that he makes a great deal of noise at night and becomes aggressive if he is spoken too.

Sean   We can all get a bit drunk sometimes. Let's both go and see what we can do with him.

Phil and Sean go off to find Derek still standing in the square and making attempts to cross the road. They take him by the arm and walk him gently back to his flat. They give him coffee, lie him on the bed and go off to their respective homes.

Phil   Not a word to Tom in the morning. Derek has enough trouble at work as it is.

Sean   No, we all like a bit of a drink.

Friday morning, 9 am.

Claire, David, Michael, Philip and Sean meet outside Tom's office.

Claire   Derek's not here. There will be trouble again. We're all making this into a big problem because we are not facing up to the issue.

Sean   What is the issue?

Claire   The man is not working properly. I don't think that he's working at all. He's late. He's asleep. He's missing. He's everything but at his desk, working.

Philip   He's like the rest of us – he drinks.

Claire   The rest of you don't behave like that. He has a drink problem. Tom has to be told because this really is an issue for management.

Sean   That just gets the guy into trouble.

Philip   I am unhappy about hiding matters. Tom tries to let us run as a team, and that means that we have to trust each other – including him.

Tom opens his door and calls the team in.

Tom   How are we doing with the bank project?

Brian   It's coming along. We just need to get another iteration on the evaluation and then we can run the system.

Tom   I thought that there were a couple of hundred hours more work to be done before we could even begin to think about evaluation.

Brian   There's more work to be done, but we've had a look at what is outstanding and think we can complete by next week. It means a few more late nights, but we'll be there.

Tom   Can we get the system up and running so that I can see it?

Brian   Phil will get things moving and give you a ring when it's ready to look at.

Tom   Where's Derek? Everyone else is here. Why is Derek missing again? The delays are down to him. He is never around when he should be!

Brian   Let's go round everyone here to see what progress has been made, what still needs to be done and where we go from here.

Michael   I think that we are ready to go with this. We could demonstrate our prototype to the customer with the design that we have. Phil has done what he can – it's just that Derek hasn't evaluated them in any way. If the customer thinks that the icons are wrong, they will tell us and then we can go back to look at the issue of coherence. This way we are waiting for Derek and he's not making progress.

Tom   OK – good, let's go for it!

Brian   That's fine as far as it goes, but our selling point is our capacity to work as a multidisciplinary team – we ought to have been able to provide a rationale for the design and we can't. If the customer believes that there is no coherence or that the training task is too complex or, worse, that the operators can't perform well when they are using the system, then it looks as though the system is badly designed. The design has to work for the operators – not just be clever graphics. These are all things that should be advised by the psychologists, and we just don't have their full input.

Tom   I hear what you say, but we have to sort something out. I think that we have to deal with Derek's performance separately and directly. What have the team got to say to me about Derek?

Claire   Well, he has a drink problem. He'll say that he hasn't. He comes in sober in the morning – late, but he does come in sober! – and he does get in! The problem is that somehow he gets worse during the day.

Tom   Are you telling me that he's drinking while he's at work?

Claire   I am – but there is no proof other than his odd behaviour. He only looks really drunk late in the evening, and he's usually gone home by then.

David   He does have a bottle of tonic water on the filing cabinet most of the time. Last week I heard that the cleaners had to deal with several dozen empty bottles that had been pushed into the disabled toilet area. They complained about the smell in there. The bottles must have had gin in them at some time. By the time you have several dozen empties, there is quite a strong smell. This lot must have accumulated over several weeks.

Tom   He has to be drinking while he is at work. Let's look at it. He falls asleep. He forgets things. He fails to complete his work. There are bottles in great quantities secreted away. His behaviour gets more erratic as the day goes on. He has problems at home. His neighbours complain about him making a noise at odd times. You don't have to be a rocket scientist to see that the man has a drink problem. What does the Personnel Department have to say about workplace drinking? I will see Oliver and ask what the policy is.

Oliver, the Personnel Officer tells Tom that the policy on drinking at work is to give the individual concerned a formal warning about conduct and about the dangers involved, to offer admission to counselling and rehabilitation or to face dismissal if no treatment is obtained and the drinking continues. The problem with rehabilitation is that people have to voluntarily enter the process in a sober condition that has been maintained for 2 days. Pressure can be exerted to get the individual just to resign if he does not take up the treatment, but this is risky since it can be construed as amounting to constructive dismissal.

Tom calls in to the Counselling and Rehabilitation Centre in town. He presents the issues to the duty counsellor.

Counsellor   Your man has a serious problem. He has probably been an alcoholic for several years, but he'll deny that he has a problem. He'll not only deny it, but also manipulate those around him so that he can maintain his drinking pattern without threat. He'll keep doing this to the point where his body gives him problems. The trouble with the neighbours is probably caused by Derek having delirium tremens – his body cells will be crying out for alcohol. He has a physical dependency. If we get him in to treatment here it will take about 6 weeks to 2 months to detoxify him. He'll need supportive counselling for 2 years or so before he establishes a pattern that is based on sobriety. I don't know to what extent you will be able to establish a decent work pattern at the level at which he is placed. He'll need help and support, but first he'll have to be jolted from the state that he is in. He has to realise the need for treatment and the damage that he will do to himself if he fails to get help. Eventually, he'll kill himself with drink if he carries on in this way.

Tom returns to his office and calls the team together.

Tom   We have to deal with this together. Everyone has to make Derek know that there is a real problem that has to be dealt with. There has to be no way in which he may collude with others in the team so as to avoid dealing with the problem he has. We have to work together to confront him with his drinking and get him to seek help. I'll speak to him first, and Brian can stay with me. We'll let you know what has happened and what needs to be done as soon as we can. OK. Go back to your work now. I'll see you later.

Derek is called in to see Tom.

Tom   Come in, Derek. As you know, Derek, we have not been happy with you for some time. You are not working well. You may not be working at all. The bank project is behind schedule and lacks the input that we expect from you. Brian and I are worried about you. We think that you are drinking during your time at work and that you are ill.

Derek   That's over the top! I'm perfectly well. I come in at the weekend when no-one else does. I work hard. Where is the evidence that I'm drinking? I'm not drunk now. I'm never drunk.

Tom takes Derek through the issues raised during the past week. Derek blocks and denies for over 1 hour. Tom goes to Derek's desk and finds a tonic water bottle that smells of gin. He brings it to Derek and shows it to him. Still Derek denies that he is drinking at work. He becomes distressed and angry. He complains about his colleagues and about Tom's lack of support for him. He complains that the work he does is not appreciated.

Tom   You're not well. You need treatment. Take it and we'll see what can be done about your work. If you don't take it, we'll have to get rid of you.

Derek breaks down and shouts, 'You're all against me. I'm going home!'

Tom tells Brian to let the team know that if Derek wants to talk to any of them, they are to refer Derek to him. He rings Personnel to let them know that Derek has not taken any of the routes they suggested.

Derek stays at home for 3 days. He returns saying that he wants to leave International Communications as soon as possible.

Tom   Give me your resignation in writing immediately. You can have 2 weeks' holiday now. Just don't come back to work. Is there anyone at home who can be with you?

Derek   My girlfriend is coming over. I will be with her for a bit.

Derek writes out his resignation and hands it to Tom.

Later that month Tom receives a telephone call from the Rehabilitation Centre telling him that Derek has admitted himself and has begun treatment.

the exercises

This case study is a much-abbreviated account of a possible incident concerning alcohol at work. It is probable that any group involved in such an incident will have to work through a series of questions once the problem person (in this case, Derek) has been dealt with. People close to the issue will seek to interpret their own actions long afterwards. Class discussion of the role play could explore some possibilities. There will not be conclusive answers to the questions raised by those possibilities. There will be many points that remain at the level of speculation. It is important that the issues are reviewed so that some learning takes place and that guilt does not overwhelm those who were affected by Derek's behaviour.

Identifying the problem

In terms of the way in which work was being done at International Communications, it is worth asking whether the difficulties between Education and IT may have contributed to the problem of Derek's drinking being overlooked until it became too late.

Would an earlier confrontation have helped, and if so, on what grounds might there have been such a confrontation? How many levels of disguise can be identified in Derek's behaviour?

Could Tom have identified a drink problem earlier? Could Derek's behaviour have been different had the problem been spotted earlier? What about the team members' part in this? How much did they handle before Derek's poor work performance became an issue? Could he have discussed the matter with any team members informally and outside the meeting?

The team's handling of Derek

How will the team feel now that Derek has left International Communications – relieved, concerned, defensive, guilty...? Is Tom feeling that he could have done more? How should he now relate to the team? Who owns the problem – both the drinking and the working difficulties? Can the problems be defined in ways that lead to solutions? How is the behaviour of Derek and the team interpreted at different points in the development of an incident? Could the team have handled Derek's behaviour in any different way prior to the meeting with Tom? Was Claire given an opportunity to put her views on Derek to the team?

General problems with alcohol in the workplace

What evasions or distortions are evident in the incident? Is there a failure on anyone's part to understand the consequences of behaving in a particular way? Is there a hesitancy or unwillingness to act on new perspectives on anyone's part? Could Tom have taken a less confrontational approach to Derek's behaviour? What of Derek himself? His behaviour is not untypical of people with an alcohol problem. What general lessons can be learned from this case? What recommendations would you make to Tom now that he has gone through this experience? What recommendations would you make to International Communications in terms of their alcohol at work policy?

FURTHER READING

The literature that effective confrontation is based on concerns individual counselling rather than help in the workplace.

Egan, G. (1994) *The Skilled Helper – A Problem-management Approach*. Brooks/Cole, California.
Nelson-Jones, R. (1996) *Effective Thinking Skills*. Cassell, London.
Special Committee of the Royal College of Psychiatrists (1986) *Alcohol: Our Favourite Drug: A New Report on Alcohol and Alcohol-related Problems*. Tavistock, London.

Students would do well to read these works in conjunction with the case study.

CHAPTER 6

Consulting

Binna Kandola

OBJECTIVES

The objectives of this chapter are to:

▶ give some insight into the consultancy process
▶ gain some understanding of the skills used in undertaking consultancy work
▶ provide the opportunity to practise using some of those skills.

INTRODUCTION

There are three exercises:

◆ Exercise 1 involves writing a proposal.
◆ Exercise 2 involves analysing data.
◆ Exercise 3 involves putting forward recommendations to the client.

All the information you require to complete the case study is provided – there is no need to make up anything!

Haven Lloyd plc

Structure

Haven Lloyd plc is the second largest retailer of children's toys in the UK. It employs about 1,200 people throughout the country. It has 47 outlets throughout the UK, mainly in England. Of these, 16 outlets are 'superstores' employing between 25 and 40 personnel. The remainder are high street stores employing between 8 and 22 personnel. The head office is located in Leeds and employs 276 people.

The organisation is structured into four regions: Scotland; northern England and the Midlands; south of England; and Wales. Each region has a director who has an input into organisational policy and has full accountability for his or her region. Each region is made up of approximately four areas, each holding several stores plus one warehouse, and is headed up by the Area Manager who reports directly to the Regional Director. Every store and warehouse has a Store/Warehouse Manager and two Assistant Managers, the remainder of the staff being sales assistants/warehouse personnel.

Head office is small and concerned mainly with policy formulation; it includes the Equal Opportunities Unit. The CEO, Human Resources Director, Finance Director and Sales and Marketing Director all work at head office. Responsibility is devolved to the Regional Directors as much as possible. Departments based at head office include marketing and sales, finance, human resources and training, corporate planning, purchasing and logistical planning.

the exercises

Putting together a proposal

You need to produce a short proposal outlining how your consultancy will tackle an equal opportunities audit. Your proposal should include:

◆ *Methodology* – what research methods will you use to get the necessary information? Where will you look for the information, for example with which groups of people, which documents and so on?
◆ *Other considerations* – are there any other issues which you need to consider?

The information you have includes:

◆ The invitation to tender (Figure 6.1)
◆ The case study, with background information on Haven Lloyd plc (the client).

Do not spend too much time considering the financial constraints, although, obviously, a consideration of resources is necessary so that your proposal is realistic.

Questions to consider are provided for you to complete your proposal. Do not worry about detailing every point here as long as you can explain the points in your group.

You should consider all this information when drawing up the proposal.

Haven Lloyd plc

8 September 1995

Dear

Further to our recent telephone conversation, I would like to formally invite you to tender for the proposed Equal Opportunities audit. We have identified four key questions which we need to address.

- How much have we achieved so far?
- How fair are our existing systems and procedures?
- How effective are our monitoring systems?
- What must we do next?

Our focus in the past has been consistent with a traditional equal opportunity approach, however, we are keen to broaden this to a managing diversity approach.

We need to receive the proposal by 15 September, and we will make our decision by 22 September. The project must be completed by 23 January next year.

Yours sincerely

Julie Fahey
Human Resources

Figure 6.1   Invitation to tender

QUESTIONS TO CONSIDER (1)

What research methods and sources of information will you use?

Are there any other factors that you need to take into account in conducting the project?

Analysing data

Your proposal has been accepted. You have completed the data gathering and are in a position to analyse the data.

Overleaf you will find a selection of:

◆ interview transcripts
◆ transcripts from group discussions
◆ sample documents
◆ a set of monitoring data from one region.

Based on these data, you should draw out the major themes, trends and patterns emerging and make a note of them. Remember:

◆ Think about what managing diversity means in practice before you try the exercise. What sorts of evidence will you be looking for?
◆ Remember to look at what interviewees do not say as well as at what they do.
◆ Try to illustrate your findings with quotes and other evidence.
◆ Try to organise your findings around the original four questions in the tender letter.

How you approach this data analysis is up to you. It may be helpful to split your group and have some people concentrating on the monitoring data and documentation, while others work on the transcripts.

Note: It should be assumed that the data presented here are representative of Haven Lloyd plc as a whole.

Jean Barlow

Scotland, Regional Director

Interviewer   What does EO mean to you?

JB   I think it's very important to be seen to be fair. I'm very aware of the cost of recent tribunal cases. Also of course, it's only right to give women and ethnic minorities a chance to get on, don't you think?

Interviewer   So what are you doing to promote this?

JB   Well, most of the EO initiatives seem to come from below. We have one person in every area who liaises with the EO officer in the HR department at head office in Leeds. I've heard some encouraging things about childcare schemes, and we have run some race awareness courses.

Interviewer   I see. What else?

JB   We've decided to write Equal Opportunities into the business plan for each area. Each one contains a sentence along the lines of 'It is part of our strategy to continually promote Equal Opportunities'.

Interviewer   What does this mean in practice?

JB   Well, obviously, it's early days yet, but I think I've mentioned some of the things already, like childcare.

Interviewer   What is the state of EO at the moment? For example, do you know the numbers of minority groups at various salary levels?

JB   Ah! You're talking about monitoring now, aren't you? I'm not so sure about monitoring – it rather hints at positive discrimination. Some people seem very keen on it, but I don't have any figures. Our staff are a pretty open-minded lot. I'm sure that there's no overt discrimination going on. Everything else is just 'icing on the cake', like the... childcare arrangements.

Interviewer   What involvement do you personally have in EO?

JB   Well, not an awful lot really. But the area managers are a wonderful bunch and seem to know what they're doing. I just deal with things at the regional level.

Interviewer   Is there anything else you would add?

JB   No, I don't think so. It will be interesting to see the results of this audit.

Michael Rothman
South East, Area Manager

Interviewer Can you tell me your views of the Equal Opportunities policy?

MR You should really ask Human Resources – I don't really know very much about that kind of thing, to be honest.

Interviewer I see, but I'd like your personal views on the matter. What do you see as the main issues?

MR Well, it's difficult to say really. As an Area Manager, I'm not the one who has to 'sell' EO. For Area Managers, it's not our specific responsibility. EO issues rarely come up at my team meetings, and I have very little personal involvement in it. It's just not my domain, and besides, it's not a priority. I see monitoring figures about once a year, maybe. Things seem to be chugging along just fine.

Interviewer So you're happy with Haven Lloyd's progress on EO to date?

MR Our record seems fine – I certainly haven't heard any complaints or cases being brought to tribunal. I think we're pretty good.

Interviewer Which initiatives do you think have been successful?

MR Well, now that the superstores open on Sundays, we've found that we have had to offer more flexible working to our sales assistants. Personally, I thought it would be really messy, but actually we've had a very positive response to it all. One store manager has started to advertise vacancies in local community newsletters. She's received applications from a much greater range of people, so that's worked well for her.

Interviewer Are any other store managers doing the same?

MR Not that I'm aware of... it's really up to the managers to decide how they go about these things.

Interviewer Any other things?

MR No, I don't think so.

Interviewer What about other human resource systems, for example appraisals, promotion and development.

MR I think we have guidance on all of those in the staff manual... though you will need to check with Human Resources. I'm not quite sure what that has to do with equal opportunities though!

Interviewer Anything else to add?

MR No, I don't think so.

Interviewer Thanks.

John Ho

West Midlands, Area Manager

Interviewer   What do you see as the main EO issues?

JH   Well, do you mean my personal view or the view commonly held here? Personally, I feel that it's good sense to make sure we develop and use all of our staff, no matter what. We need a loyal and committed workforce, so we have to give a little as well as take – this means helping those who need it.

Interviewer   Like who?

JH   Those people returning to work after childcare who need to update their skills, those who find it hard to learn, those who can't use our normal equipment... the list goes on.

Interviewer   You said your view weren't shared by others...?

JH   No, I think that most people do not have the same view. It's not really surprising; it's a difficult area and we need guidance on what is OK to do. It's a potential minefield out there.

Interviewer   What guidance do you have currently?

JH   I think EO has been written into the business plan, but it's just a cosmetic exercise. There are no guidelines or examples. I sometimes wonder if the Board's heart is really in it. We've got to decide if we're serious or not about this.

Interviewer   What do you see as your role in all of this?

JH   Managers should be aware that they are accountable for all the things that go on in their area of responsibility. This should include EO. My job should be to make sure this happens, to provide support and to act as a role model.

This isn't easy, but I have tried to make public statements about EO whenever possible. I also instigated an EO Charter, which my Regional Director and other Area Managers bought into and signed, as I did. This is definitely a local initiative, though. I haven't heard of anything similar elsewhere in the organisation. I think we've still got a long way to go.

Interviewer   How can the organisation progress?

JH   I think we really need a show of commitment from above. Also I feel that many of the initiatives have been fragmented... we really don't seem to have much of an idea about what we're trying to achieve here.

Interviewer   Have you any other comments?

JH   Just that I look forward to the results of this!

Interviewer   Thank you for your time.

TO26661

Robert Small

Oxfordshire, Warehouse Manager

Interviewer   What do you see as the role of EO at Haven Lloyd?

RS   EO is obviously important. I certainly don't want to be taken to court. We're doing our bit here, but I'm rather working in the dark.

Interviewer   What kinds of guidelines have you been working to?

RS   Well, I'm getting confused signals. We've only limited resources, and I don't know which EO initiatives to give priority to. And I'm not sure who I'm supposed to listen to... who has the power and authority on EO issues. Sometimes I feel like the rules are being made up as we go along.

Interviewer   What about the EO policy statement?

RS   Do we have our own policy statement?

Interviewer   What actions have you taken in this district towards the goals of EO?

RS   Well, we've introduced after-school care teams, which have been very successful. We've also started a liaison project with one of the schools in the town here. It has a mainly ethnic catchment area, and we wanted to try to attract more of them to apply. I think we've been seen as a 'white employer' for a long time. We've also pushed the part-timers idea. It's been very popular with both men and women with children, particularly married couples who both work here. We're thinking about a crèche next.

Interviewer   What is your personal role in this?

RS   Well, EO is driven by Human Resources up in Leeds – I try to give my support. I also try to support local initiatives. Sometimes you feel HR are too detached from us in the warehouse to really understand the issues.

Interviewer   What about ethnic monitoring data – do you see it?

RS   I'm sure we collect monitoring data, but I've never seen it. I don't even know who does it or where it's kept, come to think of it. Maybe it's a head office thing. I suppose at the end of the day, numbers speak loudest. I haven't actually seen any numbers myself... mmm, I'd never thought of that before.

Interviewer   Any other comments?

RS   No, I don't think so.

Interviewer   Thanks.

Sara Simms

Head office, EO Officer – Human Resources

Interviewer What do you see as your role?

SS Good question. Broadly speaking, my aim is to ensure that EO is continually promoted in the regions and here at head office.

Interviewer What does that mean in practice?

SS Well, the way it's working at the moment, it's been up to HR to get anything done. If we don't take a lead, then nothing happens. Our managers haven't really taken EO on board. To be honest, I don't see a lot of commitment from them. They spend a lot of time talking about EO, but they never do anything. Like I said, if we don't do anything, no-one will.

Interviewer What kind of things have you done, then?

SS Well, we've a pretty comprehensive childcare scheme operating at head office. We've also got a good record on job-sharing. We have a temporary promotion scheme, where people can gain experience at higher levels, although their pay is frozen. I think some of our women might benefit from this as there aren't too many of us at managerial level. There was a big push on the ethnic monitoring of the staff last year, but only about 70 per cent responded and the project died away.

Interviewer Do you monitor anything else? Recruitment, promotion, training opportunities?

SS We don't monitor recruitment. We use psychometric tests and interviews, so our selection is quite rigorous. I'm not sure that we need to monitor promotion.

Interviewer Anything else?

SS I'd like to check out the appraisal system, but managers tend to get a bit edgy about that. They don't think it's any of our business. It makes it more difficult that we have no real status or authority.

Interviewer Anything else to add?

SS No, I don't think so.

Interviewer Thank you for your time.

Roger Lewis

Head office, Director of Sales and Marketing

Interviewer Thank you for your time, Roger; I know you are very busy. I'd like to ask you some questions about equal opportunities here at Haven Lloyd.

RL   Fine. Fire away!

Interviewer   How familiar are you with the equal opportunity policy?

RL   I'm familiar with the essence of the policy, although I couldn't quote you the policy.

Interviewer   What would you say is the essence of the policy?

RL   Well, simply that everyone gets the same opportunity to be selected, developed and promoted irrespective of anything other than ability – is that right?

Interviewer   Is that philosophy something that you see being put into practice?

RL   Well, I think my own team resemble a fairly balanced workforce – I've got about a 50–50 split of men to women, and a few people of ethnic minority origin. Below my team, it's difficult to say. Certainly, in the stores, we employ a high proportion of women sales assistants – we find they are good with the kids and the mums.

Interviewer   What about the store managers?

RL   Ah, now I think we've probably got a higher proportion of men managers than women.

Interviewer   Why do you think that is?

RL   Two reasons. Obviously men are more geared to having a career than are women. Women tend to come for a few years, then leave when they start a family. They're not so interested in a career.

Interviewer   How many of the women return following maternity leave?

RL   Well, I couldn't really tell you... mmm, who could I wonder?... I suppose Human Resources would know. My impression is roughly half return, most of these part time, which obviously limits their career opportunities.

Interviewer   In what way does it limit career opportunities?

RL   Well, working part time is fine for shop assistants but beyond that level it becomes difficult because of problems with continuity, especially when you have responsibility for people. We found that actually here, in head office, where we had a marketing officer... Laura; she came back following maternity leave, part time. It was a hopeless situation. We work in project teams here. Laura was supposed to be heading one up, but of course couldn't make all the meetings. People got pretty fed up with the situation. It was fairly obvious that her commitment was affected by her home-life situation.

Interviewer   Thank you for your time, Roger.

Group discussion

Members of staff, Cardiff

Interviewer   How have the EO initiatives implemented by Haven Lloyd affected you?

Hanif   Oh, I don't think managers are too bothered about EO.

Jo   What about all the part-time working? That's a step in the right direction.

Hanif   That's good for women, but what about the ethnic minorities? That's all we ever hear from managers; part-time working equals new opportunities. Everyone knows that they needed to bring that in because of the staff shortages. And it saves them money.

Rebecca   There are a lot of part-timers now, but I don't envy them. I think they get a bit of a rough deal, and they can forget about promotion. 'Obviously not very committed,' my boss says about them. 'Can't even put in a full day's work.' It's not on – they really shouldn't be coming out with those sorts of comment!

John   That's right. Even getting on a training course isn't easy when you're a part-timer.

Jo   I suppose so. Not that there are many courses available at the moment. Then there's no point putting in the effort to get skilled up because there's no promotion anyway. Well, not for most of us anyway!

Rebecca   You see, promotion at our level is really down to how you get on with your manager. If you don't, then you can forget it. Most of the managers are white males, and they tend to get on better with other blokes like them, who they can have a pint with down the pub after work and talk football.

Jo   I'm quite lucky. My manager's really switched on and does his best to encourage and support everyone in the team. But he's definitely an exception.

Rebecca   Didn't he join recently from another organisation?

Jo   Yes, that's right. He's not your usual Haven Lloyd manager!

John   I'm registered disabled. In my appraisal, I was marked 'not fitted' for promotion. That really hurt – I'd the best performance record in the unit. So I appealed through the complaints procedure, and I won. That was my first mistake. I still can't get promoted, and the word is that I've been marked because I complained.

Hanif   Yeah, I'd never dare use the complaints procedure. They'll hold it against you forever.

Group discussion

Members of staff, head office

Interviewer How have the EO initiatives implemented by Haven Lloyd affected you?

Louise I think some of the things that have been done have worked extremely well. Last year, they ran some assertiveness courses for women. I went on one of the courses, and I found it quite useful.

Harshida I've never heard of those... though I'm not sure whether I would have gone on one or not. I think my manager would say that I'm as assertive as he'd like!

Gary To be honest, I'm struggling a bit with the question because I don't feel as if I know a great deal about this topic.

Harshida But that's probably not true because we all work for the same organisation and we are all subject to the same procedures... like the appraisal system and promotion...

Duncan Well, that rather depends on your line manager. It might be the same system, but they all seem to work it differently.

Omar I'd agree with that. I know people in the same job as me who get the same performance rating for doing work of a lower quality than mine.

Gary There's a lot of that actually... how well you get on with your line manager makes a difference. I've heard that, in some departments, you can tell who'll get the highest ratings by who's down the pub with the managers!

Louise It's not that different with promotion. It also makes a difference if you work part time.

Omar Yes, managers always think that they have to work around part-timers, they have difficulty in dealing with them... personally I think it's a problem of attitude rather than practicalities.

Gary It must be true, though, that working part time can break up the continuity in departments, and they can't feel the same commitment that a full-time worker feels?

Louise I'm not sure about that... I think that it should make no difference, especially when many of the part-timers at head office are women returning following maternity leave. They've got a lot of experience, and the organisation's probably invested a lot of money in their training.

Harshida Training – that's another hot potato! You're lucky if you have any development plan here, let alone actually get any development!

Gary Again, it comes down to the relationship that you have with your manager and whether he thinks that you have potential – whatever that means.

Harshida So, when are you going to tell us what the organisation is doing about all this?

SAMPLE DOCUMENT 1

Extract from Haven Lloyd's guidelines for recruitment

This is an extract from the guidelines produced by head office, which all recruiting personnel departments use when they are recruiting. It is a substantial document, running to 50 pages, covering everything from recruitment advertising to writing acceptance letters.

The extract below is the only reference made to EO.

'**Haven Lloyd plc is an equal opportunities employer. We aim to develop systems and procedures that will ensure equality of opportunity for all.**'

The EO policy statement above refers to 'systems and procedures', into which the recruitment process falls. We do not want to recruit unfairly. Two important concepts must be understood:

Direct discrimination
Direct discrimination occurs when a person treats another person less favourably on grounds of race or sex than he or she would treat someone else.

Indirect discrimination
Indirect discrimination occurs when the same mandatory rule is applied to everyone, but:

- a considerably smaller proportion of people from a particular group can comply with it

- it cannot be justified on grounds other than those which relate directly to the job

- it causes detriment or loss to those who cannot comply with it.[1]

It is, therefore, important to ensure that our recruitment and selection procedures do not produce direct or indirect discrimination.

---

[1] From *Psychometric Tests and Racial Equality*, CRE, 1992.

SAMPLE DOCUMENT 2

Extract from guidelines on appraisal procedures

The guidelines on appraisal procedures is a document originally prepared 6 years ago by head office. One day's training was originally offered (on a voluntary basis) to all managers involved in appraisals. Training is now given to all managers, although there is a waiting list of 6 months.

The areas of work/performance that are appraised are outlined here. Guidance for running an appraisal is outlined below.

Guidelines for managers

Before the actual appraisal interview, take 5 minutes to jot down some ratings about your appraisee, using the following scale:

1. *Present performance*

| 1 | 2 | 3 | 4 | 5 | 6 | 7 |

Very
unsatisfactory

Very
satisfactory

2. *Potential for management position*

| 1 | 2 | 3 | 4 | 5 | 6 | 7 |

Will never
make a
manager

Good
management
material

■ The ratings are intended for the appraisee's personnel record and should not be revealed to the appraisee.

■ Confine the appraisal interview to pointing out any areas for improvement.

SAMPLE DOCUMENT 3

Grievance procedure – outline of the procedure

Stage 1	Complaint received.
	Line manager considers the case to decide appropriate action.
Stage 2	Case addressed informally. An informal warning may be given.
Stage 3	If conduct does not improve, the case may be addressed formally.
	A formal warning may be given.
Stage 4	If conduct does not improve, formal disciplinary procedures may be instigated at the manager's discretion. The employee should maintain right of representation.
Stage 5	If conduct does not improve, the charge may result in dismissal. Authorisation for dismissal must be sought from a level of authority two grades above that of the line manager and in consultation with the Human Resource Department.

MONITORING DATA

One region in particular had kept up-to-date monitoring data of their staff relating to gender and racial background. These were felt to be typical of the organisation as a whole, and are shown below.

Grading structure

1	Clerical
2	Secretarial, administrative, sales assistants/warehouse personnel
3	Skilled administrative, assistant store/warehouse managers
4	Professional managers
5	Area managers
Personal contracts	Directors

Table 6.1   Workforce composition by grade, gender and ethnicity

	Male		Female		Total
Grading	White	Ethnic minority	White	Ethnic minority	
1	5	2	23	7	37
2	47	17	54	9	127
3	33	2	3	–	38
4	12	1	2	–	15
5	3	–	1*	–	4
PC	1	–	–	–	1
Totals	101	22	83	16	
	123		99		222

*Temporary promotion.

QUESTIONS TO CONSIDER (2)

What have Haven Lloyd achieved so far?

How effective are the existing systems and procedures?

Did any other points arise from the data?

Making recommendations

The final part of this exercise is to draw up recommendations for action. Using the information from Exercise 2, consider the issues listed below. Again, you need only record your recommendations in list form, although you should be able to explain them to the group.

Recommendations for action should be realistic – replacing management is not an option!

QUESTIONS TO CONSIDER (3)
Vision and strategy
System and procedures
Communication
Other issues

FURTHER READING

Conyne, R.K. and O'Neil, J.M. (1992) *Casebook of Organisational Consultations*. Sage, London.

Cookman, P., Evans, B. and Reynolds, P. (1992) *Client-centred Consulting: A Practical Guide for Internal Advisers and Trainers*. McGraw Hill, Maidenhead.

Lippitt, G. and Lippitt, R. (1978) *The Consulting Process in Action*. University Associates, US.

Nicholson, N. (ed.) (1995) *The Blackwell Encyclopedic Dictionary of Organizational Behaviour*. Blackwell Business, Oxford.

Tobias, L.L. (1990) *Psychological Consulting to Management: A Clinician's Perspective*. Brunner/Mazel, New York.

CHAPTER 7

Counselling

John McLeod

OBJECTIVES

The objectives of this chapter are to:

▶ examine the role and value of counselling in the workplace
▶ give some experience of using counselling skills
▶ consider different ways of providing effective counselling in work settings.

INTRODUCTION

It has always been part of the role of a good manager, supervisor or team leader to be able to respond constructively to the emotional and interpersonal difficulties of members of his or her team or department. In recent years, however, an increasing number of organisations have sought to augment the counselling skills of their managers by making professional counselling available to employees. This chapter looks at the counselling skills required by those working within organisations, as well as at some of the issues that can arise when an organisation utilises specialist professional counselling services.

There are two exercises in this chapter. First, there is a role play simulation that illustrates some common counselling dilemmas faced by people working in positions of responsibility within organisations. Second, there is a decision-making exercise that explores the issues that arise when an organisation sets up a counselling service for staff. The aim of these exercises is not to teach participants how to be counsellors – this is a skilled professional role that requires specialist training – but to examine the use of counselling skills and principles within an organisational context.

The nature of counselling skills

Counselling is a helping process, usually carried out in an individual face-to-face relationship, that has the aim of assisting a person with a problem to make some progress in the direction of resolving that problem. In the context of a counselling relationship, 'progress' can involve off-loading feelings and emotions, centre around achieving some new understanding or insight into a situation, or entail discussing new ways of acting or behaving. Counselling is a fundamentally 'person-centred' activity in that the goal is to help the person to arrive at the outcome that is right for him or her as an individual. It is a mistake to use the term 'counselling' to describe any activity that tries to persuade or control the person being counselled. For example, it can be confusing for staff if an organisation uses the term 'counselling' to include disciplinary warnings.

Counselling is a complex skill, and professional counsellors receive extensive training and ongoing supervision. However, it is possible to identify two basic rules that can be used by anyone who wishes to become more effective and sensitive in this area of their work.

Be clear about boundaries and limits

Someone coming to you for counselling basically needs a space in which to talk about whatever is bothering them. Your task is to make that space. You might want to check out that what the person wants is to 'talk through' something that concerns them rather than coming to you for some other purpose. It is helpful to be clear about how long you have by saying something like, 'Why don't we just look at this situation and see if we can make sense of it? I've got about 20 minutes today. If it needs longer, we can set up another meeting tomorrow...'.

Be as open as you can about the limits of confidentiality. It is often helpful if the person knows that whatever is said is 'off the record' or 'within these four walls'. On the other hand, you may need to point out that, for example, 'You know that I would have to act on anything you say to me that has a safety angle to it...'.

When you get close to the end of the time you have with the person, say something like, 'Well, we only have another couple of minutes... maybe it would be useful to just sum up what we've discussed.'

Listen to what the other person is trying to say

One of the main assumptions behind counselling is that most people have the capacity to sort out their own problems, if given support and encouragement. If you jump in too soon with advice or with your own theory of what has happened, you will cut across the person's ability to work things out for themselves. Because you are probably perceived as a powerful figure, this will have the effect of shutting them up and preventing either of you getting to the root of the problem.

The key skills here include *reflecting* back your understanding (for example, 'Let me just check out that I'm understanding what you're saying about this... it seems that...') and the use of *open-ended* questions (for instance, 'You said that you get most stressed out when the auditors are visiting... could you tell me more about that?' or 'You've talked a lot about the difficulties in the team... how would you like things to be different?... what's your feeling of how the team should ideally function?').

To summarise, it is useful to think of counselling as a conversation with someone who is accepting, honest and can be trusted, and who is genuinely interested in what you have to say.

You have been passed over for promotion – again. This is the third time this has happened, and you are really cut up about it. You feel confused because you have done all the right things to put yourself in line for promotion. You feel angry because of the kind of people who have been getting better jobs. You feel frustrated, desperate and angry because time is running out. However, you also feel some relief because you like working where you are now and are anxious about the increased demands that would be associated with a promotion. Your husband/wife/partner is putting a lot of pressure on you. You have got to the point at which you really need to air the problem with someone senior.

A colleague with whom you work closely, and need to depend on, has been under a lot of pressure and has been dealing with it by drinking too much. You are worried about how their drinking is affecting their ability to do the job. It's also causing problems for them at home. But you don't know how to confront this person. You are desperate to talk to someone about the whole problem and how you should deal with it, but you are worried about keeping it a secret.

You were the only person working late in the office when there was a break-in. Three raiders forcibly locked you in a cupboard while they stripped out the department's computers. At the time, you felt terrified and frightened, but you seemed to get over it. Now, you realise that you just don't want to go into the office at all and are looking for excuses to stay off sick. When you do go into work, you get distracted very easily, as if you were always hyperalert, and you get very tired by the end of the day.

the exercises

The above case studies illustrate some typical workplace counselling issues. These can be discussed in a group, but it is better to use them as the basis for experiential practice.

Divide the group into sets of three. Within each triad, take it in turns to be the counsellor, counsellee and observer. The role of the counsellor is to respond as helpfully as you can to the needs of the person being counselled. The role of the counsellee is to enter the role as fully as possible, perhaps adding some details drawn from personal experience of similar situations. The role of the observer is to keep time and to offer feedback at the end. Spend 10 minutes counselling, followed by 10 minutes feedback and discussion. During the feedback/discussion portion of the exercise, it is important to focus on the counselling skills of the person in the role of counsellor rather than to turn it into an extended therapy session for the counsellee. The counsellor should speak first, reviewing what they felt was helpful or hindering about their performance. The counsellee reports next, and finally the observer.

Choosing a counselling service for your organisation

You may be called on to participate in decision making around the type of counselling or 'staff care' package your organisation might use. This exercise explores some of the issues raised by this kind of decision. Your tasks are:

1. Break into groups of four or five.
2. Take 5–10 minutes to generate, individually, a list of what you would want a counselling service to achieve for your company or organisation. For example, you might wish to reduce sickness absence, improve morale and so on.
3. Share the items on your list with the other group members. What does this tell you about the contrasting counselling needs of different organisations?
4. There are essentially three models of counselling provision:

   (a) EAPs (Employee Assistance Programmes). An external company contracts to supply counselling (usually 6–8) sessions to your staff. Often staff contact the EAP via a telephone helpline and then meet with a counsellor based near to their home.
   (b) An in-house counselling service. Your organisation employs professional counsellors, often attached to the welfare or occupational health departments.
   (c) Peer counselling. A variant of (b), but in this case the counselling is carried out by members of the organisation, who receive counselling training.

Given the counselling needs of your organisation, what would be the advantages and disadvantages of each of these models? Spend 5–10 minutes individually on this question and then share your thoughts with the group. On a flipchart or whiteboard, list the plus and minus factors in relation to each model. Finally, look at the models in the context of the counselling needs of your organisation. Which model (or hybrid model) would be most appropriate in your organisational setting?

FURTHER READING

Carroll, M. (1996) *Workplace Counselling: A Systematic Approach to Employee Care*. Sage, London.

Carroll, M. and Walton, M. (eds) (1997) *Handbook of Counselling in Organizations*. Sage, London. Parts 1, 2 and 3 are particularly valuable.

Feltham, C. (1997) *The Gains of Listening: Perspectives on Counselling at Work*. Open University Press, Buckingham. Particularly refer to Chapters 1, 10, 11 and 12.

Highley, C. and Cooper, C. (1996) Counselling in the workplace. In Bayne, R., Horton, I. and Bimrose, J. (eds) *New Directions in Counselling*. Routledge, London.

Megranahan, M. (1989) *Counselling: A Practical Guide for Employers*. Institute of Personnel Management, London.

Megranahan, M. (1997) Counselling in the workplace. In Palmer, S. and McMahon, G. (eds) *Handbook of Counselling*, 2nd edn. Routledge, London.

CHAPTER 8

Crisis Management

Clare Allen and Morag Maddocks

OBJECTIVES

The objectives of this chapter are to:

▶ consider some examples of crises at work
▶ give experience of applying principles and skills to the effective management of crises
▶ apply learning gained from the exercises to one's own work context.

INTRODUCTION

This chapter examines ways in which crises may arise in the workplace. Three different scenarios are presented for study. They cover a range of situations that present different challenges and highlight how crises may vary in their potential impact on organisations and individual managers. The fourth exercise provides the opportunity to apply what has been learnt from working on the earlier scenarios to one's own work context. This is intended to facilitate effective implementation of learning.

Advice in using the exercises and supporting material is available in the Tutor's Notes. This includes a 'process for working through' and systematic approaches applicable to aspects of managing crises (some adapted from other areas of management and organisational theory), with relevant reading. You are encouraged to apply the approaches to inform analysis and in planning responses to the crisis situations, with tutor guidance.

Traumatic incident crisis

The setting is a health service community-based outpatient clinic. This is a relatively small building, that is, not a large hospital, and does not have its own security on site. It is staffed by a receptionist and various health professionals – doctors, health visitors, district nurses, and so on – who come and go depending on the particular clinics they run at different times in the building. Much of the time, they are working in the community so are not permanently on site.

This clinic provides a wide variety of health services to the public, normally by appointment. It does not provide care for people with drug or alcohol problems. The aims are to be accessible, to provide a friendly environment, and to encourage people to use these important resources in an area where there are considerable health needs most appropriately met in community settings.

Day 1

A man comes in and starts to argue with the receptionist in a threatening way – he is demanding to see a doctor, he has no appointment and he is demanding drugs. The receptionist tries to explain to him that he needs to go elsewhere to see a doctor for help with drugs, but he will not listen and becomes aggressive, shouting and pushing her over the counter and trying to get hold of her saying, 'Get me a doctor, now.' She rings through to the consulting room and asks a doctor who is in the middle of a consultation to come through to assist. While the doctor tries to calm the man down, the receptionist quietly telephones the police. The man becomes increasingly aggressive with the doctor, grabbing hold of him. He then takes out a knife and a struggle ensues, the doctor being seriously wounded. The man runs from the department, hitting two other staff (a health visitor and a district nurse) who have come out on hearing the noise. By the time the police arrive, the man has left. The doctor is rushed to hospital and has to undergo emergency surgery. The receptionist and other assaulted staff are severely traumatised. One is crying hysterically and another is shaking uncontrollably, while a third is wandering around with a glazed expression. Members of the public in the waiting area, including young children with their mothers, are clearly also upset. Meanwhile, people are continuing to arrive for their appointments. The manager covering this part of the service arrives on the scene after being contacted by the police.

Subsequently (in the days and first couple of weeks following the incident), severely traumatised, the receptionist refuses to return to work. Morale falls among staff who work at this and similar clinics, many expressing fears and resentment about the lack of security provision in their workplaces.

It is normal procedure in the organisation to make a report whenever there has been an accident to any member of staff or patient. The manager is responsible for the investigation and the report writing.

the exercises

exercise

1

How should the manager respond to this crisis?

Study the scenario and make brief notes on your analysis of and response to the situation. Work in a group to clarify the situation, analyse the problem and develop an action plan and a review process. The action plan should include ideas on how to deal with the immediate and short-term issues, as well as how to avoid future problems.

Use the 'process for working through' as a guide and include systematic approaches from Exercise 2 to inform analysis and planning (see Tutor's Notes for guidance here).

case study ▶

Critical absence crisis

It is Monday morning. Alan Haynes, Chief Executive of Hampton Health Trust, a large acute hospital, comes into work having had a shock telephone call the previous night informing him that David Smith, one of his senior managers, has been arrested and charged with manslaughter following a fatal car accident. He had been drinking and was well over the legal limit.

David Smith has carried responsibility for strategic planning and major service developments. He has three operational managers who report directly to him, one of whom, Alice Jones, only joined the Trust the week before. John Peters has worked with David for several years and is a close friend of his. The third manager, Michelle Wright, has a more difficult working relationship with him and has recently complained about aspects of his management style to the Human Resources Director, Jane Patterson. She spoke of his irritability and aggressive attitude, losing his temper with staff inappropriately. Although she has not reported it to anyone, Michelle has also been convinced on several occasions that David has been drinking at lunchtime. Some mornings he has come in late, muttering that he has had a 'heavy night' and looking as if he is suffering the after-effects of heavy drinking.

Alan Haynes had cause to raise concerns with him earlier in the previous week. Despite his putting in longer hours at work, David's performance was not satisfactory. He had missed deadlines and made careless errors in his presentation of reports. Morale around him seemed to be poor, and Jane Patterson has been concerned about his impact in the organisation. However, both she and Alan Haynes have been aware that David has had some family problems. They had hoped that, once these were resolved, his performance and attitude at work would improve. Nevertheless, the Chief Executive laid it on the line that, while he wanted to support him, given his level of seniority in the organisation, he could not allow standards to fall and expected to see some progress. David was contrite and assured Alan that it was only that he was under pressure at home and was sure he would be on top of things again soon.

In David Smith's office today, his secretary, Mary Francis, is in floods of tears, and people are suggesting that she should go home. The office is chaotic. There are piles of papers in a state of disorder on David's desk. Mary says he was never an organised person and would not let her file things regularly as he liked to hold on to current papers himself. The telephone is ringing with people wanting to know if the rumours about David are true, some asking if anyone has spoken to his wife and volunteering to go to see her on behalf of the Trust. The Press have been on, wanting confirmation and a comment from the Trust: 'This is the organisation that has been involved in health promotion about drinking and healthy living. Has it any comment?'

David Smith's diary for this week is very full. It includes among other things:

Today

1. A very important meeting as lead person for the Trust with the health authority, social services and other local Trusts to negotiate an agreement involving a potential joint development worth £1 million to the Trust. This meeting has been very difficult to set up because of co-ordinating the diaries of senior people in these organisations. As there are national development monies involved, the negotiations are constrained by tight, externally set deadlines. No-one else in the Trust has been involved in the preparation for the meeting, apart from David having consulted one or two clinicians. However, it is not clear with whom he has spoken.

2. A disciplinary meeting with a member of staff. An HR representative is also involved.

Tomorrow

3. A job-planning meeting with Alice Jones, who is still in her period of induction.

4. A meeting with the senior doctors to hear their grievances about nurse staffing levels on the wards. Mary Francis says that this meeting was difficult to arrange around doctors' clinics, and they have been pressing for it for several weeks.

---

the exercises

How should the organisation respond to this crisis?

Study the scenario and make brief notes on your analysis and response to the situation. Work in a group to develop an action plan. Again, use the 'process for working through' as a framework. Include different time scales, that is, ideas on how to deal with the immediate demands and forthcoming meetings, as well as preventive action planning.

Home–work interface crisis

Sally Mohammed is a senior manager with responsibility for children's services in Walford City Social Services. She lives with her partner, Anil, and two teenage children. Anil's job involves quite a lot of travelling away from home, but the family are used to this, and the children are now relatively independent. Her elderly widowed father lives 20 miles away in a neighbouring borough, on his own, and Anil's parents live 200 miles away.

Sally enjoys her job and felt pleased when she gained promotion to this post only 6 months ago at the age of 36, a considerable achievement given the average age of her (all male) colleagues at this level, which is 47. The job is very demanding. There are, as always in local authorities, constant pressures and uncertainties about budgets. Her predecessor took early retirement after a major enquiry into one of the children's homes revealed abuse. One of her priorities is to implement new policies for staffing and recruitment in residential care. This is proving very challenging as there are entrenched attitudes among staff and managers. Last week, a complaint landed on her desk from a member of staff about standards of care in one of the homes. This was followed by a warning from a shop steward that he believed people were trying to stir up trouble for his members in the same home by making false allegations. Sally senses this is going to need careful handling if she is going to avoid it escalating and creating barriers to the development work she is taking forward. She has arranged to see both the member of staff making the complaint and the shop steward separately today.

Meanwhile, Sally is increasingly worried about her father, Abdul. He seems to be having lapses of memory and getting confused. He is a stubborn, fiercely independent man and has always refused any suggestions that he might move into sheltered accommodation. Two weeks ago, she had a real scare when one of her father's neighbours telephoned her to say that he was concerned to see Abdul wandering round the garden in his pyjamas on a cold winter's day. She had driven over to see what was happening. By the time she got there, her father was back inside but was still in his pyjamas and seemed oblivious to anything being wrong. Indeed, he did not seem to recollect having been outside. She had previously noticed little things like his forgetting to turn off the gas and looking unkempt and untidy compared with how he used to be. She has begun to worry that one day he will have an accident.

Sally has discussed the problem with Anil and talked about whether her father might come to live with them as they have a small spare bedroom. Anil is not very keen, having had difficulties with her father in the past. He also worries about it placing another pressure on Sally, given the demands of her job and the children. The children are both studying for exams and have their bedrooms set up as studies. Like most teenagers, they feel strongly about their privacy.

Sally has been losing sleep, worrying about her father and what to do. She wishes he were nearer so she could pop home and check he is all right, but she knows that to have him live with them could be quite difficult. When she gets home, she just needs to collapse and recover from a stressful day. Recently, it has been hard to do that.

At work, she is aware that some people are jealous of her promotion, and there has been muttering about 'women not being up to the demands of the top jobs', which she has tried to ignore. She is now beginning to worry about her capacity to cope and has had the occasional crisis of confidence. She has been finding it difficult to concentrate and has made one or two mistakes recently, which is not like her. For example, she missed a recent meeting about the new staffing and recruitment policies as she had simply forgotten to check her diary. She is determined to prove herself in this job: it is what she has set her sights on for so long.

It is half an hour before her meeting about the complaint, and, just as she is about to study her notes in preparation, the telephone rings. It is her father's neighbour again. Abdul has set a chip pan on fire and the fire brigade has been called: 'Can you get over here right away?' Today of all days. Anil is away and will not be back until the weekend. She has given her word she will meet the staff member and union representative today. That situation has been getting very tense, and she does not want it to blow up.

the exercises

What is she going to do now and in the future?

First, study the scenario and plan for coping with the immediate crisis (Steps 1–3 in 'process for working through'). Reflect on the experience from Sally's point of view. In a group, discuss the alternative options and their possible implications.

Second, in the group, consider what recommendations you would make to Sally (and others if appropriate) about ways of reducing the likelihood of such a crisis recurring (Step 4 in 'process for working through').

Note: Proceed to Exercise 4 only after full discussion of Exercises 1–3. This is an individual exercise and can be supplemented by paired discussion with a colleague.

Personal application of learning to your own work context

During your exploration of the previous exercises, you will no doubt have found yourself making reference to your experience in your current or previous workplace. The following exercise will help you to consolidate your knowledge and understanding of the key principles that underlie effective crisis management. It will also increase your potential for its effective implementation in and application to your own work as a manager. Once you have completed it on your own, it is useful to discuss it with a colleague who, ideally, has undertaken the same exercise (Step 4).

Step 1
Identify what you anticipate might be common or potential crisis situations that could arise in your own organisation, based on your knowledge and past experience of it or similar organisations. For example, did you identify with any of the situations in the exercises?

Step 2
Identify what personal–work interface crises could theoretically arise for you, at some point in the future, that could have an impact on you and your organisation.

Step 3
Given what you have learned from your discussion of the previous exercises, and bearing in mind the principles that have been identified for effective crisis management, consider:

◆ How might you handle these potential crises on the day they were to occur?
◆ What would you find most difficult?
◆ What could you or your organisation do *proactively* to reduce the potential impact of such crises, through planning ahead, making contingency plans, developing systems, procedures and policies for good practice, and so on. Is there any further training or development that might help you personally feel more confident in handling crises effectively?

Step 4
Discuss your responses with a colleague or fellow participant. Help each other to identify options, particularly for dealing with those situations you anticipate being most difficult for you.

FURTHER READING

Fisher, R. and Ury, W. (1983) *Getting to Yes: Negotiating Agreement Without Giving In*. Penguin, Harmondsworth.

Morgan, G. (1986) *Images of Organization*, Chapter 6. Sage, Beverly Hills, California.

Parry, G. (1990) *Coping with Crises.w* Problems in Practice Series. British Psychological Society/Routledge, London.

Reason, J.T. (1993) The human factor in medical accidents. In Vincent, C., Ennis, M. and Audley, R.J. (eds) *Medical Accidents*. Oxford University Press, Oxford.

Regester, M. and Larkin, J. (1997) *Risk Issues and Crisis Management*. Kogan Page, London.

CHAPTER 9

Decision Making

Chris Clegg

OBJECTIVES

The objectives of this chapter are to:

▶ introduce 'how decisions happen' in organisations
▶ give some experience of decision making
▶ gain insights into decision-making skills
▶ give some experience of using those skills.

INTRODUCTION

This chapter is concerned with the ways in which people make decisions in organisations. It is organised around a role play exercise, which is itself based on a set of real organisational problems. The exercise involves people taking on various roles in a small manufacturing company and holding a management meeting at which to plan and agree some actions for improvement. More detailed advice on how to set up the role play exercise is given in the Tutor's Notes. The rest of this chapter is organised in three parts.

First, there is a description of a set of problems facing Loco Ltd, a medium-sized manufacturing company. Second, there is a description of a role play exercise based in the company. To prepare for this exercise, the participants need to refer to some literature; this is listed at the end of this chapter.

Loco Ltd – a company facing problems

Loco Ltd is a medium-sized capital engineering company that makes diesel locomotives to customer specification, usually for large corporations that have their own railway sidings. Customers include corporations involved in the extraction, processing and distribution of petroleum, steel and mineral products.

Loco Ltd either make new locomotives to order (usually in batches of one, although exceptionally in twos or threes) or rebuild (renovate) a customer's existing locomotive.

The company is based in the north of England and employs around 250 staff. It was family owned until recently, when it was bought out by a large multinational engineering holding company. The holding company encouraged Loco Ltd to increase its manufacturing capacity, and this was financed internally.

Loco Ltd has been hard hit by the latest recession and is struggling to survive. The local management team is coming under increasing pressure from the Divisional Director of the holding company, who is insisting on improvements.

Loco Ltd is organised in five main functions, as shown in Figure 9.1. The Sales Director is responsible for getting the business and for commissioning finished products on the customer's premises. Because of the recession, he has persuaded the company to hire a new Export Manager, who is responsible for developing business abroad, especially in the developing countries. This new manager reports directly to the Sales Director. The Design Director is responsible for the design of new locos and for any design work associated with rebuilds. He employs a small skilled team of experienced designers. The Purchasing Director is responsible for ordering and controlling parts for new locos or rebuilds. He is always under pressure from the Managing Director to keep stock levels low (too low, say the people in Manufacturing). The Manufacturing Director is responsible for building and rebuilding locos. His workshops are organised in several different areas, for example including a fabrication area, assembly bay, electrical shop and paint shop. Many of his staff are time-served, skilled workers. The Accounts Director is responsible for putting together any financial quotes and for billing customers, as well as for normal accounting reporting and good practice.

Figure 9.1   Organisational structure

To get some idea of how the company works, we can visualise work flowing through the company, first as a tender or bid for business, and then as a confirmed order if it gets the business. The principal workflows are represented in Figure 9.2.

Thus the Sales team visits potential customers trying to ascertain forthcoming demand. If a new loco or rebuild is required, the team asks the customer for a statement of their requirements. It develops a customer specification that it passes on to the Design team, which prepares a set of outline drawings for any non-standard parts (which are passed to Manufacturing) and a list of parts (which is given to Purchasing). Purchasing costs out the materials required (from the list of parts), and Manufacturing budgets for the hours it needs, at the same time estimating when it could fit the product into its build schedule. Accounts pulls together the estimated costs of parts and labour, adding in estimates for administration costs, overheads and profit. The Sales team can then go to the customer with a price, delivery date and guarantee of quality. On this basis, the Sales function negotiates with the customer.

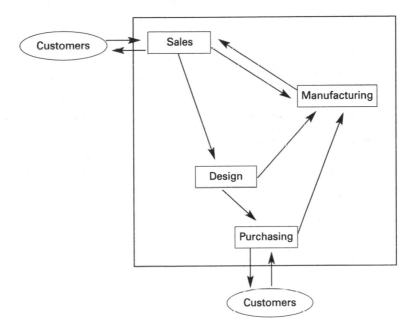

Figure 9.2   Principal workflows

Several additional points should be noted here. First, the actual process is more 'negotiable' than the above description suggests. To get business, especially in the current climate, the Sales team may promise tighter deadlines and lower costs (or lower margins). Second, it is not uncommon for customers to change their minds late in the process, for example preferring a rebuild to a new loco, perhaps because of their own financial problems.

If the company gets the order, the same sequence is followed, except this time in more detail. The Sales team prepares a full specification, which goes to Design, which prepares a full set of drawings for Manufacturing and a list of parts for Purchasing. Purchasing orders all the necessary parts. Manufacturing fits the loco into its build schedule and makes the product, in theory beginning work when it has the necessary drawings and the required parts. Accounts gathers the necessary information to charge the customer. When the loco is finished, Sales delivers and commissions it on the customer's premises.

Again, several additional points should be noted. First, the time lags in the system can be quite substantial. For example, it can take 18 months to make and deliver a new product from receipt of the confirmed order. Second, the impact of a decision made in one area can have substantial repercussions further on in the process, sometimes immediately, sometimes much later. For example, a decision not to work overtime in Design may slow down the drawings for a new loco and may mean that the people in Manufacturing are waiting for work. Similarly, a decision in Purchasing to keep low stock levels may result in a production delay on a critical path, that leads to a delay in the delivery of a product. Third, the management information systems in the company are not good. It is often difficult to trace the causes of delays and problems, especially when they have resulted from decisions in other functions. Indeed, the information systems tend to be organised within each function rather than across them.

In practice, the major sources of uncertainty are experienced by Sales, which finds the market hugely difficult to predict, and by Manufacturing, which experiences uncertainty at the hands of the other functions within the company. Manufacturing sees itself very much as the 'dustbin' at the end of the line, the place where earlier problems and decisions become visible. Needless to say, the other functions do not agree. Nevertheless, Design and Purchasing especially tend to 'pass on' their difficulties; for example, Design will say, 'We know we are behind but we can't do everything; so what do Manufacturing want us to do next?' Similarly, Purchasing will restrict the numbers of suppliers it uses, largely to make its own work more manageable.

To give some idea of throughput in the system, the company may at any one time be involved in preparing 20 bids or tenders, and be at various different stages in processing and manufacturing around 10–15 orders.

There are two mechanisms for integrating the work of the different functions, each involving weekly meetings. The first is a meeting of the heads of function (production supply meetings). This meeting is to discuss the progress of each tender and each product to try to ensure a smooth and integrated flow of work. Unfortunately, the Directors are often too busy to attend and usually send a deputy, and the meeting often discovers the problems too late for their avoidance. The second is a production meeting attended by the Manufacturing Director, his supervisors and the Parts Controller from Purchasing. This meeting has the same function as above, but is restricted to a concern for those products currently under manufacture. Again, the Manufacturing Director often cancels these meetings because he is too busy to attend. Without him, they do not take place.

Aware of the need for improvements, the Managing Director of Loco Ltd has hired a management consultant to undertake a study of its internal management and operational problems. In particular, the MD has asked her to look at two sets of 'organisational' problems, one focused on relationships between the different functions (the issue of integration), the other concerned with communication and 'employee morale'.

The consultant has used a range of techniques and sources to gather data, including interviews with managers and others, the observation of various meetings, the scrutiny of company accounts and documentation, and the administration of a company-wide opinion survey.

Attendance by the consultant at one of the management meetings has proved especially interesting. The Managing Director opened by asking why a particular loco was overdue: the customer was angry and penalty costs were being incurred. The Manufacturing Director said that the delay was largely due to receiving essential drawings too late. The Design Director accepted that this had occurred on this occasion, but he was short-staffed; his staff spent too long undertaking work for tenders that they seemed unlikely to obtain. The Sales Director re-stated his policy that they had to chase all available work given the economic climate. At this stage, a senior supervisor from Manufacturing interrupted: the problem wasn't just drawings. His staff were also often waiting for parts, picking up and putting down work in a way that prevented efficient operation. The Purchasing Director chose to remind the meeting that inventory costs had to be kept down; the days were gone when spares of everything could be kept in stock. Better planning and organisation were required. And so the meeting went on.

Venturing around the factory, the consultant has found that almost everyone she meets complains of low levels of co-operation and co-ordination between the different functions, each seeming to be pursuing their own goals, often suboptimally. Function heads are seen as 'empire builders', protecting themselves and covering their backs. Inter-personal relationships are largely satisfactory, but conflicts are high between the Director of Manufacturing and all the other function heads. To the others, Manufacturing is the major source of the company's problems.

Looking at the hierarchical dimension, management are complaining of the low commitment, motivation and effort invested by their staff. They do not seem to care. For their part, people on the shopfloor and in the offices are fiercely critical of the quality of management and of their communications. 'Mushrooms' are frequently mentioned. The only point of agreement is that morale is indeed very low.

Seeking some 'harder' facts, the consultant has found that performance is indeed poor. On average, for the preceding year, each new loco and rebuild ran over budgeted cost by 5 per cent, and each was delivered on average 8 weeks late. Profit margins, already under pressure, are inadequate.

In interviews, members of the management team all agree that Loco Ltd is good at designing new products, at manufacturing high-quality products and at satisfying customers' technical needs. Technically, the company remains very capable. But they also report some major weaknesses: at meeting date and cost targets, at co-operating between departments, at planning ahead, at predicting events outside the company and at keeping their employees happy. Managerially, they perform badly.

The Management team says things like 'We often don't have time to make good decisions', 'We spend a lot of time firefighting', 'Some things just don't get done, they seem to fall through the cracks', 'There is a lot of grumbling behind the scenes', 'People here have to defend and cover themselves' and 'Differences of opinion tend to get smoothed over rather than resolved.'

Furthermore, managers, foremen and indeed others report high levels of stress and pressure. For example, managers feel under pressure to make improvements, especially when the Managing Director holds them personally responsible for achieving a target in their area of responsibility.

For their part, people in clerical and shopfloor jobs complain that their views are not taken into account, that they are not given enough responsibility and that management keeps them in the dark. Levels of job satisfaction and morale are low.

The Managing Director has called a meeting to discuss what needs to be done and to make improvements to the performance of the company. The participants should now take up their roles.

the exercises

exercise 1

Role play

This is effectively a meeting of the company's managers. The task is to decide what should be done to improve the performance of the company, in particular to resolve the problems concerned with integration between the different departments and with communication and employee morale. The output of the meeting will be a set of decisions mapping out the way forward for the company. The meeting should last around 2 hours.

Students are asked to take the part of members of the management team addressing their problems. The principal roles are as follows:

- ◆ Managing Director
- ◆ Sales Director
- ◆ Design Director
- ◆ Purchasing Director
- ◆ Manufacturing Director
- ◆ Accounts Director
- ◆ Management Consultant.

There should also be two non-participant observers. More details of these roles are given in the Tutor's Notes.

The non-participant observers observe the ways in which the team makes decisions. They should attend all meetings set up by the role players, including for example any preparatory meetings of any subgroups. After the role play is completed, these observers report back to the group in a plenary session, describing what they have observed.

ESSENTIAL READING

List for non-participant observers only

These help the observers to consider decision-making processes and skills.

Gilhooly, K.J. (1990) Decision making and judgement. In Eysenck, M.W. (ed.) *The Blackwell Dictionary of Cognitive Psychology*. Blackwell, Oxford.

Klein, G.A., Orsanu, J., Calderwood, R. and Zsambok, C.E. (1994) *Decision-making in Action: Models and Methods*, Chapters 1, 5 and 23. Ablex, New Jersey.

March, J.G. (1991) How decisions happen in organizations. *Human–Computer Interaction*, **6**: 95–117.

Pugh, D.S. and Hickson, D.J. (1989) *Writers on Organizations*, 4th edn, Chapter 4, Decision-making in organisations. Penguin, London.

List for participants in the role play only

These help the participants to derive ideas for how the company could be reorganised and restructured.

Galbraith, J. (1973) *Designing Complex Organizations*. Addison-Wesley, Reading, MA.

Morgan, G. (1986) *Images of Organisation*, Chapters 3 and 4. Sage, Beverly Hills, California.

CHAPTER 10

Managing Diversity

Catherine Cassell

OBJECTIVES

The objectives of this chapter are to:

▶ introduce the concept of 'managing diversity'
▶ explore the significance (both psychologically and practically) of notions of 'difference' for individuals
▶ encourage participants to connect notions of individual difference to organisational strategy
▶ develop skills in applying managing diversity concepts to the construction of organisational action plans
▶ outline a workshop in which these issues can be addressed.

INTRODUCTION

The skills of managing diversity

Organisations are increasingly becoming more diverse in their composition. Examples are the growing number of women entering the labour market and the general aging of the working population. Managing diverse groups is now perceived as an important management skill. This chapter introduces a workshop designed to encourage participants to explore the variety of dimensions along which individuals differ and the ways in which diversity within a workforce can be effectively managed. The workshop is in two stages, as outlined below.

There is considerable debate over whether the skills associated with the successful management of diversity are essentially the same as the skills of 'good management'. It is indeed difficult to generate a precise list of the distinctive skills that a manager needs in this area. They would include, for example, being perceptive to the distinctive needs of individual subordinates, listening, delegating, negotiating and those skills associated with encouraging learning among employees.

A key theme, however, is that the manager needs to be aware of the range of characteristics in which individuals differ and the significance of those differences for their contribution in the workplace. For example, the stereotypes that particular differences such as age or sexuality may create within the minds of others may have an impact on an individual's work performance and experience. The Stage 1 exercise presented in this chapter seeks to address these issues by addressing the meaning of 'difference'.

The successful management of diversity is also about being able to design and implement policy within this area. The Stage 2 part of the workshop focuses on designing diversity interventions in a range of organisations. Given that a key underlying theme of the management of diversity approaches is the business case, it is important that such interventions can be linked into an organisation's overall business strategy. This forms the focus of Stage 2.

the exercises

Stage 1: The meaning of difference and diversity

This part of the workshop aims to consider the significance of difference for the individuals involved. The group as a whole is asked to consider the following question:

◆ How different are you? Take some time to think and then write down on a piece of paper five reasons why you feel different from the rest of the group.

After a few minutes, the tutor will ask participants to generate a list of the reasons why they may feel different. A list is then written up on a flip chart or board so that all participants can see. Some comment is made about the wide range of differences that are apparent within one group of people. A question is then posed for general discussion:

◆ What does this list of differences tell us about approaching the concept of diversity generally?

The group is then divided into smaller groups as the tutor deems appropriate. These small groups work through the following questions and report back after each:

◆ What do you think are the psychological consequences of these differences? How do they impact on people's behaviour at work?
◆ What are the organisational consequences of these differences? For example, how do they impact on the organisation achieving its goals?
◆ Are some of these differences more important than others? Do some have more significance for the individual or the organisation?

◆ Some people argue that these differences are irrelevant and that managers should focus on managing each individual in the same way. What are your views on this?

◆ To what extent can, or should, all of these differences be taken into account in the development of a managing diversity strategy?

The end of the discussion on these questions represents the end of the first stage of the workshop. Participants should now have thought through a number of the more individual issues associated with the management of diversity and should now be ready to think about these issues at a strategy-making level.

Stage 2: Designing a diversity intervention

At this stage, participants are divided into three groups, each of which is to act as a 'Diversity Planning Committee'. The task of this committee is to design a diversity intervention for one of the three organisations – Evans Cards, Simons Educational Publishers and Bubble-beautiful Cosmetics – described in the case studies below.

As an alternative, if the participants are all members of the same organisation, they may wish to design an intervention for their own organisation.

Evans Cards

Evans Cards was started by William Evans in 1874. Evans had an artistic talent that he used for drawing individual greetings cards for his family and friends. As demand for the products he made increased, members of William's family joined him in creating the more intricately decorated cards. As the products of the firm grew in popularity, Evans Cards began to expand, investing in its first printing press in the early 1900s. The business continued to grow and moved into the mass production of greetings cards for the family market. William, as Managing Director, was keen that some element of the origins of the company remained, and, despite the focus on mass production, a small sideline in the design and production of handmade cards remained.

After William Evans died in 1934, the firm remained in the family and is now managed by the Chief Executive, James Evans, who is William's great-grandson. The company headquarters, warehouse and packaging plant are housed in the same Lancashire town where William originally started the business in his own home. Orders for the cards produced by Evans Cards come from all over the world, and the company has recently started a mail order business. The demand for handmade products continues, but these are now dealt with by a series of 50 homeworkers who make the cards in their own homes. These homeworkers are mainly women from ethnic minority groups. There is a recognition within the senior management team that the company is in a position to expand. A couple of the directors believe that there would be a considerable market for Evans' products in the European Union. This diversification of markets, however, would require a more diverse set of skills from the sales and marketing staff. In particular, there would be a requirement for staff to work from a European office and be comfortable dealing with a set of managers from a range of European cultures. James Evans, however, is also keen that the firm retains its Lancashire roots. He believes that the handmade products are just as good and as popular as the product his great-grandfather produced years ago.

The company employs about 250 people. Seventy per cent of the work-force are women who work mainly on the production line, and 10 per cent are from ethnic minority backgrounds. All the managers and senior management team, except the Human Resource Manager (a white woman), are white males. Turnover in the company is generally low, although there has been some dissatisfaction expressed by the produc-tion staff about career advancement issues and issues relating to parenting. In particular, there are problems with turnover among the homeworkers. They are generally perceived as having little loyalty to the firm and are unreliable in meeting agreed dates for production. There has been some talk within the firm of investing in a team of artists employed officially by the firm who can be based in the firm's headquar-ters. The plan is that some of the current homeworkers will be employed on this basis. Early evidence suggests that they may not be particularly interested in this option. Indeed, the majority of these workers are women who fit their drawing work in with looking after small children. However, if the company is to diversify, a key aim of the directors is to 'get the homeworkers on board'.

The HR Director has suggested that the issues facing the firm are management of diversity issues. Although the other senior managers are uncertain, they have agreed to invite in a team of consultants to consider these issues further.

Simons Educational Publishers

Simons Educational Publishers was initially estab-lished in 1902 as a publisher of educational text-books. Starting off with a small printing press in a London back street, by the 1920s the firm employed 20 people in the selling and production of high-quality educational texts. After the 1944 Education Act, the demand for educational texts increased, and Simons became one of the leaders in the market, with a name for commissioning and publishing language texts. Initially focusing on English, the senior management team, after World War II, realised that there would be an increased demand for tuition in European languages. Their proactivity in addressing this new market led to the firm successfully developing a reputation as the leading publisher of foreign language texts. During the 1960s, the senior management team, led by Henry Birtles, predicted a growth in multicultural texts aimed at schools. In advancing into this area, Simons took a large share of what was to be an increasingly important market. At the same time, Simons was taken over by a large multinational media corporation. Henry Birtles and his senior management team felt that they had done quite well out of the deal, retaining the major decision-making power over the strategic direction of Simons, while benefitting from the networks carried by the corporation.

Currently, Henry Birtles still chairs the board of 18 directors at Simons. He is a powerful, charismatic figure, who is said to inspire his colleagues and staff. Birtles currently employs 430 employees. Although 53 per cent of the managers in the company are women, only three women sit on the Board. There has recently been considerable dissatisfaction among the female staff, who perceive that there is a glass ceiling at senior management and board level. Most of the female senior managers do not have children. Combining a successful career with motherhood is seen to be a difficult option, given the long hours and travel often associated with the work. Recent company evidence from the HR department suggests that talented female managers are leaving the company to work freelance, an option seen to tie in more favourably with raising a family.

By far the majority of employees at Simons are white. This creates issues with regard to selling multicultural texts. In the past couple of years, Simons have tried to recruit a number of ethnic minority publishers and sales people. Henry Birtles' view is that they will serve to keep the company on top of the growing multicultural educational market. Indeed, a number of clients purchasing multicultural texts have commented on the lack of ethnic diversity among Simons' selling staff. Where ethnic minority workers have been employed, they have rarely stayed at Simons long, commonly complaining about the lack of access to 'real' opportunities.

Given these issues, Henry Birtles has decided to invite a team of consultants into the organisation to assess whether there are 'any real diversity issues to worry about' or whether 'We're just like any other company.'

Bubble-beautiful Cosmetics

Bubble-beautiful Cosmetics design and distribute natural-based cosmetics and toiletries derived from vegetable and fruit ingredients. The company was founded in the 1960s at Glastonbury by two hippies dedicated to animal rights and environmentalism. They recognised that many of the visitors to Glastonbury at the time could benefit from the use of such products, and were concerned not to participate or invest in what were seen to be environmentally damaging products. With the benefits of a keen family investor, Jo Wilcox and Piers Francis toured the wilds of Europe and South America, finding appropriate ingredients for their products. On their return, they set up Bubble-beautiful. At first, they were keen to maintain a collective spirit within the company, and the organisation efficiently ran as a collective of 15 people for its first 5 years. The demand for Bubble-beautiful products was increasing rapidly, and their base in Glastonbury was seen as a prime site for tourist visitors. In 1971, Jo Wilcox married, and her new husband, Will Williams, became heavily involved in the company. Over the next couple of years, the company went through a period of turmoil as Will built up a power base around his own concerns about expanding the company within a more commercial framework, including the development of a mail order business. In 1973, a key turning point emerged, with a number of the initial members of the collective leaving, suggesting that they were unhappy that the collective spirit of the firm had somehow been lost. The next few years were times of considerable growth for the company. Moving to a larger shop in Glastonbury, they also opened outlets on Carnaby Street in London, and in Brighton and Edinburgh.

Currently, Jo Wilcox still has a major role in the company, responsible for Marketing and HR issues. Piers Francis is now in charge of the research and development of new products and spends much of his time searching the globe for exotic ingredients on which to develop new products with his partner, David. Meanwhile Will Williams is MD of the ever-expanding firm. Those three key individuals still maintain much of the idealism of the 1960s, and company policies are seen to be quite liberal. Recently, however, there have been a number of instances in which staff have complained about their treatment. The company currently employs over 900 people at mail order distribution sites and shops all over Britain. Each of these sites is headed by a 'co-ordinator' whose job is to oversee the operation of the company in that outlet. Twice a year, the trio meet regularly with the co-ordinators, but they will also make site visits as necessary. In practice, the top trio rely on the co-ordinators to run their own outlets in line with the company's guiding philosophies. HR policies in each of the outlets may consequently be considerably different. The head office is still in Glastonbury, seen as the 'spiritual home' of the firm. About 20 per cent of the workforce is gay or lesbian. As a result of the company image and philosophy, and the open homosexuality of one of its founders, Bubble-beautiful has always been seen as a relatively safe place to work, free from discrimination. However, some members of this group are now asserting that they are treated less favourably than heterosexuals when it comes to management opportunities. In particular, there have been suggestions that outside the Glastonbury headquarters, there is considerable intolerance towards gay and lesbian staff.

Jo Wilcox is extremely concerned about this situation. Being deeply committed to equal opportunities, she is considerably distressed that such discrimination may be happening within her firm. Additionally, this kind of allegation could threaten the good reputation of Bubble-beautiful, which is renowned for not just its products, but also its radical philosophy. She has therefore, in conjunction with Piers Francis and Will Williams, decided to approach a group of consultants to see if they can provide some advice on developing an overall strategy on managing diversity for the company as a whole. She is keen that all employees feel that their talents are recognised and rewarded regardless of any differences that may exist between them.

---

the exercise

Each group is given 1 hour to prepare a presentation to the rest of the group. In preparing the presentation and discussing the relevant issues, participants can refer to the diversity interventions checklist (Figure 10.1).

Once the preparation time is over, each group presents its plan to the rest of the participants. After each stage, the tutor leads the whole group in an evaluation of the presentation. Key questions will include the following:

◆ What response do you think the plan will receive from diverse groups within the organisation and from the senior management team?
◆ What problems did you have in devising the plan?
◆ Are there any particular problems you would anticipate in the implementation of the plan?
◆ How does the plan link in with the overall business strategy of the organisation?

After each of the presentations is over, the instructor leads a general evaluation of the plans. Key questions at this stage are:

◆ What are the similarities and differences between the organisational situations?
◆ What are the similarities and differences between the diversity plans?
◆ How well does each plan respond to the unique situation in which it will be implemented?

The tutor concludes by leading a general discussion on what the participants have learned from the exercise. Questions here include:

◆ What were the key difficulties you experienced in devising the diversity plan?
◆ Is it possible to link in individual needs with organisational goals?
◆ Can the demands of managing diversity interventions link in with overall business strategy?
◆ Overall, what has this exercise taught you about managing diversity?

The tutor then brings the workshop to a close by drawing out the key themes that have emerged and concluding as appropriate.

1. **Research**

◆ What research do you need to conduct in order to design the intervention?
◆ What information do you need?
◆ How will you access that information?
◆ Whom do you need to talk to?
◆ What do you need to ask them?
◆ What other research is necessary (for example, an audit of company culture)?

2. **The context of the intervention**

◆ What is the motivation behind the intervention?
◆ Is there a vision?
◆ What is the scope of the intervention (for example, to all the diverse groups)?

3. **Designing the intervention**

◆ What are the objectives of the intervention?
◆ What will it consist of?
◆ Who will be involved?
◆ How will assumptions be addressed?
◆ How will systems or structures be addressed?
◆ How will the intervention be communicated?

4. **Implementing the intervention**

◆ How will the intervention be implemented?
◆ Who will be responsible for implementation?
◆ What will be the timescale?

5. **Evaluating the intervention**

◆ How will the intervention be evaluated?
◆ What criteria will be used for the evaluation?

6. **Issues in the long term**

◆ Who will be accountable for diversity issues in the future?
◆ How will they be accountable?
◆ What will be the role of the consultants in this process?

Figure 10.1 Diversity interventions checklist

FURTHER READING

Cox, J.T. Jr (1991) The multi-cultural organization, *Academy of Management Executive* **5**(2): 34–47.

Ellis, C. and Sonnenfeld, J.A. (1994) Diverse approaches to managing diversity, *Human Resource Management* **33**(1): 79–109.

Jackson, S.E. (1992) *Diversity in the Workplace: Human Resource Initiatives*. Guilford Press, New York.

Kandola, R. and Fullerton, J. (1994) *Managing the Mosaic: Diversity in Action*. IPD, London.

Ross, R. and Schneider, R. (1992) *From Equality to Diversity: A Business Case for Equal Opportunities*. Pitman, London.

Thomas, R.R. Jr (1990) From affirmative action to the effective management of diversity, *Harvard Business Review* **68**(2): 107–17.

Thornberg, I. (1994) Journey towards a more inclusive culture, *HR Magazine* February: 79–96.

CHAPTER 11

Equal Opportunities

Janette Webb

OBJECTIVES

The objectives of this chapter are to:

▶ introduce the concept of 'mainstreaming' equal opportunities in a public sector organisation
▶ give some experience of devising such an approach to equal opportunities
▶ gain insights into some of the political and practical problems surrounding the management of equal opportunities
▶ develop some of the skills of negotiating and managing equal opportunity policy.

INTRODUCTION

The chapter is concerned with understanding and experiencing a 'mainstreaming' approach to equal opportunities in public sector organisations. It is constructed as a role play exercise, using materials derived from local authorities. The exercise requires people to play the parts of councillors, officers and union representatives, prepare short presentations and hold a meeting of the Equal Opportunities Member–Officer Working Group in order to make progress on the Council's EO strategy.

Further details on the roles, associated tasks and suggested structure and content of the meeting are given in the Tutor's Notes. The rest of this chapter is organised in four parts:

◆ a description of the background to local government reorganisation
◆ a description of the Council, with particular reference to its approach to EO
◆ a description of a role play exercise and task assignments based in the Council
◆ briefing notes to support the role play.

Suggestions for further reading are included at the end of the chapter.

Local government reorganisation and the new unitary local authorities

During the 1990s, local government has been subject to large-scale restructuring. The aim has been to reduce costs, and change local government from service provider to enabler, through a variety of partnerships and contracts with private and voluntary sector suppliers. One of the major strands of reorganisation has been the progressive shift from two-tier (regional and district) to single-tier unitary councils. This case focuses on Midshire, one of the new single-tier councils, which has responsibility for education, social work, housing, roads and transport and economic development, as well as sharing the responsibility for police and fire services. In common with many authorities, it has sought a more streamlined organisational structure: a corporate management team controls strategy and finance, but operational control is devolved to service departments with fixed budgets.

New structures and budget cuts have led Midshire Council to reappraise its equal opportunities policy. It has been influenced by ideas from Europe and the USA, which suggest that the 1970s model of good practice is costly and inefficient. The old-style solution was to create a specialist EO unit, responsible to a Council committee. The new Council views this as over-bureaucratic and as creating another opportunity for empire building by officers. Midshire wants to devise a form of EO practice consistent with the corporate style of management and has decided to try 'mainstreaming', which aims to integrate EO principles into every area of activity. An EO working group, with membership drawn from councillors and senior officers, is responsible for devising the overall framework, setting targets and reviewing progress. The EO working group reports to the Policy and Resources Committee, which governs Council strategy and finance. The responsibility for implementation is devolved to line managers, whose departments have to develop an action plan and specify appropriate performance indicators for their area. There are no specialist EO officers, and mainstreaming itself is something of an unknown. Midshire Council nevertheless hopes to put itself on the map by becoming one of the first councils to exemplify the approach and to demonstrate its effectiveness.

Midshire Council

The Council serves urban and rural areas, comprising a total population of 125,000. There are approximately 50,000 households, over half of which fall into the lowest council tax band. Although the area was relatively prosperous until the 1960s, international competition and technological change have reduced the industrial base and resulted in high levels of unemployment, particularly for young people, and substantial long-term unemployment among older men. A number of small communities are suffering considerable poverty as a result of the loss of jobs in the deep-mined coal industry.

The new Council has 30 elected councillors (25 men and 5 women), with a Labour majority. The councillors are extremely concerned to tackle poverty and deprivation in the community and are acutely aware of the need to make efficient use of restricted resources. There is consequently a small management team comprising a chief executive and deputy, and directors of education, social work, housing, commercial operations, support services, community services, finance, economic development, personnel and technical services.

Midshire Council's mission statement

In order to define service priorities, the Council agreed the following statement, which was printed in leaflet and poster form for distribution in Council offices and in the community:

Midshire's Commitment

Midshire aims to be a good council to have working for you and to be a good council to work for

The council's key values are:

Quality, Equality, Access and Partnership

In serving the people of Midshire, the council will seek to:

- eliminate poverty, deprivation and unemployment
- protect the weak and vulnerable
- secure a quality environment for living and working
- strive for a society based on equality and equal opportunities.

Working in partnership with others, the council will seek to deliver good and accessible services

---

EO strategy

The next step was to agree strategy documents to guide the Council in relation to economic development, social provisions, environment and equal opportunities. The Equal Opportunities Member–Officer Working Group met to draft the EO strategy, which was endorsed by the Council's Policy and Resources Committee. The following statement constitutes the agreed summary:

As an employer and provider of services, Midshire council will promote equality of opportunity. No employee, job applicant, customer or recipient of services will receive less favourable treatment than any other because of race, religion, ethnic or national origins, disability, age, gender, sexuality, marital status, responsibility for dependants or political affiliation.

The three primary areas for action are defined as employment, service delivery and the wider community.

Employment

The Council is a highly significant local employer, with a wide range of professional, administrative, technical, secretarial and clerical, skilled engineering and manual occupations. It is therefore responsible for setting a good standard for other local employers, for the fair treatment of staff and job applicants, and for employing staff who will provide good service to the community. It aims to overcome the effects of past discrimination by positive action where appropriate and to reflect the composition and diversity of the community in the make-up of its own workforce.

The immediate responsibility for implementing the policy in relation to employment falls to the personnel department. The officers have to devise an appropriate job application form with an EO monitoring form, and specify a code of practice and complaints procedure. The Council intends to monitor the application of its policy through an audit of the workforce, giving a breakdown of staff by grade, gender, ethnicity, age and disability. It will also record and compare the profile of job applicants with the profile of those appointed and promoted. The detailed workforce audit will not, however, be available until the computerised personnel system is up and running. Meanwhile, the personnel office can report that 23 per cent (or 8 out of 35) of chief executive and chief officer level staff are women. Overall, approximately 62 per cent of the staff are women. Almost half of the women, compared with 7 per cent of the men, work part time. The vast majority of women part-time workers are in clerical/secretarial and manual grades. Women are well represented overall in the professional and administrative grades, but fare less well at senior and middle management levels. Men predominate in the technical, engineering and crafts grades, hold a high proportion of jobs in professional and administrative grades, and dominate the senior posts.

Equal pay and the manual workforce
The Council employs over 2,000 people responsible for providing cleaning, catering, refuse collection, housing repair and maintenance and gardening services. The Council is required to submit most of these services to competitive tender. It has so far maintained the contracts in-house by competitive bids and is concerned not to lose such contracts, not least because it retains control of any surpluses generated and secures the managerial and administrative jobs that might no longer be local if contracts went to the private sector. It is, however, increasingly clear that compulsory competitive tendering (CCT) has had a deleterious effect on the pay of women manual staff and has widened differentials between men's and women's pay (Escott and Whitfield, 1995). Occupational segregation remains pronounced, men having a virtual monopoly of refuse, street cleaning and maintenance jobs, and women having a similar monopoly of school and office cleaning and catering jobs, and domestic care work. An extract from the national New Earnings Survey data for 1996 (Table 11.1) demonstrates the gender impact of competitive tendering in the manual grades across the whole of local government.

Table 11.1   Full-time average gross weekly earnings of men and women in local authority manual occupations, covered by national collective agreements

	Men (£)	Women (£)
Average basic pay	175.00	149.10
Overtime pay	32.60	14.20
PBR pay	37.10	2.50
Shift pay	6.30	6.20
Total pay	**251.00**	**172.00**
Average percentage change in pay April 1995–96	-1	-12

Source: Adapted from New Earnings Survey (1996).

The summary figures show that:

◆ On average, men's pay in the manual grades continues to be higher than women's. Women's average basic pay is £149.10 per week; men's average basic pay is £175 per week. The differential is widened by the significant element of payment by results (PBR) or bonus elements included in men's pay (£37.10 per week as opposed to £2.50) and by overtime.

◆ On average, women's weekly pay was 12 per cent less in 1996 than it was in 1995, while men's pay was 1 per cent less. This statistic suggests that women manual staff have been particularly adversely affected by the operation of CCT and the use of 'market rates' to lower women's pay relative to men's.

Although Midshire Council is aware of the effect of competitive tendering on pay differentials between men and women, it has defended its strategy as producing the 'least worst' outcomes. Jobs in cleaning and catering hold predominantly by women are not well paid, but terms and conditions of employment are nevertheless better than those in the private sector. Tenders based on more favourable pay rates for women would result in the private sector being able to undercut the Council bid.

During the first year of the Council's operation, however, there was a significant industrial tribunal decision that the Council has had to take into account. Catering staff providing school dinners in the former Cleveland County Council won an equal pay case, with awards totalling £4 m. The women, members of the Unison and GMB unions, asserted that, despite carrying out work of equal value, their pay was between 20 and 40 per cent less than that of their male comparators, including gardeners and refuse collectors, because the men received significant bonus payments over and above basic rates. Midshire is now represented with other councils on a national working party to consider the implications of the tribunal decision for manual grade payment systems. In line with its EO policy, it wishes to remove the anomaly whereby bonus payments add significantly to men's earnings despite men and women carrying out tasks evaluated as equivalent (or indeed carrying out extremely similar tasks in the case of street cleaning versus building cleaning). There is, however, a difficult conundrum to be resolved. The Council's preference is to limit the bonus element in men's gross pay. The union position is that bonus payments should be introduced for women on a similar basis to those of the men: men's manual pay is not, after all, generous. The Council argue that they cannot afford to do this and that anyway, if they did, the women would lose their jobs as a result of the Council's bid for the tender for cleaning and catering services being undercut by private sector competitors, employing cheaper female labour. There may be a way forward as a result of the Labour government's plans to introduce a 'best value' system for local government services in place of CCT. The system will retain an element of cost competition, but in association with other indicators of quality. The other factor to consider is the probable impact of a minimum wage. The Midshire Council representative on the national working party on bonus payments is responsible for drafting outline proposals to present to the next meeting.

Service delivery

The legislative framework provided by the Sex Discrimination, Race Relations and Disability Discrimination Acts makes it unlawful to discriminate against any member of the public or section of the community in the provision of goods, facilities or services. Although good practice in relation to employment has been developing for at least 20 years, EO in service provision has been less actively debated. The council has outlined the following priorities that it seeks to address:

◆ *Access* – it needs to ensure that it is taking action to ensure reasonable access to services for everyone in need
◆ *Service users' charter* – it wishes to develop specific commitments to users with appropriate complaints procedures and review processes
◆ *Complaints procedure* – it needs to establish a procedure and specify how it would work, who would have executive responsibility for its implementation and how it would be monitored and reviewed.

As part of its agreed social strategy, the council aims to promote equality, particularly on behalf of women, people with disability and the black and ethnic minority communities.

Women:
◆ make up 52 per cent of the local population
◆ are 94 per cent of lone parents, two-thirds of whom are economically inactive
◆ are more likely to act as carers
◆ are under-represented in the decision-making processes of local government
◆ comprise two-thirds of the single person elderly households.

People with disabilities:
◆ are over three times more likely to be unemployed
◆ are likely to be in lower-paid jobs if they are employed
◆ suffer the effects of shortage of appropriate housing for independent living
◆ are often excluded from access to buildings and transport.

Black and ethnic minorities:
- ◆ experience harassment and institutional racism in access to employment, education, training, housing opportunities and service delivery
- ◆ are more likely to be unemployed or in low-paid jobs
- ◆ are poorly represented in the decision-making processes of local government
- ◆ are likely to be represented by organisations that are under-resourced.

In each case, specific action plans need to be determined.

The chief executive and management team have the day-to-day responsibility for developing and implementing appropriate provisions, with the Policy and Resources Committee having ultimate political authority.

The wider community

The Council perceives that it can potentially influence other organisations and individuals in the area with respect to good practice on EO. It seeks therefore to work in partnership with private and public, voluntary and community groups and individuals to challenge discrimination. The Equal Opportunities Member–Officer Working Group needs to give careful thought to using its influence proactively across the wide range of local organisations routinely using Council services or acting as suppliers of goods and services, and to make a series of proposals in a paper to be presented to Policy and Resources Committee at their next meeting.

the exercises

Roles to be assigned:

Officers
Appoint a chief executive and directors of personnel, finance, commercial operations, and social work. Depending on the number available, others could take the parts of directors of education, housing, community services and so on.

Council members
Appoint a leader of the Council (to chair the Planning and Resources Committee) and convenors of the personnel sub-committee, social work committee and commercial operations. Two participants should be assigned roles as councillors, with experience of the previous regional Council, which had specialist women's and race relations committees, and an EO unit staffed by specialist officers. These two should play the part of 'devil's advocate' during the discussion of the pros and cons of the mainstreaming approach to EO. Depending on the number of participants, others could act as convenors of housing, education and community services.

Union representatives   Appoint one or two people to represent Unison and GMB, depending on the number in the group.

Role play

During the first half of the session, the class should divide into the following subgroups and prepare short papers as set out below. During the second half of the session, the papers form the basis of verbal presentations to a full meeting of the EO Member–Officer Working Group.

1. *Chief executive and leader of the Council*
   - Prepare a short statement explaining the concept of mainstreaming and setting out the key points in the case for its adoption (see below for briefing notes).
   - Prepare to lead a discussion with the Equal Opportunities Member–Officer Working Group to establish what actions the Council can take to ensure that EO is 'built in with the bricks' rather than an 'optional extra' or a merely cosmetic operation. They should bear in mind that there is no dedicated budget and that finances are severely constrained.

2. *Two councillors sceptical about what can be achieved through the use of mainstreaming*
   - Summarise the arguments about the disadvantages and limitations of mainstreaming, to present to the Equal Opportunities Member–Officer Working Group meeting, under item 1 on the agenda detailed below (see below for briefing notes).

3. *Personnel director and convenor of the personnel subcommittee*
   - Compose outline statements describing interim measures to be adopted pending the introduction of the computerised personnel system.
   - Using the sample job application form provided (see below), devise a draft EO monitoring form as a detachable front page, which would be held centrally in the personnel department and used to produce an annual report on EO in recruitment. What other information would the personnel department need to collect in order to know whether suitably qualified applicants from under-represented groups were being interviewed or offered jobs?

4. *Director of commercial operations, convenor of commercial operations committee and union representative(s)*
   - Meet to draft proposals to resolve the gender discriminatory pay differential in the manual grades. These proposals are for presentation to the Equal Opportunities Member–Officer Working Group meeting, to be discussed before they are taken forward to the national working party on manual grades payment systems.

5. *Director of social work (and others if numbers permit) and convenor of the social work committee*
    ◆ Compose outline statements on:
      access issues
      a service users' charter
      a complaints procedure.

6. *Other officers and councillors*
    ◆ Compose outline statements on what priorities the new Council should adopt in relation to service delivery for:
      women
      people with disabilities
      black and ethnic minority people.

Second half of session

The chief executive and the leader of the Council convene a meeting of the Equal Opportunities Member–Officer Working Group. The leader of the Council should chair the meeting. He or she should announce the following agenda and appoint a minute-taker. The minute-taker should note points of agreement, points to be amended or deferred for further meetings, agreed action points and who is responsible for taking the action forward. Draft statements brought to the Group may be agreed, amended or referred back for further development. The minutes should be written up, signed by the leader and chief executive of the Council, and presented, together with agreed documents, as a public account of progress on EO strategy.

Agenda

1. Debate on strategy for mainstreaming EO – led by chief executive.

2. Employment and personnel strategy – led by director of personnel.

3. Manual grades payment systems – led by director of commercial operations.

4. Service delivery

    4.1 Draft statement on: access; service users' charter; complaints procedure.

    4.2 Draft statement on priorities in relation to service delivery for: women; people with disabilities; black and ethnic minority people.

5. Any other business.

BRIEFING NOTES ON MAINSTREAMING EO

Mainstreaming seeks to promote equality of opportunity through the integration of an EO dimension into all strategic analysis, policy development and implementation. It also seeks, through monitoring and review processes, to assess the effects of strategy on specified groups.

Mainstreaming has been a recognised approach since the EC's Third Action Programme and is a central facet of the Fourth Action Programme. In 1996, EU President Jacques Santer asked all Directorate Generals of the EC to report back on progress towards equal opportunities, and the Council of Ministers announced that the Commission intended to mainstream EO in all its activities and policies. There is, however, limited practical guidance available in EC documents.

Arguments for mainstreaming

◆ It enables the cost-effective use of resources – no special budget is needed and there is a limited upfront expenditure.

◆ Mainstreaming seeks to tackle the broad institutional environment and the culture of organisations by 'building equality in with the bricks', requiring every line manager to be proactive in identifying the EO implications of every strategy, to set appropriate 'performance indicators' and to report progress at least annually.

◆ It protects initiatives against cuts when finances are under pressure and councils have to find areas in which to cut back. EO specialists are 'easy targets' for cuts in spending, whereas mainstreaming EO makes initiatives integral to all services.

◆ Mainstreaming may smooth the path for initiatives perceived as unpopular or politically contentious. For example, in relation to gay and lesbian issues, if proposals are seen to be emanating from an EO committee and/or specialist unit, they may be more easily dismissed than if they are legitimised through an integral commitment to equality.

◆ EO specialisms are perceived as producing cumbersome, bureaucratic and inflexible procedures and are seen as relatively ineffective in challenging broad patterns of occupational segregation or social division.

◆ EO units may become 'ghettoised' and ignored by service departments.

◆ There are likely to be significant financial penalties linked to the failure to mainstream EO, given the pattern of increased awards in recent industrial tribunal decisions.

Arguments against mainstreaming

◆ There is a danger that a lack of specialist expertise in EO will result in poorly formulated, ineffective strategies.

◆ Mainstreaming may result in nothing more than a 'tick the box' cosmetic approach to EO. The strategy provides an incentive to departments to devise non-risky, easily achieved performance indicators, so that they are able to report 'positive' results in the annual monitoring round, but this may boil down to little more than 'appointing an extra tea lady'.

◆ It is notoriously difficult to devise meaningful performance indicators, much less measure progress towards them or their attainment.

◆ The consultative, inclusive style entailed by mainstreaming may paradoxically raise the expectations of targeted groups, which, if not met, cause resentment and hostility, and a subsequent loss of political support for the council members.

◆ There is an argument that mainstreaming results in a watered-down version of EO: the disadvantages faced by women differ from those faced by disabled people, which differ from those faced by black and ethnic minority people. Sympathy is more easily generated for 'visible' disadvantage, such as that experienced, for example, by wheelchair users. This may produce a hierarchy of 'good causes' with disability at the top, while other groups gradually disappear from view unless they have an effective political presence on the council.

SAMPLE JOB APPLICATION FORM

Midshire Council
An Equal Opportunities Employer

APPLICATION FOR EMPLOYMENT   *Confidential*

Please use black ink and block letters, or typescript, and return to the address shown on the accompanying letter.

(Please refer to notes for guidance)

---

1   POST DETAILS   POST REFERENCE NUMBER:

Department: Post Title:

---

2   PERSONAL DETAILS: This information is contained in Part A

FOR OFFICE USE ONLY	Do you hold a driving licence?
Applicant Number	Yes ☐ No ☐
	State Class of Licence

---

3   QUALIFICATIONS:
Please give details of qualifications held or awaited (include band of pass wherever relevant)

---

4   SPECIALISED TRAINING:
Please give any details of specialised training, for example apprenticeship, shorthand, typing, youth/government training courses, in-house training and so on that you consider relevant to this post

---

Initials box ☐

5   MEMBERSHIP OF PROFESSIONAL BODIES

Please give details of any professional bodies (including class of membership, method of entry and dates of admission) that you consider relevant to this post

6   CURRENT EMPLOYMENT   (or most recent employment)

Name and address of employer:

Dates from   To

Basic salary/wage   £   Per week/year

Additional supplement/bonus etc.   £   Per week/year

Notice required:

Position Held:

Please give a summary of duties and responsibilities

If you are not currently employed, please give the reason:

7   PREVIOUS WORK HISTORY

Please give brief details of your previous work experience in addition to that described in no. 6 above

List in order, with the most recent employer first

Employer	*Dates*	*Post held*	*Reason for leaving*

8   STATEMENT IN SUPPORT OF APPLICATION

Please state why you are applying for this post; refer to any knowledge, skills, experience or other factors that you would consider relevant to this position

Please continue this statement on a separate sheet if required.

9 REFEREES

Please give name, address and occupation of two referees, one of whom should be your current or most recent employer or has known you in a work capacity, if previously employed. Please advise clearly if you object to a referee being contacted prior to an interview

1   Occupation   2   Occupation
     Telephone   Telephone

10 JOB SHARING

Do you intend to apply for this post on a job-sharing basis?   Yes/No

If yes, please indicate your preferred work arrangement:

11 HEALTH

1   How many periods of absence have you had as a result of illness in the past 2 years?

2   Have you been absent through illness for more than 2 consecutive weeks during the past 2 years?   Yes/No

3   Are you aware of any medical condition that could affect your performance in the post applied for?   Yes/No

12 DISABILITY:

Disabled persons who meet the essential criteria will automatically be interviewed

Do you have a health problem or disability that you consider has a substantial or long-term adverse affect on your ability to carry out normal day-to-day activities?   Yes/No

If yes, please provide details:

If called for interview, please state any help you may require (for example, signer, wheelchair access and so on)

13 ADVERTISEMENT SOURCE

Where did you see this vacancy advertised?

14 REHABILITATION OF OFFENDERS ACT 1974

The Rehabilitation of Offenders Act 1974 (Exceptions) Order 1975 as amended applies to many posts within the Council, particularly in those departments that provide education or social work services.

If selected for interview, you will be required to complete a Criminal Convictions Form.

15 WORK PERMIT

Do you require a work permit to take up employent in this country?   Yes/No

ACKNOWLEDGEMENTS

The case is derived from ongoing research on gender relations and local government restructuring, funded by the ESRC and EOC. The members of the research team are Esther Breitenbach, Alice Brown, Fiona Mackay and Janette Webb, all of Edinburgh University. The case, while describing a fictional council, concerns real dilemmas and problems encountered by councils in our study of reorganisation. I wish to thank all of the local authorities, agencies and trade union officers who have greeted the research team with generosity and openness despite enormous pressure on their time and resources. I am particularly indebted to East Ayrshire Council for copies of relevant background documents and material.

REFERENCE AND FURTHER READING

Cockburn, C. (1989) Equal opportunities: the short and long agenda, *Industrial Relations Journal* **20**: 213–25.

Escott, K. and Whitfield, D. (1965) *The Gender Impact of CCT in Local Government*. EOC, Manchester. A summary pamphlet is also available from the EOC.

Liff, S. and Dale, K. (1994) Formal opportunity, informal barriers: black women managers within a local authority, *Work, Employment and Society* **8**: 177–98.

Solomos, J. and Back, L. (1995) *Race, Politics and Social Change*. Routledge, London.

Stewart, J. and Stoker, G. (eds) (1995) *The Future of Local Government*. Macmillan, Basingtoke.

Webb, J. (1997) The politics of equal opportunity, *Gender, Work and Organization* **4**: 159–69.

CHAPTER 12

Information Overload

Paul Sparrow

OBJECTIVES

The objectives of this chapter are to:

▶ convey the range of problems that surround 'information overload' in a modern organisation

▶ provide students with some analytical skills that will enable them to identify the root source of much information overload, that is, the design of jobs

▶ gain insights into the types of decision and action in the organisation that lead to excessive information overload, and some simple changes that can help to manage it

▶ provide an exercise that can be adapted to most real-life situations and provide tutors with hard data around which to construct critical discussion.

INTRODUCTION

This chapter is concerned with the problems of information overload that face many employees and many managers responsible for designing the jobs of other people. Information load is defined as 'a complex mixture of the quantity, ambiguity and variety of information that people are forced to process. As load increases, people take increasingly strong steps to manage it' (Weick, 1995, p. 87). Load is typically measured in terms of:

◆ the number and difficulty of decisions and judgments that the information requires
◆ the time available to act
◆ the quality of information processing required
◆ the predictability of the information inputs.

Overload implies an excessive burden and encumbrance that is sustained with difficulty. The chapter is organised around an analytical exercise that can be used to identify and characterise the interactions that form a major part of many jobs and a major source of information overload. Detailed advice on how to manage and adapt the exercise is given in the Tutor's Notes. The rest of this chapter is organised in three parts. First, a scenario is laid out which enables students to understand the nature and scope of the problem. Second, there is a set of instructions on how to conduct an interaction analysis on a target job. Third, in order to prepare for this exercise, and to be able to critically analyse its results, essential reading is outlined.

case study ▶

The problem scenario

July 1999

Lawrence Segal had just been appointed as HR Director. His new organisation had been through all the traumas of the 1990s. It had survived and prospered, and was now a 'lean, flat, empowered, nimble firm focused around core processes that make it capable of delivering customer delight'. And, of course, people were its biggest asset. He smiled at the language the strategy documents used, but he knew that considerable effort had been devoted to putting most of these changes in place. New employees had become knowledge workers. They worked long hours, were committed to their jobs and kept the organisation in profit through their ingenuity and efforts. But, in talking to employees, he wondered how this was possible. They complained that at times the work seemed like chaos. They worked under intense pressure and felt that the organisation was sinking under the weight of information it generated, jobs were poorly co-ordinated, no-one seemed to do what they should with the information that was generated, they spent much of their time checking and rechecking data, often for no other reason than internal politics, and they knew that by the time it was filtered, most of the information that was passed on was not worth the paper it was written on. Even the information that was powerful never seemed to get to the person who could or would do something about it. The biggest favour Lawrence could do them, he was told, was to redesign their jobs and get rid of the 'information overload' that they faced before either they or the organisation began to crack. A lot of good people were talking about getting out of the madness.

He sensed that they were right, but where to start? What was 'information overload' anyway? He did some research, starting with the Internet. Clicking his way through his favourite search engine, he entered 'information overload' as key words and got a list of 327 entries. However, many of these were obviously not to do with his interest. They were small press articles, technical telecommunications reports and library journal articles on personality. So he put the printout in his briefcase to look at when he had more time. The next day, reading it on the train, he noticed that one of the sources was a home page for a professor from an HRM group and looked relevant. He asked his secretary to access the page and download whatever looked interesting. As he was listening to his voice mail later that day, a beep on his computer alerted him to an incoming e-mail. Attached to the message from his secretary was a document lifted from the professor's home page. This document made it clear that information overload was one of the biggest problems facing managers today. It pointed to a number of problems:

◆ Managers are bombarded with a considerable volume of both data and information, which is often of poor quality and low value.

◆ The 'information load' on managers has increased because of the need for managers to assess the value of the information they come across, to analyse contradictory data and to devote time to improving poor-quality data.

◆ Information overload is leading to more dysfunctional behaviour. As load increases, managers start to make more errors and misinterpret important messages.

But so what, Lawrence thought? What could he or his managers do about this? Could they develop an instrument to help to assess the level of information load on some important jobs? He knew that time management and prioritisation skills, stress management skills, developing a learning company and improving decision-making processes and creative problem-solving skills would all be part of the solution. But to Lawrence, these were all reactive changes designed to cope with the aftermath of the problem. Reading the review from the home page, he was clear that he wanted an analytical exercise that would help managers to understand the scale of the problem in the first place and then identify the root cause of the information overload. He was sure that redesigning the organisational structure and changing job designs would form a major part of the solution. Someone had to redesign the 'interactions' that took place within the organisation so that the information load they carried was more manageable. Lawrence decided to contact the research group.

August 1999

A month later, Lawrence has a number of reports and documents from the research group. These have proved helpful in shaping his thinking. One of the documents specifies an exercise that can be used to review the interactions that take place around a key job. Given the amount of job analysis, evaluation and business process re-engineering that is always taking place in the organisation, adding a small pilot exercise to conduct an interaction analysis would be easy enough and something that the HRM team could easily handle. Whoever handled this exercise needed to do a thorough job and would have to show some leadership and originality in the task. The team could sort out the detail of exactly what would be analysed, but Lawrence wants a critical report on their findings in a month's time.

the exercises

exercise

Interaction analysis method

You are part of the HRM team that has been asked to analyse the problem of information overload. You have access to the article about information overload on the professor's home page. The research team has also provided you with details of a method that can be used to examine the problem, a technique known as interaction analysis. A simple way of describing interaction analysis is that it enables the job analyst to identify 'who says what, to whom, how often, and why'. Interactions occur in many forms – a meeting, conference, telephone call, sales call, informal conversation, access to the office groupware, sending a report, memo, letter or an e-mail, or a data search. The variety is almost endless, but each medium is associated with a different load and richness of information. The data that the exercise produces can be used to generate a more efficient job design, that is, one that reduces *unnecessary* information load. The exercise to be followed here is a simple one. Its purpose is to enable you to:

◆ analyse the interactions that take place within an individual job
◆ gather empirical data that will help you to evaluate the information load involved in this job
◆ devise recommendations on how any problems, peaks or overload may be dealt with by the job holder and his or her manager.

The first task is to identify the job and the job holder(s) that should be analysed. In essence, you will require the job holder to record data about all the different types of interaction that are involved in their work at a number of different time points over a number of days. To do this accurately, you will have to attend first to the following four tasks:

1. negotiating the purpose of the exercise and the use of the data with the chosen job holder(s)
2. devising a customised form that you can use to record the information load that is associated with the interactions
3. setting up a method for data collection
4. considering how you wish to analyse the data.

Preparing the interaction analysis form

The most important task is to devise a proforma that you can give to job holders so that they can record the types of interaction that take place around their job. This proforma should help you to identify who was involved in the interaction (the initiator and target), what communication medium was involved (the type of interaction), the frequency and duration of the interactions, and the information load or strain associated with each type of interaction. A sample form is provided as guidance in Figure 11.1.

Identifying the likely sources and targets of an interaction
It will help the job holder immensely if they are given some guidance on how to complete the interaction analysis form. Before designing your form, you should investigate the nature of the work carried out and create a list of typical *initiators* of the interaction (that is, the people or units who send the

interaction to your job holder), as well as the targets for the interaction (that is, the people or units to whom they send information if they have initiated the interaction). To identify probable targets, you can either interview senior managers to find out the anticipated interactions that will take place, run a focus group with job holders or get a group of job holders to brainstorm ideas. You might chose to recombine the 'interactors' into more easily identified groups; for example, a 'financial officer' and 'accounts clerk' may be grouped into the 'accounts department' for the sake of simplicity.

Deciding the frequency of recording

As with any job analysis technique, you must decide on how often you will ask people to record their activity. This decision has to balance the inconvenience to the job holder with the need for an accurate recall of what has happened. The recommended time interval is to ask job holders to break off work and record their activity every hour. They can usually recall the telephone conversations, messages and meetings in which they have been engaged over the period. They might time themselves, use an alarm beeper to time intervals or perhaps be telephoned by you as a reminder.

A related decision is to decide over how long a time period you should gather data. Some jobs are highly routine, and every day is the same. Others may suffer from information overload at particular periods of the day or week. Perhaps there is a critical period that occurs sporadically that you need to capture. Again, some interviews before the exercise or piloting can ensure that you gather a valid picture.

Designing the recording forms

The recording forms should be designed so that all the necessary information can be recorded and coded quickly. The form should be user friendly, quick and relatively simple. Each job or role you analyse is different, so you need to customise your data collection accordingly. However, the main principles and types of data to be recorded and outlined are the same (see the sample form in Figure 11.1).

The job holder should complete a form for *each type of interaction* that occurs in the recorded time period, for example one to cover telephone calls, one for a meeting and so on.

You will need to devise a rating sheet that measures some important qualities in relation to information load associated with the job. These measures should enable you to make an assessment of the load carried by the interaction and the importance of the information being brokered. Some sample questions for which rating scales could be developed are listed in Figure 11.1. These cover the information load or strain, the meaningfulness of the interaction, and its criticality. Not all questions may be deemed relevant or practical for your job holder.

Deciding who collects the data

The interaction form may be designed to be completed by the job holder. However, you might be the person who codes the data if you actually observe the person or arrange to interview/telephone them at set intervals.

Training the job holders

The job holders may clearly need to be trained and counselled by you. Each item on the form should be explained beforehand. You may also wish to observe job holders at some stage or find some other way of validating the data.

Interaction analysis exercise: analysis of data

The exercise has been designed to enable a range of useful analyses. The information revealed by the interaction analysis can provide detailed insights into the information load associated with a particular job. The data can be used to calculate the total volume of interactions, by type and by nature. A calculation of the average level of information load and types of information demand can be made. A plot can be made of peak time periods or blockages. The data may be used to identify highly redundant or irrelevant information, especially if the data are collected across a number of job roles. The possibilities and areas for critical evaluation are quite wide.

INTERACTION ANALYSIS FORM

Time of recording:

◆ Day, hour

Type of interaction (please tick one):

Interpersonal sources:
◆ Formal face-to-face encounter/conversation
◆ Informal grapevine

Company sources:
◆ Company publication, for example newsletter
◆ Bulletin board, notice board

Communication media:
◆ Reading of printed material, for example article, newspaper, computer printout
◆ Telephone call
◆ Written letter or memo
◆ Written report
◆ Meeting/conference
◆ e-mail
◆ Computer, for example access to a database, contribution to a project via groupware computer program

---

Other:

Role played in the interaction (please tick one):
◆ Sender of the information/initiator of the interaction
◆ Receiver of the information/recipient of the interaction

Frequency of this type of interaction in last (hour):
◆ Number

Duration of the interaction:
◆ Number of minutes occupied

Interaction qualities:
Reason for the interaction (tick one):
◆ Needed as part of an information enquiry
◆ Needed for job holder to complete an information analysis
◆ Requirement for job holder to develop or add value to the information covered by the interaction
◆ Simple dissemination or forwarding to other people

Information load/strain:
◆ How predictable was the information? 'Quite predictable' to 'Very unexpected'
◆ Quality of initial information involved? 'Very low quality/highly ambiguous' to 'Very good quality/clear'
◆ Level of information processing or thought required by the job holder in the interaction? 'None' to 'High quality of thought and analysis'
◆ Number of decisions or judgments required by the job holder as a result of the interaction? 'None' to 'Several'
◆ Number of information elements/interdependencies with other people or actions to be considered? 'All information elements clear' to 'Need to consider several possible dependencies'
◆ Time available to act? 'No real urgency' to 'Immediate decision/action'
◆ How long will the information involved be relevant or current? 'Situation will change almost instantly' to 'Relevant for a long time to come'

Meaningfulness of the interaction for either the job holder or the person they interact with:
◆ Provides a specific directive about the tasks necessary to complete their work? 'Not at all' to 'Clear directions given'
◆ Helps to explain the rationale behind a job or make a decision transparent? 'Not at all' to 'Very much so'

◆ Explains or conveys the nature of the company and the nature of its policies? 'Not at all' to 'Clear explanation'
◆ Provides some feedback on work performance? 'No feedback involved' to 'Strong feedback'
◆ Provides information that could help the organisation to set its goals? 'Of no use' to 'Potentially very relevant'

Criticality:

◆ Consequence to you or the organisation if the interaction had never taken place? 'Absolutely none' to 'Very serious ramifications'
◆ Consequence of an error being made in the information you received or sent? 'Absolutely none' to 'Very serious ramifications'
◆ Centrality to your role? 'Need to know who to contact about the information' to 'Need to have personal and detailed knowledge of the data'

Figure 11.1   Sample interaction analysis form

ESSENTIAL READING

Butler, P., Hall, T.W., Hanna, A.M. *et al*. (1997) A revolution in interaction, *McKinsey Quarterly* **1**: 5–24.

Daft, R.L. (1995) *Organisation Theory and Design*, 5th edn, Chapter 9. West Publishing, St Paul, MN.

Finke, R.A. and Bettle, J. (1996) *Chaotic Cognition: Principles and Applications*. Lawrence Erlbaum Associates, Hillsdale, NJ.

Finke, R.A., Ward, T.B. and Smith, S.M. (1992) *Creative Cognition: Theory, Research and Applications*. MIT Press, Cambridge, MA.

Fisher, D. (1993) *Communication in Organizations,* 2nd edn. West Publishing, St Paul, MN.

Heyer, S. and Lee, R. (1991) Rewiring the corporation, *Journal of Business Strategy* **12**(4), 40–5.

Huber, G.P. and Daft, R.L. (1987) The information environments of organisations. In Javlin, F.M., Putnam, L.L., Roberts, K.H. and Porter, L.W. (eds) *Handbook of Organisational Communication*. Sage, Newbury Park, CA.

LaBarre, P. (1996) Knowledge brokers, *Industry Week* **245**(7): 50.

Norman, D. (1985) Twelve issues for cognitive science. In Aitkenhead, A.M. and Slack, J.M. (eds) *Issues in Cognitive Modelling*. Lawrence Erlbaum Associates, London.

Weick, K.E. (1988) Enacted sensemaking in crisis situations, *Journal of Management Studies*, **25**: 305–17.

Weick, K.E. (1995) *Sensemaking in Organisations*. Sage, London.

CHAPTER 13

Innovation

Nigel King

OBJECTIVES

The objectives of this chapter are to:

▶ give an understanding of the skills involved in initiating and managing innovation in organisations
▶ provide experience of using some of these skills, through practical exercises
▶ encourage a critical awareness of the complexity of innovation processes.

INTRODUCTION

This chapter focuses on one of the most difficult challenges facing organisations: the management of innovation. The importance of innovation is widely recognised and, in the past few years, has been the subject of major policy initiatives at national and international levels. There is an abundance of advice available to managers on how to manage innovation successfully, in the form of popular texts, training courses and organisational change consultants; in fact, a veritable innovation industry has come into existence since the appearance of best-sellers such as *In Search of Excellence* (Peters and Waterman, 1982) and *The Change Masters* (Kanter, 1983), in the early 1980s. However, there is probably no area of management education in which overgeneralised and oversimplified advice can offer such traps for the unwary. My aim here is not to detail a set of specific skills that will *all* be required in *all* innovation management. Instead, it is to enable you, through the experience gained from practical exercises, to recognise the range of skills which – to different degrees in differing combinations – is likely to be needed when managing an innovation process.

Two quite different exercises are provided: the first, a role play and discussion; the second, a comparison of contrasting group idea generation techniques. Both are linked to a case study, based on a real-life example of managing innovation.

Tipper and Watkins

Tipper and Watkins Ltd is a small engineering company that specialises in manufacturing machine parts for the textile industry; it is based in the medium-sized northern industrial town of Kirksbury. It is an old family firm, established in 1884, and until recently top management positions were always filled by family members. Two years ago there was a major break with tradition when old Mr Tipper, then Managing Director, was succeeded on his death by an 'outsider', Mike Falmer, who had formerly worked for a rival firm. The Tipper family were forced into this radical step by difficulties that the firm was facing, losing out to competitors for its share of a shrinking market. The company shed a third of its workforce at this time, leaving it at its current size of 42 employees.

Mike Falmer immediately saw the need for major change at Tipper and Watkins. The company was very hierarchical, with virtually no communication across departments except at the top level. It made no real efforts to scan its environment for potential new markets, preferring to concentrate on its very good relationships with a relatively small number of long-established customers. Managers at all levels had little or no formal training in managerial skills; the emphasis was entirely on understanding the technical side of the company's business. Although there was a recognition of the need to innovate in order to compete, the product innovation process invariably followed the reactive model shown in Figure 13.1, below. The notion that more effective product innovation might necessitate organisational and managerial changes was scarcely even considered. Overall, the culture of the organisation reflected the values of the production department, by far the biggest department in the company, comprising almost half the employees. Production emphasised stability, continuity, quality control and the imperative to avoid any disruption to the manufacturing process at all costs.

Falmer took things slowly during his first year, thinking it best to 'get his feet under the desk' before introducing any major changes. In the last year, however, there has been quite a shake-up: top and middle managers have been sent on a variety of training and management development courses, cross-departmental project teams have been set up to work on the development and marketing of new products, decision-making powers have been devolved and democratised, and a small group of managers and senior engineers has been established to begin exploring the possibilities of diversifying into new areas outside the textile industry. The old product development division of the production department has become a separate research and development department, enlarged from three to seven members, including staff moved in from marketing and finance. Mike Falmer himself has participated in the Mercurius Innovation Program run by Lewis Lear Consultants (LLC), a management consultancy firm with strong links to manufacturing industry in the region. The program covers idea generation techniques, leadership skills and team building.

Reactions to Mike Falmer's initiatives have been mixed: staff at all levels are uncomfortable about changing the nature of the firm, but there is a widespread recognition that, without change, the future for Tipper and Watkins looks bleak. The strongest resistance has come from two of the

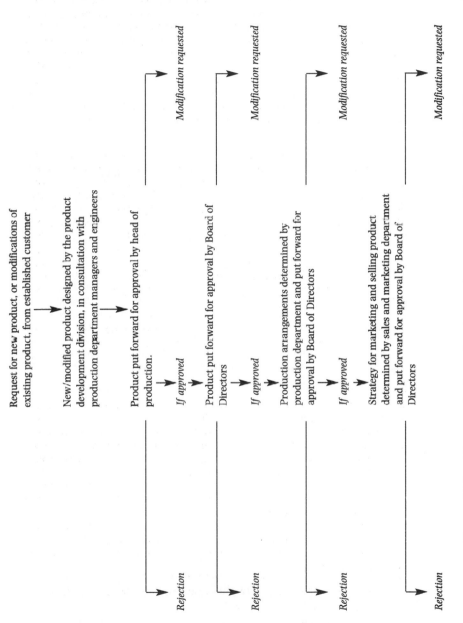

Figure 13.1 The standard product innovation process at Tipper and Watkins

older senior managers – Martin Wilkin, Production Manager and Brian Williams, Quality Control Manager – who attempted to appeal over Falmer's head to the firm's owners. The ensuing power struggle has recently been resolved, with Wilkin being forced to accept early retirement, and Williams agreeing to co-operate with the changes. Falmer knows that he has the owners' confidence 'for the moment' – but they expect to see positive results in the not-too-distant future.

the exercises

Setting up the Innovation Team

This exercise requires participants to work in small groups (5–7 members).

One member of each group should act as non-participant observer; their task is described below. The remaining members are to play the role of a team of management consultants who have been asked by Mike Falmer to provide advice on one specific aspect of organisational change and innovation in Tipper and Watkins:

> The diversification group – which Falmer himself chairs – has identified a promising new area into which the firm might move: the manufacture of plastics moulding equipment. They wish to develop a prototype range of products that they could show to potential customers, and intend to set up an Innovation Team whose time would be solely devoted to developing this. However, this would necessitate diverting resources (both human and financial) from routine production activities; resistance is expected from managers and supervisors who would 'lose' staff to the Innovation Team.

exercise

The team's task

You have 1 hour to consider the questions below and report back to Mike Falmer. Your report should be in the form of a 10-minute presentation, which will be followed by 5 minutes for questions.

1. What skills should Mike Falmer seek in potential members of the Innovation Team?
2. What strategies would you suggest to maximise support for, and minimise resistance to, the introduction of the Innovation Team, at various levels of the organisation, from the shop floor to the firm's owners?
3. What extra resources might be needed to help the Innovation Team to function effectively?
4. Are there any alternative methods of facilitating product innovation that Mike Falmer should consider in place of, or in addition to, the Innovation Team?

The observer's task

The goal for the observer is to examine the team's discussion in the light of the research literature on innovation at work. You are required to make a brief report on this (no more than 5 minutes in length) following the team's report. This should be structured around the following two headings:

1. *Theory and evidence* – what theoretical areas and what empirical evidence did the team draw upon in their discussion? Were there other areas of theory, or other examples of evidence, that they might usefully have considered?
2. *Assumptions* – what, if any, assumptions did members of the team make about the innovation process and the responses to it? For instance, did they assume that particular people in Tipper and Watkins would react to the Innovation Team in particular ways, on the basis of characteristics such as age, gender, tenure, departmental affiliation, or professional/occupational group? Were these questioned or challenged in the course of discussion?

You should also comment briefly on the process of the discussion. Consider questions such as these:

◆ Was there any attempt to impose formal structure (such as turn-taking rules or a timetable) on the discussion?
◆ Did all members participate fully, or did some individuals contribute much more than others?
◆ Were decisions about what to include in the report made on the basis of consensus, majority opinion, or the power and persuasiveness of particular team members, or by other means?

After the team and observer presentations have finished, your tutor will sum up the main points arising from this exercise.

Idea generation techniques

An important component of the Mercurius Innovation Program in which Mike Falmer participated was training in idea generation (or 'creativity enhancement') techniques. The program leaders argued that such techniques offer the potential to 'unlock the creativity' of people at all levels of the organisation and thus to stimulate innovation. One only has to look at the continued popularity of creative thinking courses and texts aimed at managers to realise that the Mercurius Innovation Program is by no means unusual in emphasising this aspect of innovation training.

For this exercise, you will be working in the same groups as in Exercise 1, to gain experience of probably the best-known creativity enhancement technique: brainstorming. First presented by Alex Osborn in 1953, the technique has spread so widely that it has entered common usage, although often what people call 'brainstorming' bears little resemblance to what Osborn or subsequent developers meant by the term. It is frequently used to describe any attempt by a group of people to come up with original or unusual ideas without consideration of the method used to achieve this, other than a vague notion that participants should avoid criticising each other. While 'ruling out criticism' is one of Osborn's rules of brainstorming, there are three other rules that also must be adhered to in brainstorming sessions. We will come to these shortly, but first we will look at the two major principles upon which brainstorming is based:

◆ *Principle 1: Deferment of judgment* – the production of new ideas and their evaluation should be kept as separate as possible. According to Osborn, one of the main inhibitors of creativity is our tendency to judge new ideas (our own as well as those of others) too swiftly and critically.
◆ *Principle 2: Quantity breeds quality* – the best way to get more good ideas is to get more ideas overall. Given that only a minority of ideas is ever likely to be truly creative (appropriate as well as novel), it is more efficient to produce a very large number of ideas and then select the few creative ones than to concentrate on producing only good ideas from the start.

In order to operationalise these principles, four rules for idea generation in brainstorming have been devised:

1. Criticism is ruled out – you are not allowed to voice criticism of others' (or your own) ideas, no matter how daft they may sound.
2. 'Freewheeling' is welcomed – you are encouraged to let your imagination run as freely as possible; no idea should be considered too wild or impractical to suggest.
3. Quantity is wanted – you are explicitly encouraged to come up with as many ideas as possible.
4. Combination and improvement are sought – you are encouraged to build upon ideas that arise during the session, for example by combining the elements of two or more previous ideas.

A very common misconception about brainstorming is that it is simply a process for generating a large number of ideas. In fact, Osborn detailed two stages subsequent to idea generation. The second stage is that of 'evaluation'; in this, the skills of critical thinking, barred from Stage 1, are brought to the fore. The group decides on the criteria on which ideas should be judged and then evaluates them all carefully and systematically. In the final stage, 'idea selection', the group strives to reach a consensus on which idea(s) should be adopted, but if this cannot be achieved, a majority vote of the group is allowed. For evaluation and selection, Osborn recommends a group of five, compared with the usual size of about 12, for the idea generation group. This may be a subgroup of the latter or it may include members not involved in generating ideas, but Osborn argues that members should have some direct responsibility for the problem being addressed in order to ensure their stake in the quality of the decision arrived at.

The current exercise has three aims:

◆ to provide you with experience of participation in a formal brainstorming session
◆ to encourage you to consider the issues that arise when using brainstorming in a real-world setting
◆ to compare the effectiveness of two different forms of the brainstorming technique.

Half the groups in the exercise will be using a version of the brainstorming technique very similar to Osborn's original formulation (the 'classic' condition), and the others will be using a modified version called the I-G-I technique ('Individual-Group-Individual'), first proposed by Van de Ven and Delbecq (1971). The task for both groups is the same, and is based on the Tipper and Watkins case, above.

Very soon after he began to introduce structural changes, such as setting up cross-departmental teams and devolving decision making, Mike Falmer realised that these alone were not making a very big impact on the problem of communication within Tipper and Watkins. There remained little spontaneous and informal interaction across departmental groupings, and the cross-fertilisation of ideas in formal meetings was often inhibited by mutual suspicions. He has therefore selected a group of managers from across the firm – all of roughly equal status – to suggest *three new ideas for improving internal communications* at Tipper and Watkins.

Playing the role of this group, you are to use the brainstorming technique described on your instruction sheet to produce the required ideas. Your tutor will assign you to a group and provide you with the appropriate instruction sheet. Groups in both conditions will have 15 minutes to generate ideas, and 45 minutes to evaluate them and select the best three.

Evaluating the brainstorming session

The purpose of this evaluation is, first, to compare the performance of the two forms of brainstorming, and second, to decide whether brainstorming (in either form) is a suitable technique to use when addressing the kind of problem presented in the case study.

Quantity and quality of ideas

The performance of groups in the two conditions should be compared in terms of the quantity and quality of ideas produced. It is a simple matter to calculate the quantity of ideas in each condition; just count the number of ideas suggested in each group, discarding any duplicates, and divide by the number of members in the group to obtain a score of the mean number of ideas per member. If there are two or more groups in each condition, the average of the group means can be taken to obtain an overall condition mean.

The quality of ideas is much more difficult to assess and is often ignored in experimental studies; however, as Osborn argued that brain-storming increases not only the quantity of ideas produced by a group, but also the quality, this aspect should not be avoided. It is generally agreed that the most valid approach to assessing idea quality is to use a panel of expert raters who have personal experience of the kind of problem that the brainstorming task was addressing and of the organisa-tional (or other) context of the problem. However, because in the current exercise it is necessary to have the idea quality assessment completed within the class to allow the comparison between conditions to be carried out, groups will be asked to rate each other's ideas. Your tutor will hand you the three selected ideas from one of the other groups (anonymised) and instructions for how to carry out the rating. You will have 15 minutes to agree ratings for each of the three ideas. Try to reach a consensus if possible; if not, a majority vote is permissible.

Your tutor will compile and present to you the quantity and quality scores for each group, and calculate the overall mean scores on each crite-rion for each condition as a whole.

Discussion of suitability

Once the quantity and quality scores for the conditions have been presented, there will be a general discussion of whether brainstorming (in any form) seems an appropriate technique to use in the kinds of circum-stance described in the Tipper and Watkins case study, and if so, which of the two forms you have tried is preferable. In considering the latter issue, do not be driven purely by the statistical comparison of scores – your task is to think about what would be likely to happen in the organisational setting of Tipper and Watkins. In order to structure the discussion, your tutor will ask you to cover the following four points, but will allow free time for any additional issues that emerge:

1. How well were the participants able to keep to the rules of brain-storming, in particular the exhortation to avoid criticism of oneself or others? Did participants really feel able to suggest any idea that came into their heads? Again, were the two conditions different in this respect?

2. How happy were the individuals in each group with the three ideas that were selected by the group to be put forward to Tipper and Watkins? What, if any, were the sources of dissatisfaction?
3. How stimulating and/or enjoyable was the brainstorming exercise? Do there appear to be any consistent differences between the two conditions in these experiential reports?
4. What barriers to accepting the ideas generated through brainstorming might occur in Tipper and Watkins? How might they be prevented from arising, or overcome if they did arise?

REFERENCES

Kanter, R.M. (1983) *The Change Masters*. Simon & Schuster, New York.
Peters, T. and Waterman, R.H. (1982) *In Search of Excellence: Lessons from America's Best Run Companies*. Harper & Row, New York.
Van de Ven, A. and Delbecq, A.L. (1971) Nominal versus interacting group processes for committee decision-making effectiveness, *Academy of Management Journal* **14**: 203–12.

FURTHER READING

For general reading on innovation, try the following texts:

King, N. and Anderson, N.R. (1995) *Innovation and Change in Organisations*. Routledge, London.
Mabey, C. and Mayon-White, B. (1993) *Managing Change*, 2nd edn. Open University/Paul Chapman Publishing, London.

Reading on resistance to organisational change can be found in:

Kotter, J.P. and Schlesinger, L.A. (1979) Choosing strategies for change, *Harvard Business Review* March–April: 106–14.
Meston, C. and King, N. (1996) Making sense of 'resistance': responses to organizational change in a private nursing home for the elderly, *European Journal of Work and Organizational Psychology* **5**(1): 91–102.

Brainstorming is described in:

Kabanoff, B. and Rossiter, J. (1994) Recent developments in applied creativity. In Cooper, C.L. and Robertson, I.T. (eds) *International Review of Industrial and Organisational Psychology*, Volume 9. Wiley, Chichester.
Osborn, A. (1953) *Applied Imagination*. Scribner's, New York.

CHAPTER 14

Interviewing

Carolyn Axtell

OBJECTIVES

The objectives of this chapter are to:

▶ introduce some basic skills for both selection interviewing and being interviewed
▶ provide some experience in the use of these skills
▶ raise awareness of the process and issues surrounding selection interviewing.

INTRODUCTION

Why interview?

Interviews are a popular method of selection. They allow a two-way exchange between the organisation and the candidate so that both can gather and give information. As such, the emphasis is on gaining 'evidence' about whether the candidate is suitable for the job and whether the job is suitable for the candidate. The type of interview is also important as structured interviews, using pre-planned job-related questions, are better predictors of a candidate's subsequent behaviour than those which are *ad hoc* or have little structure (Cooper and Robertson, 1995). An interview can also act as a public relations exercise for the organisation, as candidates will form an impression of the organisation from such interactions. Both parties usually want and expect some form of interview so that they can meet each other face to face. They feel that it brings a personal element to the selection process (Anderson and Shackleton, 1993).

Structure of this chapter

This chapter is organised into a series of five activities dealing with the preparation of interview schedules and the social skills of interviewing and being interviewed (within a selection context). These activities include discussions, a case study and a role play. The final activity enables delegates to think about broader issues than the interview itself and to consider the process of selection and other selection techniques.

The objective of this case study is to initiate discussion on the basic skills of interviewing and being interviewed. The case study describes an interview for a telesales officer. Read the case carefully and answer the questions at the end.

Interview for a telesales officer

The candidate arrives. The receptionist takes her to a noisy corridor and quickly rushes off. The candidate sits patiently for quite some time. She wonders what is happening. Meanwhile, the interviewer arrives back at his office late. He picks up the candidate's CV and then notes the time. He is already 10 minutes late. He has no time to go over the CV or interview questions. The interview questions were those he thought of last night while he was watching TV. His office looks quite messy, so he moves a pile of papers away from the centre of the desk. He goes to fetch the candidate but does not introduce himself. The candidate is quite nervous. She has her eyes down and doesn't give much eye contact. When seated, she shuffles around a lot and fidgets. The interviewer sits opposite her, on the other side of the desk, and slumps back in his chair. He's thinking that the candidate looks smart but isn't sure about her. He thinks she looks quite a 'mumsy' type.

Interviewer   OK, I just need to ask a few questions. Um, I see you're married, do you have any children?

Candidate   Um, no I don't.

Interviewer   Oh, do you think you might have children in the near future?

Candidate   Um, no, not for a while yet.

Interviewer   Oh, OK, it's just that you sometimes have to work odd hours in this job. Have you done this type of work before?

Candidate   Yes, you'll see on my CV, that...

Interviewer   (interrupting) Ah yes, I see now.

Interviewer   This job can get a bit stressful. Can you cope with stress?

Candidate   Oh, yes.

Interviewer   Do you like talking to people, although, obviously you can't just talk to your colleagues all the time, or else you wouldn't get any work done would you?

Candidate   Um, yes..., I mean no... yes to the first bit but no to the second.

Interviewer   How would you deal with customers on the phone?

Candidate   Oh, well I'd start off by trying to build a rapport with the customer. I would just try to persuade them to buy the products, you know, tell them what is in it for them.

129

Interviewer   Right, you have experience of building rapport with customers in your old company then?

Candidate   Yes.

Interviewer   Have you had to meet targets before?

Candidate   Yes, in my old job we had to meet a group target.

Interviewer   Oh right, and I guess that was usually met, was it?

Candidate   Yes (internally – Oh, I should have told him about me getting the highest sales in our group for the year!).

Interviewer   Right, yes, good. What would you say your weaknesses are?

Candidate   Oh, well, apart from chocolate, I guess sometimes I get carried away with a sale, if you know what I mean.

Interviewer   Yes, I see (internally – mmm, I wonder if she means she keeps trying to persuade the customer and doesn't let them go easily? I'll make a note of it and come back to it later).

This is the only bit of note taking that the interviewer does.
There is a knock at the door. The secretary brings in a letter.

Interviewer   Ah, thank you, Beryl.

Interviewer   Right, where was I? Ah yes, do you know much about our products?

Candidate   Um, well, what does this organisation actually sell?

Interviewer   We sell music tapes and compact discs.

Candidate   Oh, right, yes, well, I guess I know quite a lot about music. I buy music magazines quite a lot, and I've got quite varied tastes, although really I like pop music better than jazz or classical. But, I don't mind anything really, I'm sure I'd get used to all the different artists and stuff when I'm selling it. Anyway, I don't suppose it matters what music you're into, when you're selling it, as long as you know the basics?

Interviewer   Well, yes, I guess so. (Pause – glances through the candidate's CV.) I suppose I should ask you about what hobbies you have?

Candidate   I play football.

Interviewer   Oh, really? Tell me about that?

Candidate   Oh well, I just play with a group of women.

Interviewer   What is your position?

Candidate   I play attack usually.

Interviewer   Is that what you prefer?

Candidate   Yes.

Interviewer   What do you like about it?

Candidate   Well, I just enjoy trying to get a goal for the team.

Interviewer   Ah, right that's very interesting. Well, I think that's about it then. We'll let you know (internally – mmm, maybe she's a 'team player' at work as well then – that's good).

Candidate   Oh, OK. Can I just ask when I'll hear?

Interviewer   Um, well, I'm not sure, maybe tomorrow, maybe next week. Do you have any other questions?

Candidate   No, I don't think so (internally – but I wish he'd asked me more about my experience of telesales at my old company).

Interviewer   OK, well, you can find your own way out?

Candidate   Yes, thanks, goodbye.

Interviewer   Goodbye.

---

the exercises

After reading the case study, consider the ways in which the interviewer and candidate handled the interview:

◆ Identify the main problems.
◆ How could the interviewer and interviewee have improved this interview?

Discussion of learning points

The objective of this exercise is to introduce some basic points regarding the preparation and conduct of interviews, as well as some basic points about being interviewed.

Discuss the learning points presented at the end of this chapter. Consider the case study and your own experience in relation to the learning points (if appropriate):

◆ Is there anything you would add?
◆ Are there any suggestions within the learning points with which you disagree?

Role play

The objective of this exercise is to provide some practical experience in the basic skills of interviewing and being interviewed.

Content of the role play

Split into groups of three. You will be interviewing one person in your group, and one of them will be interviewing you. While the interview is being conducted, the third person will observe. After the interview, the observer will give feedback to the interviewer and interviewee about their performance. Rotate the roles of 'interviewer', 'interviewee' and 'observer' so that you all have the opportunity to play each role once. Decide who will be interviewing who in your group. Each interview will last 15 minutes, and feedback after each one should last approximately 10 minutes.

Documents required
You will need copies of the:

◆   job description and person specification (Figure 14.1)
◆   learning points (given at the end of the chapter).

You will use these to help you devise a selection interview schedule.

Preparing the interview
Start your preparations for the interviews in your group of three:

◆   Use the job description and person specification to identify some of the important general areas (job-relevant criteria) on which you want to gain information (or evidence) about the candidate.
◆   Think about *two or three general areas* you want to ask about (such as leadership skills) rather than specific questions.

Discuss this for 10 minutes.

As a candidate
After the above discussions, you will have 15 minutes to write a brief summary of your career history (no more than one page of A4 paper):

◆   Include any qualifications, work or leisure interests and experiences that you think might be relevant to the job.
◆   Write a draft CV in bullet point form, perhaps under headings that relate to the important job-relevant criteria you have identified. This will help you to think of how you might answer questions in these important areas. The CV will not be detailed but will help your interviewer prepare for the interview. For the purposes of this exercise, you should assume that you are suitably qualified for the position.
◆   Think about how you will practise some of the learning points for candidates (see below), such as being interviewed, non-verbal behaviour and active listening.

As an interviewer
After you have given your CV to your interviewer and have received one from the person you will be interviewing, you will have 25 minutes to prepare the interview schedule (now thinking of the specific questions and structure). It is important that you write your own interview

schedule so that the candidate does not know exactly what questions he or she will be asked. For the purpose of this exercise, it is advisable to ask questions on the candidate's *past experience*, rather than possible future behaviour.

◆ Focus on gaining evidence in two or three main areas so that you have time to practise the questioning techniques, particularly funnelling (see learning points below).
◆ Use the CV to formulate questions based on: missing information or areas not fully covered; any areas for clarification; alternative hypotheses you may have about the candidate (for example, did they make a conscious decision to go in this career direction, or were they just unsuccessful in other directions?, and so on).
◆ Ensure that your interview is well structured and make sure you have time to run through your questions before conducting the interview. Try to keep the interview focused on the main areas on which you want to gain evidence, without making the interaction too stilted.
◆ Think about how you will practise process skills, non-verbal behaviour, active listening, note taking and dealing with the interviewee (see learning points).

Observer's feedback
After allowing the candidate and interviewer to express how they felt the interview went, the observer will give his or her feedback using the lists below for guidance. Feedback should be constructive and helpful and concentrate on the following areas for interviewers (see learning points):

◆ structure (for example, the opening, core and closing)
◆ questioning techniques (were they able to gain suitable evidence?)
◆ process skills
◆ non-verbal behaviour and active listening
◆ note taking
◆ dealing with the interviewee.

For the interviewee, the areas of the learning points to concentrate on are:

◆ being interviewed (for example, speed, conciseness and enthusiasm)
◆ non-verbal behaviour and active listening.

Important note
It is important to ensure that the contents of the CV, interview and feedback are kept confidential (and not discussed outside the workshop without the individual's permission).

Background information

Pasta Products is a division within the Italian Foods section of Multi-Foods plc, which is a fast-growing organisation with several offices in the UK and USA. The current post will be at the Head Office in Leeds. The Pasta Products division deals with a great variety of fresh (and dry) pastas and sauces, as well as frozen pasta-based meals.

Job and person specification

Marketing Manager for Pasta Products
Salary: £22,500–£27,500 plus benefits

The job

The Marketing Manager will lead the Pasta Products marketing team in the research, development, planning and implementation of innovative marketing activities.

Responsibilities

Reporting to the Manager of Italian Foods Marketing, the successful candidate will be responsible for:

- Leading the development of the marketing plan for pasta foods (encompassing advertising, sales, promotions, sales force priorities and PR issues)
- Developing, with input from key contacts and research, strategies for defending and enlarging the Pasta Products market
- Co-ordinating and participating in projects with other divisions of the Italian Foods section
- Leading the Pasta Products teams in specifying, briefing and implementing marketing plans through specialist advertising, direct marketing, sales promotion and PR agencies
- Specifying pricing, product specification and product development needs within the Pasta Products area to reflect customer needs and applications
- Recruiting, training, motivating and developing the Pasta Products team members, setting clear objectives related to skills, and identifying and encouraging opportunities for improvement.

The person

- Degree or MBA calibre. Professional marketing qualification preferred
- Ability and confidence to deal effectively at senior director or board level both internally, and externally with marketing agencies and customers
- A good understanding of marketing and sales
- Experience of motivating, leading and working in teams
- Excellent interpersonal, influencing and communication skills; the ability to express ideas clearly in both written and verbal formats
- Analytical skills combined with the ability to resolve problems and make decisions under pressure
- The ability to think creatively
- High degree of numeracy
- Computer literacy.

Figure 14.1   Sample job description and person specification

Discussion of the interviews

The objective of this activity is to allow delegates to reflect upon the practical experience of the skills of interviewing and being interviewed.

Discuss what you have learned about being an interviewer and being interviewed in a plenary session with the other delegates and tutor. Consider the following:

- How well do you think the interviews were structured?
- Did you feel that appropriate evidence was gained about the candidate in the interviews?
- Who did the talking?
- How you would have felt if this had been a 'real' interview?

Pick out some other elements of the learning points to discuss (if appropriate).

Other elements of selection

The objective of this activity is to raise awareness of the process and issues surrounding selection interviewing.

Discuss the following in a plenary session with the other delegates and tutor:

- What other parts of the selection process need to be managed and administered?
- What needs to happen before and after you interview someone (that is, activities that are not mentioned in the learning points)?
- Is it enough just to interview? What other techniques can be used to gain evidence about a candidate?

LEARNING POINTS FOR INTERVIEWER

These learning points are intended for discussion and practical use within the workshop and will be useful for future reference. This list is not exhaustive and is necessarily brief. Delegates are advised to refer to the references at the end of the chapter for fuller explanations of these points and to find out about activities that occur prior to and after those described here (for example, job analysis, decision making and so on).

Preparation

Good preparation is the key to interviewing.

- Develop or decide a rating procedure and decision procedure (from an analysis of the job).

◆ Devise an interview schedule based on job-relevant criteria, for example, from the job description and person specification. (See also the sections on structure, questioning and process below.)
◆ Decide when and how to communicate your decision to the candidates.
◆ Familiarise yourself with the interview schedule, job and person specification, and CV or application form.
◆ Devise any additional questions or clarification relating to the particular application form, for example about qualifications, the content of previous jobs and so on.
◆ Ensure communications with the candidate – time, place of interview and so on.
◆ Prepare a timetable, the room (seating, paper, pens, water and heating) and the waiting area, and avoid any interruptions.
◆ Deal with your own nerves – to be just a little nervous can facilitate your performance, but if you are very nervous, try deep breathing exercises or positive thinking. Remember that you probably won't be as nervous as the candidate.

Structure

◆ Introduction – greeting, names, domestics, ice-breaking chat, building rapport, outline and purpose of interview, length of interview, what will happen next and so on.
◆ Core – gather and give information related to the job, start with straightforward non-threatening questions, structure to gather information or evidence on main criteria for the job.
◆ Ending – summary, ask if there are further questions from the candidate and whether the candidate has anything to add, next steps (when the candidate will hear and so on)

Questioning techniques

These seek evidence of behaviour:

◆ Open – Why?, What?, Who?, 'How did you organise...?', 'Tell me about an occasion when you...?'
◆ Closed – 'Do you have a driving licence?'. This encourages a 'Yes/No' answer and is only appropriate if you want this type of answer, that is, when you are checking facts
◆ Probing/follow-up, for example 'Who did what?', 'What was your role?', 'Can you give me a specific example?', 'In what way was it successful?' and so on.
◆ Reflection (paraphrasing or restating candidate's statement): 'So you felt that...'.
◆ Summarising or checking understanding: 'So let me summarise/check my understanding...', 'Do you mean that...?'.
◆ Funnelling – open questions to probing/reflection to summarising/moving on.

   Avoid:
      Leading questions 'Do you agree that...'
      Non-questions/multiple questions
      Vague questions, which will invite non-specific answers/evidence
      Irrelevant side tracking (which wastes time)
      Discriminatory questions (concerning race, gender, sexuality and so on)

Personally intrusive questions

Theoretical questions – 'What causes employee dissatisfaction?' won't gain evidence of actual behaviour, just 'textbook' answers.

Process skills

These improve with practice.

◆ Interpreting and probing candidates' answers
◆ Recognising the relevance of information
◆ Testing understanding
◆ Pacing or keeping to time.

Non-verbal behaviour and active listening

◆ Eye contact. Look at the interviewee when you meet and part, most of the time that they are talking and some of the time when you are talking.
◆ Smile (frequent use of positive facial expression).
◆ Relax. Adopt an open posture, sit comfortably, don't fidget and avoid over-animated gesticulation.
◆ Attentive. Sit fairly upright and lean slightly forward.
◆ Non-threatening stance/position. Consider the seating position, for example a 90° angle, barriers or desks.
◆ Nodding and verbal reinforcers such as 'Mmm...', 'Yes, I see', summarising and checking understanding (see above).

Note taking

◆ Tell the candidate you will be taking notes to help you remember accurately what has occurred.
◆ Keep notes brief using key words, one-liners or incidents
◆ Be careful that your note taking does not indicate good or bad responses.

Dealing with the interviewee

◆ Be courteous and efficient.
◆ Build a rapport with the initial ice-breaking chat, for example asking about their journey, whether the interview structure sounds OK, whether the interviewee minds if you take notes and so on.
◆ Deal with the interviewee's nervousness by reassurance and encouragement.
◆ Deal with long-winded or chatty candidates by reinforcing concise answers, summarising and moving on: 'We have rather a lot to cover, so could you just briefly tell me...' and so on.
◆ Handle reticence – give time for a response, encourage, prompt and don't appear irritated.
◆ Ensure that the candidate does most of the talking, for example speaking for two-thirds of the time.

Use of information

Be aware of and try to avoid:

◆ Premature decision making – wait until the end of the interview
◆ The over-weighting of negative information
◆ Bias and prejudice
◆ The 'Halo' effect, in which one favourable aspect clouds your judgment of all other aspects (that is, you then feel everything is favourable even if it is not)
◆ Dispositional errors – de-emphasising the effect of the situation on behaviour
◆ Information overload, especially when only one interviewer (you may wish to have more than one, although panel interviews are costly).

Additional notes

Behaviour description and situational type questions/interviews

Behaviour description type: for example, 'Can you give me an example of a time when you had to do X? Describe to me exactly what you did and what your role was.'

Situational type: describe a full and specific scenario and ask what the candidate would do or say in that situation. Follow up with probing etc...

The purpose of these additional notes is to raise an awareness (for future reference) of behaviour description and situational questions that are characteristic of some forms of structured interview. They are based on a thorough job analysis, which identifies key examples of good and poor performance on the job. These questions are most useful when candidates' answers are scored on specially formulated rating scales that use good and poor behaviour as rating points. This is particularly effective when trying to assess candidates on job-relevant areas. Both types of interview, when used with appropriate rating scales, can produce valid predictions of behaviour on the job. Instructions on how to design these interviews, with their accompanying rating scales, goes beyond the focus and timescale of this workshop. Further details can be gained from Anderson and Shackleton (1993), and Cooper and Robertson (1995).

LEARNING POINTS FOR THE CANDIDATE

Advice on completing application forms and further information about these learning points can be found in Fletcher (1981).

Preparation

- Practise being interviewed.
- Photocopy your completed application form or CV to help you to prepare for the interview.
- Find out about the organisation and job (company brochures, job descriptions and so on).
- Prepare answers for likely questions, that is, based on the skills, abilities, knowledge and personal qualities associated with the person specification, job description, application form or advertisement information you have available.
- Be prepared for questions on strengths, weaknesses, career, other jobs applied for, education, training, work experience, motivation and aspirations, leisure interests, current affairs relevant to the job/organisation, specialist questions (applying your skills to the job/previous project work and so on).
- Prepare questions to ask the interviewer regarding the job, working conditions, promotion prospects and so on.
- Plan your appearance – clean your suit or interview outfit, look neat, tidy and clean and feel comfortable and good.
- Get a good night's sleep.
- Allow plenty of time to get there and know your route.
- Attitude should be confident but not overconfident or brash.
- Nerves – to be just a little nervous is good (as it facilitates attention and performance). If you are excessively nervous, try deep breathing exercises and positive thinking about the interview.

Being interviewed

- Make a good first impression – smile, have confidence, be neatly dressed, polite, positive and enthusiastic (see points below).
- Take your time before answering (a second or two).
- Watch your speed of speech (not too fast).
- Speak in a clear, confident, audible voice.
- Be enthusiastic even if the interviewer looks tired or bored.
- Be concise but informative, and don't ramble.
- Be positive but honest in your answers.
- Sell yourself without bragging, for example subtly drawing attention to your strengths in the course of answering questions.
- Check and clarify ambiguous questions or misunderstandings.
- When faced with too many inappropriate closed questions, try to answer more fully than 'Yes' or 'No' to get more information about yourself across.
- Try to get over all the information you want the interviewer to know about you, that is, by asking questions related to the area of expertise you want them to know about, pulling this information in to answering a question about another related topic or volunteering it at the end of the interview.

- Do not volunteer negative information about yourself.
- Don't let a bad interviewer provoke you.

Non-verbal behaviour and active listening

- Eye contact – look at the interviewer when you meet, when you leave, most of the time when he or she is talking and some of the time when you are talking.
- Smile (but keep it natural).
- Posture – sit comfortably and fairly upright, or slightly forward; don't fidget, and try to relax.
- Gesticulation – avoid being over-animated.
- Be attentive, nod and so on.

Follow-up

- If you are not successful, ask for feedback.
- Learn from this feedback for your next interview.

REFERENCES AND FURTHER READING

Anderson, N. and Shackleton, V. (1993) *Successful Selection Interviewing*. Blackwell, Oxford.

Cooper, C. and Robertson, I.T. (1995) *The Psychology of Personnel Selection: A Quality Approach*. Routledge, London.

Fletcher, C. (1981) *Facing the Interview: A Guide to Self-Preparation and Presentation*. Unwin Paperbacks, London.

Rae, L. (1988) *The Skills of Interviewing: A Guide for Managers and Trainers*. Gower, Aldershot.

CHAPTER 15

Learning Company

Mike Pedler and Kath Aspinwall

OBJECTIVES

The objectives of this chapter are to:

▶ introduce the idea of the learning company (or learning organisation)
▶ give some 'glimpses' or examples of this idea in action
▶ offer a model of the Eleven Characteristics of the Learning Company
▶ provide opportunities to practice diagnostic, analytical and implementation skills.

INTRODUCTION

This chapter is concerned with the idea of the learning organisation or learning company. It takes the form of a series of mini-cases or 'glimpses' of this idea in practice and contains a formal model of the Eleven Characteristics of the Learning Company. Following this, five exercises are provided to help participants explore and apply these ideas to organisations with which they are familiar.

A short list of further reading is also given and this is expanded in the Tutor's Notes, which also offers some ways of using the exercises.

The learning organisation arrives

Leaders in today's organisations face one overriding challenge – to ensure that their companies learn quickly and continuously enough to cope with rapidly changing times. Managing change is the number one task in schools, hospitals and cities as much as in business and commerce. Where quality and excellence were once the limits of corporate ambition, learning has become the new organisational frontier. The learning organisation seeks sustainable performance and development through being flexible, adaptive and responsive to change.

For business, this is a major source of sustainable advantage:

Learning has become the key developable and tradable commodity of an organisation. (Garratt, 1987, p. 10)

The accumulated knowledge and know-how in a company amounts to its 'intellectual property'; the essence of what it has to offer, sell, trade or exchange. Public service organisations such as schools, health organisations, local authorities, the police, the armed forces and the emergency services supply the indispensable basis for a civilised society. Yet the pressure to learn and respond to changing needs, demands and circumstances is just as great here as in the commercial sector. The economy may grow, but the welfare state is shrinking, a 'grateful generation' is being replaced by far choosier 'consumers', and if public services cannot change themselves, they will be changed via the blunt instruments of privatisation, outsourcing, compulsory competitive tendering, local management of schools, purchaser/provider splits, 'best value' contracts and so on.

Much of the same applies to voluntary organisations and the not-for-profit sector who are faced with both overwhelming demands for their services and highly competitive fundraising. Here the new skills of tendering, contracting, selling, public relations and managing rather than administering are urgently needed.

We use the term 'learning company' instead of learning organisation, not to indicate a preference for the private sector but to recapture the old meaning of company – as in 'good company' – of people who are engaged in a joint enterprise with a shared purpose and values.

What does the learning company look like?

There is no blueprint for the learning company – you cannot go and visit one or buy a programme to install it. However, you can learn from what others are doing, and create a plan and a vision that fits the unique mix of the people, products, processes, history, aspirations and culture of your organisation. The following 'glimpses' or mini-cases are based on actual organisations and illustrate various aspects of the learning company idea. From these glimpses and the published literature, it is possible to build up a model or 'identikit' for the learning organisation.

Rover

The car maker Rover Group has a history studded with famous names: Austin, Morris and MG, for example. Yet by the 1980s, a new direction was needed. As a smaller company in a global market dominated by giants, it would soon disappear if it did not change. A collaboration with Honda of Japan was a radical step and challenged many of the assumptions of the Rover people. But it stemmed, as the then MD said, from a critical need to learn:

As a company we desperately needed to learn. We thought there was only one way to run a car-manufacturing plant. Our collaboration with Honda taught us differently.

To help with the learning, Rover established the Rover Learning Business, a business within a business, to provide learning and development opportunities for all employees. The message is that everyone needs to be up to date and to keep on developing, and also that the company supports the learning of all employees and not just a few 'high flyers'. Everyone is entitled to a Personal Development Budget to follow a Personal Development Plan agreed with their manager, and increasing numbers of people are taking up this offer. Learning has become an important part of company image, and the activities of the Rover Learning Business are widely published both inside and outside the company.

This transformation was fuelled by a major shock to the system and paved the way for Rover's later merger with BMW of Germany. This latest merger suggests that either Rover thought it could learn more from BMW than Honda at this juncture, or that issues other than learning were dominant in this decision.

(Adapted from Pedler *et al.*, 1997, pp. 143–4)

Organisations, like people, can get set in their ways. When this happens, it may take a shock or a crisis to shake them up to the point where they decide to change. As the Rover case study shows, the learning organisation puts learning at the heart of the enterprise. Rover set out to get everyone involved in the learning business in order to support the changes that they thought needed to happen.

However, this requires high trust; learners are open and vulnerable, easily misled by those acting in bad faith. One litmus test for a learning organisation is how it deals with mistakes; does it suddenly drop the learning rhetoric and punish or crush people, or does it really live up to its values? Another test is whether organisational leaders are learners themselves.

At Woodmill School, the head teacher sets a good example for the staff.

The learning school

Do good teachers first have to be good learners? Woodmill was an old-fashioned school – the teachers respected each other's space and didn't talk about work much in the staffroom, sticking to safe topics like homes and holidays. New teachers found it a tough school to learn in. If they asked for help, they were likely to be told, 'We had to learn how to teach for ourselves!'. They rarely stayed longer than their probationary year if they could help it.

The new head teacher, Mrs Oakley, brought in one or two new staff and some new ways of behaving. Although this would be her last school before retirement, she was currently following an Open University course in the teaching of reading to young children. One day, she burst excitedly into the staffroom to say, 'Look, I've just discovered this research which shows that children naturally look at each page of a book as a whole picture and not as lines of print. This habit is hard to break, and that is why it takes so long for them to learn to follow each line along from left to right. It's obvious when you think about it, but how could I have been teaching all these years without realising it?'.

While deprecating herself for not knowing such an 'obvious' thing, Mrs Oakley was not embarrassed; it was all part of her enthusiasm for learning. This was typical of her, and gradually her openness to learning proved to be catching, and a new atmosphere developed in the school. However, some teachers did not like these new ways and thought that Mrs Oakley did not behave 'properly'. In particular, one senior teacher consistently sought to undermine her efforts.

Three behaviours were central to Mrs Oakley's leadership of learning:

◆ Be a learner yourself.
◆ Share and demonstrate your new learning.
◆ Persist in confirming learning as a central value, make it normal and encourage others to do it.

Putting learning at the centre should include upholding each person's human rights – to learn at their own pace, to disagree with the direction of change and not to learn or change against their will. However, when organisations are going through periods of rapid change and development, these rights can be hard to uphold, and decisions not to learn may carry serious consequences. In this case, the senior teacher who had sought to undermine Mrs Oakley's efforts eventually left as her influence declined.

Given the necessary courage and humility, it is possible to make learning a central value in a smallish company of learners like a school, but what about a multinational giant?

The networked learning organisation

Electrical engineer ABB was created in a 1987 Swedish/Swiss merger to transform two national institutions into a new kind of company able to operate successfully worldwide. ABB set out to decentralise radically while operating globally. Recognising that its 200,000 people were mainly committed to their local companies, these were made into 1,200 separate legal and trading entities, with a further subdivision into 4,500 profit centres, each with an average of only 45 people.

Promoting the continuous exchange of learning in ABB is a core value, and each member company is expected both to learn from elsewhere in the group and to make contributions to the learning of other units. Benchmarking within business areas is easy in ABB because of the widely available reporting data, and it is the job of both business area leaders and country CEOs to facilitate these processes of learning between the companies.

These processes of learning are part of the design for holding this radically decentralised organisation together. At ABB, strong, centralised reporting goes hand in hand with local autonomy. Abacus, a monthly reporting system, provides performance data on all profit centres that are instantly communicated via electronic data interchange. Other powerful structures and processes link the units together in various networks, including the Global Networking Hubs in which managers link by business area and country. Great efforts are made to communicate via overlapping information systems.

The minimisation of cultural barriers is a major part of improving communication. Chief Executive Percy Barnevik has noted that European managers in particular tend to be selective about sharing information. Such habits must be challenged in order to realise the vision of speeding and facilitating communication and learning in ABB.

(Adapted from Pedler *et al.*, 1997, p. 93)

So even huge companies can aspire to be learning organisations by seeking to maximise local knowledge while maintaining parochialism, holding themselves together with a common culture of networking that encourages learning and communication as the 'corporate glue'.

It can be noted at this point that the learning organisation strategy may not be all sweetness and light. The vision may be accompanied by much less enticing realities and the sort of mayhem that led someone to invent the truly awful term 'tough love'. Here, Tom Peters comments on a speech given by the same Mr Barnevik of ABB:

he commented that during the first year of Asea's owning Brown Boveri they had managed to modestly trim the corporate staff of Brown Boveri back from its prior 4000 people down to 100. Now some of you snicker when I say that, some of you weep. Some of you become ill at your stomach. All three responses are appropriate. My simple comment, whether you are a middle manager, whether you are a chief executive officer, is if you look at that number and think it is amusing, you do not understand what is going on around you. (Peters cited in Burrell, 1997, p. 172)

There may thus be a dark side even in companies aiming to be learning enterprises. Such a strategy rests on a long-term trust in the individual and collective learning of the people in an organisation as a way of preparing for uncertain futures. If this trust is contradicted by ruthless or cynical decisions, management by fear is likely to prevail, and compliance, rather than commitment, will be the order of the day. On the other hand, a learning approach to strategy may enable the company and the individuals within it to be better prepared for the consequences of change and 'downsizing'. So much depends on how you do it.

Enacting a learning company vision can start by looking for ways of enhancing learning for individuals and for the organisation as a whole. Although this is easily said, it cannot be emphasised too often that this vision must fit the people and their circumstances. Here is an example of a printing company with a very particular vision.

Keatings

Keatings, of Mold in North Wales, is a specialist printer producing high-quality packaging for household name clients such as Cadbury's and Marks & Spencer. Having previously been the Managing Director of a much larger printing company, Mike Keating was determined not to make the mistakes he saw in action there. Because of his experiences, he was determined *not* to have managers, trade unions and wage differentials, or to let any plant get much bigger than 50 staff.

Curiously, it was these 'noxiants' that he wanted to avoid which first began to define the learning organisation vision for the company. For example, everyone was paid the same high flat rate of pay, and there were no designated managers apart from Mike and his co-director, Phil. Some of the other elements of the vision were:

◆ All people to have a picture in their minds of how our business should work – even when it doesn't.
◆ We should always know what others are doing in the industry – worldwide.
◆ Learning is part of what everyone is paid for.
◆ It feels as if everyone is responsible for their own business.
◆ Everyone should talk to the customers when necessary.
◆ 'Mutual adjustment meetings' are a normal part of working through conflicts.
◆ There is more humility and less arrogance between departments.

Keatings has a strong vision, unique to itself and largely defined by what it doesn't want to be like.

These glimpses show all the organisations seeking to maximise both individual and corporate learning as a vital part of carrying out their business and fulfilling their purpose. What else do they have in common?

The Eleven Characteristics of the Learning Company

According to Pedler *et al.*, those organisations seeking to become learning companies tend to share some common characteristics, as described in their model of the Eleven Characteristics of the Learning Company (adapted from Pedler *et al.*, 1997, pp. 15–18):

1. A learning approach to strategy

Where policy and strategy formation are consciously structured for learning purposes – for example, deliberate pilots and small-scale experiments are used to create feedback loops for learning about direction and the creation of 'emergent strategy'.

2. Participative policy making

Where all or most members of the organisation have a chance to contribute and participate in policy making. Ideally, they do this together with other key stakeholders so that policy reflects and supports a diversity of ideas. This was an aspect of Mrs Oakley's style at Woodmill School that some staff found hard to accept.

3. Informating

In the learning organisation, information technology is not just about automation but is used to inform people about critical aspects of the business in order to encourage and empower them to act on their own initiative.

4. Formative accounting and control

A particular aspect of informating in which systems of budgeting, reporting and accounting are structured to assist learning in all members about how money works in the business.

5. Internal exchange

The Keatings vision aims for a high degree of internal exchange, in which learning from other departments is normal practice, in which internal units see each other as customers and suppliers in a supply chain to the end user, and in which all are fellow learners in a company-wide network.

6. Reward flexibility

Greater autonomy and empowerment for staff leads to a need for more flexible rewards. Here, there is a flexibility in both monetary and non-monetary rewards to cater for individual needs and performance.

7. Enabling structures

A wide concept not only covering networked organisational structures such as ABB's, but also including many other aspects of roles, processes and procedures, seen as temporary structures, easily changed to meet job or customer requirements.

8. Boundary workers as environmental scanners

Environmental scanning is carried out by people who have contacts with the outside world of users, suppliers, business partners, neighbours and so on. Processes for bringing back and disseminating information in the organisation are also important.

9. Intercompany learning

As again clearly demonstrated by ABB, the organisation meets with others for mutual exchange and learning through benchmarking, joint ventures and other alliances.

10. A learning climate

A primary focus of Mrs Oakley's efforts at Woodmill School, a good learning climate is one in which leaders and managers facilitate their own and other people's experimentation and learning from experience, through questioning, feedback and support.

11. Self-development opportunities for all

The purpose of the Rover Learning Business – making the resources and facilities for self-development available to all members of the organisation rather than just the favoured few.

These Eleven Characteristics of the Learning Company give a clear picture of the practices that you would expect to see in an aspiring learning organisation. Of course, this is an 'identikit' rather than a real company or organisation, but it can serve as a useful template against which to make comparisons.

---

the exercises

Five learning company exercises

The following exercises are designed to help you to:

◆ explore your own ideas about the idea of the learning company or learning organisation
◆ create a definition of the learning company that suits the particular people and circumstances in any given organisation
◆ audit your own organisation against the Eleven Characteristics of the Learning Company
◆ develop ideas for encouraging learning and development in an organisation
◆ question the surface gloss of the learning company idea by focusing on some of the problematic and unresolved issues.

Learning and anti-learning organisations

Purpose:

To explore the organisational conditions that are conducive to learning – individual and collective – and those which are not!

Step 1:
Brainstorming (15 minutes). Split the group into two. One half takes a flip chart to another room and brainstorms all their ideas to the starting question 'What sorts of thing would you expect to see and experience in a learning organisation (or company)?'. The other group works with a flip chart to brainstorm their responses to the question 'What sorts of thing would you expect to see and experience in an organisation that sets out to minimise, prevent and punish learning?'.

Step 2:
Presentations (10 minutes each). Each group presents their findings to the other, using any examples from personal experience to enhance the performance.

Step 3:
Discussion. What can be done to bring about the good conditions for learning (and avoid the bad ones)?

Creative variation
1. Before Step 2 and after they have finished their brainstorm, give each group 15 minutes preparation time to present their findings to the other group in a more dramatic medium. For example, they could use pictures or drawings, poems, parables or stories to get their message across. They could even produce a short play, a mime or a skit on a TV programme. Encourage them to use their imagination.
2. After both presentations have been suitably applauded, each group can comment on what they liked and appreciated about the other group's presentation.

Defining your ideal learning organisation

In the notes accompanying this case in the Tutor's Notes, we have given some of the definitions of the learning company or learning organisation that we like. Now you might like to think about which of these best fits the aspirations of the people in your organisation. Perhaps you have a different way of looking at things? As there is no blueprint, the vision and the reality of the learning organisation are developed from within.

Purpose:

Exercise 2 aims to help you to create a definition of the learning organisation to suit your situation. You can do this alone, but it is much better done in company with others from the same organisation. If you are a full-time student, you could apply this idea to any organisation you know well. In a group, you need to choose one which you all have in common, such as your university or college.

Step 1:
Interview pairs (15 minutes). Take turns to interview each other: 'From what you have just read and your experience in general, what characteristics would you ideally want to see in your organisation if you were aspiring to turn it into a learning organisation?'.

Write all the other person's idea or statements on sticky notes and put them up on a flipchart or wall.

Step 2:
Group discussion (15 minutes). Now look at all the sticky note statements and sort them into three groups. What are the essential, desirable and possible characteristics of your ideal learning organisation?

Essentials	Desirables	Possibles

Variation:
Noxiants. Similar to Exercise 1, where the groups brainstorm the negative as well as the positive aspects of the learning organisation vision, you could have a fourth column of 'noxiants' – poisons that will kill off your vision before it can be realised. Visions are sometimes easier to arrive at by deciding what you do not want as much as by what you do want to see there.

Step 3:
Group discussion and decision (15 minutes). Now tidy up your essentials list (including any desirables that you can manage to fit in without sacrificing too much elegance and simplicity) to complete the following sentence:

> *In _____ (your organisation's name), what we mean by the learning organisation is...*

Your aim should be to complete this in as few words as possible while capturing your key ideas or statements.

Step 4:
If you are a part-time student, you may wish to apply this activity to your own work organisation.

The learning company audit

Purpose:

To audit your organisation and see how it measures up to the model of The Eleven Characteristics of the Learning Company. Again, although you can do this on your own, it is far better to involve others in the exercise as there is then the opportunity to discuss where you agree and disagree, which is the best way of making use of this sort of model.

Another good way to use this exercise is as a survey before holding a discussion on the topic. Distribute the questionnaire to all the people in a team, department or whole organisation, collect the anonymous replies, score them and then feed them back as a way of starting your discussion. This might lead to some good ideas for improving the learning in your organisation.

Step 1:

Questionnaire: The Eleven Characteristics of the Learning Company. Give your organisation a score out of 5 for each statement listed below. Giving 5 points would mean that your organisation is very much like this statement; a score of 1 would suggest that it is not at all like this:

Very much like this	*Mostly like this*	*Somewhat like this*	*Not much like this*	*Not at all like this*
5	**4**	**3**	**2**	**1**

1. We regularly examine the social, economic, political and market trends that affect our business ☐

2. Everyone here plays a part in policy and strategy formation ☐

3. Access to organisational information and databases is open to all ☐

4. The financial consequences of actions are fed back to those concerned as soon as they are known ☐

5. Departments and units understand each other's purposes and values ☐

6. There are many different ways of rewarding good work, both monetary and non-monetary ☐

7. Structures are very flexible and change frequently to suit different tasks and purposes ☐

8. People bring in and share information about what's happening out there from our customers, business partners and so on as a way of life ☐

9. We engage in joint ventures to develop new services and to learn about new methods and ideas ☐

10. People are not blamed for raising bad news ☐

11. Everyone is encouraged to learn new skills and abilities ☐

12. We find new directions by experimenting with practice and by setting up pilot projects ☐

13. Important policies are widely discussed before they are adopted ☐

14. Information technology really helps us to do new things together and is not just seen to be useful for automating processes ☐

15. People understand the importance of money and resources and also how such things work in this organisation ☐

16. Different sections and units share information and skills, and help each other out as a matter of course ☐

17. Most people have a say in the nature and shape of reward systems ☐

18. People are encouraged to come up with different ways of organising work ☐

19. There are effective channels of communication for collecting and sharing information from outside the organisation ☐

20. We often meet with other organisations in our business to share ideas and practices ☐

21. The central focus of our appraisals is the exploration of the person's learning and development needs ☐

22. There are lots of opportunities, materials and resources available for everyone's learning on an 'open access' basis ☐

The full and validated version of this questionnaire is available from the Learning Company Project, 28 Woodholm Road, Sheffield S11 9HT. Telephone and Fax: (0114) 262–1832.

Step 2:
Scoring. Now find your scores by adding the responses to two questions for each of The Eleven Characteristics of the Learning Company. For example, Characteristic 1 – A Learning Approach to Strategy – is scored by adding together the points for questions 1 and 12:

Totals

1. A learning approach to strategy — Q1+Q12= ☐
2. Participative policy making — Q2+Q13= ☐
3. Informating — Q3+Q14= ☐
4. Formative accounting and control — Q4+Q15= ☐
5. Internal exchange — Q5+Q16= ☐
6. Reward flexibility — Q6+Q17= ☐
7. Enabling structures — Q7+Q18= ☐
8. Boundary workers as environmental scanners — Q8+Q19= ☐
9. Intercompany learning — Q9+Q20= ☐
10. A learning climate — Q10+Q21= ☐
11. Self-development opportunities for all — Q11+Q22= ☐

Step 3:
Analysis and discussion. Looking at the scores, what do you see? There will typically be a range of scores, with higher scores on some items than on others. This is where it is useful to have some discussion in order to make sense of what these scores may mean. Do these high and low scores represent your strengths and weaknesses as a learning organisation?

◆ Are there weaknesses that you would like to improve or strengths that you wish to build up further?
◆ Once you have done the analysis, what actions are indicated in your particular company?

Transforming the non-learning company

Purpose:

To develop ideas for encouraging learning and development in a company.

Step 1:
Brainstorming (15 minutes). Split the group into two. One half takes a flip chart to another room and brainstorms all their ideas to the question 'What could be done to develop the idea of the learning company in organisation X?. As in Exercise 2, you can apply this idea to any organisation you know well, including your university or college.

Step 2:
Presentations (10 minutes each). Each group presents its findings to the other.

Step 3:
Discussion. How can we bring about the learning company?

Step 4:
Action. Each person choose some small step to take as a result of the activity.

Critical questions about learning companies

Purpose:

To question the surface gloss of the learning company by focusing on some of the problematic and unresolved issues.

Step 1:
(10 minutes) Each person writes some notes in response to the following questions:

◆ What do we mean by learning?
◆ Who benefits from the learning in an organisation?
◆ How is learning rewarded?

- ◆ Why should individuals and groups share their knowledge with 'the organisation'?
- ◆ In what sense can organisation be said to learn?
- ◆ Is the learning company a worthwhile vision or just the latest in a long line of managerial fads and manipulative human resources strategies?

Step 2:
Discuss. What other questions are raised?

REFERENCES

Burrell, G. (1997) *Pandemonium*. Sage, London.
Garratt, R. (1987) *The Learning Organisation*. Fontana, London.
Pedler, M.J., Burgoyne, J.G. and Boydell, T.H. (1997) *The Learning Company: A Strategy for Sustainable Development*, 2nd edn. McGraw-Hill, Maidenhead.

FURTHER READING

For a further list, see the Tutor's Notes.

Argyris, C. and Schön, D. (1978) *Organisational Learning: A Theory of Action Perspective*. Addison Wesley, Reading, MA. Chapter 1 of this seminal book, entitled 'What is an organisation that it may learn?', remains a classic statement of organisational learning from a systemic perspective.
Casey, D. (1993) *Learning in Organisations*. Open University Press, Buckingham. A very readable little book with many wise insights from a reflective practitioner; fits in your coat pocket.
Dixon, N. (1998) *The Organizational Learning Cycle: How We Can Learn Collectively*. Gower Press, Aldershot. Perhaps the best book to date on the organisational learning process, with lots of corporate examples.
Pedler, M.J. and Aspinwall, K.A. (1998) *A Concise Guide to the Learning Organisation*. Lemos & Crane, London. As promised, a 25,000 word encapsulation; the ideas of Senge, Dixon, Argyris and Schön, Pedler, Burgoyne and Boydell and so on, and a survey of what can go wrong.
Pedler, M.J., Burgoyne, J.G and Boydell, T.H. (1997) *The Learning Company: A Strategy for Sustainable Development*, 2nd edn. McGraw-Hill, Maidenhead. From the UK; strong on ideas, models and suggestions for enacting the ideas.
Senge, P. (1990) *The Fifth Discipline: The Art and Practice of the Learning Organization*. Doubleday Currency, New York. From the USA and a best-seller; good on ideas, stories and vision but less so on implementation.

Other material, including the full and validated version of the Eleven Characteristics of the Learning Organisation, is available from the Learning Company Project, 28 Woodholm Road, Sheffield S11 9HT. Telephone and Fax: (0114) 262–1832.

CHAPTER 16

Listening and Questioning

A. Lavender and V. Martin

OBJECTIVES

The purpose of this chapter is to provide a plan for a workshop, the objectives of which are to:

▶ develop an understanding of why listening and questioning are important for managers
▶ enable individuals to appraise their listening and questioning skills
▶ enable individuals to discover the principles behind effective listening and questioning
▶ enable individuals to enhance their listening and questioning skills.

INTRODUCTION

This workshop uses the experience of all the participants to meet the objectives detailed above. It draws on participants' experience of listening and questioning, encourages participants to reflect on this experience and then extracts principles of good listening in order to identify the key skills involved. Participants will then have an opportunity to practise those skills and to consider how they might utilise the learning in the workplace.

The workshop is based on the assumption that listening and questioning are fundamental to the management of people and that managers need to have a self-awareness of their skills in this area. Listening and questioning are essential skills in understanding the views and problems of staff and clients/customers. If listening and questioning skills are poor, the level of understanding developed will be affected and any solutions or plans based on poor understanding will inevitably be weak.

The workshop

The workshop is structured to enable participants to follow a sequence of stages in learning from experience based on Kolb's Experimental Learning Cycle (Kolb and Fry, 1975; Gibbs, 1988). This model is described in more detail in the Tutor's Notes, but, in brief, it identifies four distinct stages in learning from experience:

- ◆ Stage 1: The work-based experience
- ◆ Stage 2: The exploration of experience through further observations and reflection
- ◆ Stage 3: The formation of ideas, principles, concepts and generalisations drawn from those reflections
- ◆ Stage 4: The implementation of action drawn from these ideas in new situations.

The workshop is designed as a number of stages to enable participants to explore these components of the experiential learning cycle.

the exercises

Introduction (5 minutes)

Participants will be invited by the facilitator to introduce themselves and briefly describe their work role. The group may be small or large, and the workshop will involve sometimes working in pairs or small groups, and sometimes as a whole group.

Whole-group brainstorm (15 minutes)

Participants will spend a few minutes considering particular situations at work where good listening and questioning skills are important in the management and running of the organisations. Participants will also be encouraged to think why these skills would be important in those situations and to use their experience of being a member of an organisation, perhaps as a manager, as an employer and as a customer of organisations. Participants will be asked to consider:

- ◆ *Staff interaction: formal situation*
  - individual appraisals, performance management reviews
  - regular individual and group management meetings
  - presentation of proposals and assessing reactions
  - board meetings
  - selection interviewing
  - exit interviewing (that is, when a person leaves an organisation)
  - disciplinary interviews
- ◆ *Staff interaction: informal situation*
  - informal meetings with staff, for example making requests, assessing problems as they arise, assessing a crisis and arbitrating between staff
  - telephone conversations/discussions
  - informal occasions, for example lunches or dinners
- ◆ *Customer–client interaction: formal and informal*
  - assessing complaints
  - assessing requirements or needs
  - understanding feedback about products and services
  - assessing the impact of potential new products and services

and to focus on the issues that arise in listening and questioning.

Once people have had a chance to gather their thoughts, the facilitator will ask participants to share their ideas and will collate the responses on a flip chart so that everyone can briefly discuss the range of issues arising.

The experience (20 minutes)

This stage involves a role play in which participants will be asked to form pairs, ideally with someone unfamiliar to them. The role play is central to the workshop and is intended to provide a 'real-life' situation in which the manager and employee are meeting to discuss the underperformance of the employee. Each of the pair will be given instructions describing the role they are to play – one as an employee and one as a manager. Participants will be asked to assign roles, read the role briefs and take part in a 15-minute interview in these roles.

Once participants have read the role brief, they will be asked to spend a few minutes planning how to act in the interview in terms of the types of question to ask before beginning the role play.

Reflection (20 minutes)

The interview will be followed by the opportunity to discuss the role play in the pairs. Participants will be asked first to explain to each other what their role was and how they had planned to play it, and second to discuss the extent to which a mutual understanding was developed through revealing and exploring the issues. Participants will also be asked to discuss how they felt about this and whether choices were made about the direction the interview took. The following questions might give focus to this discussion:

◆ What behaviour elicited what response?
◆ What thoughts or feelings were raised?
◆ What choices did you make?
◆ What was the manager doing and feeling when he or she seemed to be listening?

Participants will be encouraged to reflect and consider:

◆ how what was planned or anticipated related to what actually happened
◆ the influence of eye contact, body language and how each was positioned
◆ the use that was made of questioning and types of questions
◆ whether either person repeated, clarified or summarised what was being said in any way
◆ whether there was a shared plan for the meeting
◆ whether trust was developed, and if so, how.

Developing principles – identifying key skills (60–70 minutes)

Each pair of participants will be asked to join another pair to make a group of four. There will be 25 minutes given to discussing the implications of the interviews in terms of the importance of listening and questioning. Participants will be asked to summarise their discussions in the fours as a set of principles or key skills (five or six) written up on a flip chart. The group should then decide who will present these to the larger group and how they derived these principles or skills.

The small groups will be asked to join together with all the workshop participants to share their findings. Each group will present its points and summarise its discussion.

Once the presentations are complete, there will be time to discuss the issues that have emerged and to consider the implications for managers.

Implementation (30 minutes)

In this stage of the workshop, each participant will have an opportunity to try out some of their recent thinking. Participants will be asked to pair up once again, this time with a different person, ideally someone with whom they have not previously worked.

One of the participants should be the interviewer and one the interviewee. Participants will have 15 minutes each to interview the other person. The task of the interviewer is to help the interviewee to develop a 5-year plan for their career development. It is not intended that participants will have planned roles for this task as it is likely to be more helpful if questioning and listening approaches are tried out for 'real'. In particular, the interviewer should try to help them to explore the direction that they would like their career to take and some of the things that they might do in order to progress in their preferred direction. The personal implications of any proposed career change should also be explored.

After 15 minutes, participants will be asked to change roles as interviewer and interviewee. The interviewer should try to question and listen in a way that helps the interviewee explore their options. The interviewee should notice how the interviewer encourages them to explain their thinking and to develop their ideas.

Review (30 minutes)

In order to complete the learning cycle, participants will be asked to reflect on the extent to which the ideas and principles developed from the original experience have been evident in Exercise 4. Participants will be asked first to do this in the Exercise 4 pairs.

Participants will be asked to consider the following:

◆ the extent to which issues were revealed and explored
◆ what went well or not so well in questioning and listening

◆ whether there are implications for questioning and listening at work as a manager.

The facilitator will then ask the participants to rejoin the whole group. There will be an opportunity to make some notes of particular issues that participants would like to remember and, more importantly, things that could be tried out at work to improve listening and questioning. Participants will be encouraged to put notes where they will be seen again in a day or two because they may be useful to add to or develop further after another period of reflection.

If participants have found the use of the learning cycle helpful in focusing attention on skill development, they will be encouraged to use it to facilitate learning about other issues at work. It can be planned into occasions when other skills could be developed, for example before carrying out a sensitive negotiation or taking part in an important meeting.

Participants will be encouraged to plan what they intend to do, take part in the event, review how it went and what they actually did and consider why anything happened differently from their plan. They may be able to get some feedback from colleagues to help them reflect on how their skills are developing. Another suggestion is to use the learning cycle to notice when their performance produces better – or worse – results than they were expecting, in either case, how their actions led to the sequence of events. Again, they may seek other viewpoints or feedback from colleagues to develop their understanding of how their skills (or lack of skills!) contributed to the sequence of events. Then they can consider how they could have acted differently and whether they need any training or practice to be able to develop appropriately different actions. Once they are ready, they should try out their new skills and review the effect.

The message to participants will be to remember – there is a big difference between people who repeat the same experience again and again – and those who learn from each experience and develop through them.

Plenary session – returning to the workplace (20 minutes)

Participants will be asked to bring paper and pen to the large group circle. When settled, participants will be asked to write down *three* things that they will do when they return to work to improve their questioning and listening. Participants will then be asked to share one of their proposed actions with the rest of the group and take contributions from volunteers.

Participants will be encouraged to reflect after a longer period and to look at their action plans tomorrow, perhaps adding another action.

It will also be suggested that the cycle of plan–act–reflect–understand can be applied at work and can be used to improve personal skills.

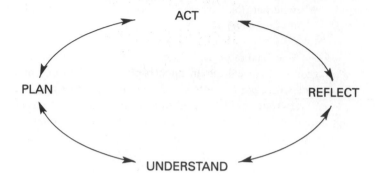

Participants will be wished good luck and the session will finish.

REFERENCES AND FURTHER READING

Gibbs, G. (1988) *Learning by Doing: A Guide to Teaching and Learning Methods*. Oxford Books, Oxford.

Ivey, A. and Authier, J. (1978) *Microcounselling: Innovations in Interviewing, Counselling, Psychotherapy and Psychoeducation*, 2nd edn. Charles C. Thomas, Springfield, IL.

Kolb, D.A. and Fry, R. (1975) Towards an applied theory of experiential living. In Cooper, C.L. (ed.) *Theories of Group Process*. Wiley, London.

Pedler, M., Burgoyne, J. and Boydell, T. (1990) *Self-Development in Organisations*. McGraw-Hill, Maidenhead.

Pedler, M., Burgoyne, J. and Boydell, T. (1994) *A Manager's Guide to Self-Development*. McGraw-Hill, Maidenhead.

Rogers, C. R. (1977) *On Becoming a Person*. Constable, London.

Sue, D. (1990) Culture specific strategies in counselling: a conceptual framework, *Professional Psychology* **21**: 424–33.

CHAPTER 17

Meetings

Tanya Arroba

OBJECTIVES

The purpose of this chapter is threefold:

▶ *to allow an exploration of the key skills of managing meetings.* The success of a meeting is often deemed to rest solely with the person who chairs it. While this may not be strictly the case, there are nonetheless particular skills that can be used to contribute to the successful management of meetings.

▶ *to encourage the identification of the key skills of participating in meetings.* The behaviour and skills used by participants in a meeting will have a major impact on the effectiveness of the meeting. It is not enough to leave responsibility for the success or otherwise of a meeting totally in the hands of the person in the chair.

▶ *to practise managing and participating in meetings.* Knowing the skills that are needed for successful meetings is helpful; however, the crucial point lies in the practice of those skills.

INTRODUCTION

Meetings are an integral part of organisational life. Much managerial time is spent in meetings. They can be held for a variety of purposes. Meetings can involve people who do not know each other well coming together for a single occasion or can involve the same set of people meeting on a regular basis. A single meeting, if unsuccessful, can have consequences for the organisation as well as the morale of the participants. However, it is when the same group of people meets regularly that the gaps caused by less skilful management and participation in meetings become most pronounced. This chapter is organised around an exercise that enacts a particular meeting of a senior management team, a group that meets on a regular basis.

Nowadays, it is often taken as an organisational given that senior managers need to meet regularly to manage an organisation effectively, and the practice is widespread. This chapter is designed to explore some of the issues that can occur when a group of people do meet regularly.

Background to case study

A description is given of the organisation, a medium-sized district council. The story of the team meetings is told, together with an extract from a hypothetical meeting that sets the scene for the subsequent exercise, followed by a short description of the members of the management team and a brief given for the exercise. No preparation is needed apart from familiarisation with the information given.

Loamdale District Council

Loamdale District Council is a medium-sized local authority. It provides the usual district council services, such as housing, environmental health, leisure, planning and technical services. There remains a two-tier system of local government in that part of the country, the County Council providing social services and education. Relations with the County Council have always been cordial.

The authority covers a mixed area, with one large urban centre and surrounding rural areas. The town, Loamington, is a popular tourist resort, with many visitors in the summer. Tourism forms an important part of the local economy. Apart from this, the town has a small light industrial sector but no major industry. The surrounding area is mainly agricultural.

The Council is hung politically and has been so for many years. The local political parties have developed a good working relationship, and there is little tension between them. There is an important minority of Independent elected members. Party politics do not impinge greatly on Loamdale. There is a spirit of working together for the local area among the elected members. The councillors generally hold the management team in high esteem.

There are 1,100 staff at Loamdale District Council. There was a reorganisation 4 years ago, bringing 10 departments into 6 multidisciplinary directorates. Each directorate is headed by a Director. The directorates are: personnel with 40 staff; finance, 120; legal administration, 30; housing and environmental health, 250; planning and technical services, 450; and leisure and tourism, 200. There is a Chief Executive who does not have a directorate but has a policy unit of 10 staff.

The culture of the organisation shows the hallmarks of a traditional bureaucracy. Communication flows up and down the hierarchy within directorates. There is not a great deal of interdirectorate working. Occasionally, working groups across directorates are called together. Matters that affect more than one directorate tend to be dealt with at Director level.

The offices of the council are in Loamington, but not all the directorates are on the same site. Each Director has offices in their directorate.

Story of the management team meetings

The management team consists of the Directors and the Chief Executive. They have been meeting regularly for many years, since the time of the previous Chief Executive.

When the present Chief Executive took up post, the meetings were continued. There is no formal document outlining the role of the management team or the purpose of the meetings, and no discussion on either topic has taken place among the team.

The management team meets regularly each Monday afternoon. The meetings start at 2 pm, and the aim is to finish by 5.30 pm. However, the meetings continue until the agenda is completed, which has been known to be as late as 7 pm.

The meetings are chaired by the Chief Executive. If the Chief Executive is away, the meetings are cancelled. If a Director is away, the deputy is allowed to attend instead. Attendance at the meetings is good, as it is expected that the Directors will attend the management team meetings.

The meetings are always held in the Chief Executive's office. The Chief Executive sits at the head of the table, and the management team members always sit in the same places.

The agenda is drawn up by the Chief Executive. All members of the team are invited to put items on the agenda, but few do. The agenda is circulated on the Friday of each week for the meeting on the following Monday. It is dominated by the common concerns that affect all Directors, such as personnel matters, the financial affairs of the Council and the political decisions taken at committee by the elected members. These are the issues that are viewed as corporate concerns. Each meeting starts with the Chief Executive going through the committee minutes in detail.

There are refreshments available at the start of the meeting but no break is taken once the meeting is underway, however long the meeting.

A year ago, a decision was taken by the Chief Executive that strategic issues were being neglected, and one meeting a quarter is now devoted to the discussion of a major strategic issue. A Director is asked to prepare a presentation on these occasions. To date, the Director of Leisure and Tourism has spoken on tourism in the area, the Director of Finance on the government's approach to local government finance, and the Chief Executive on client–contractor relationships and the move to best value. The presentations were followed by desultory discussion with no decisions being taken. They are not viewed as very successful occasions.

At a management team meeting, towards the end; the time is 6.30 pm.

Chief Executive to Director of Personnel   The item you put on the agenda, and I must say I am pleased that you did put something on as so few of you do, just says 'Review'; tell us what you mean.

Director of Personnel   I know I have not been here long, but I think that can be quite useful. It is like seeing a situation with new eyes. It seems to me that it would be a useful exercise to take an hour or so and look at these meetings of ours. We spend a lot of time in them, and I can't help but wonder if there are not some things we could do to make them more effective. Chief Executive, that is not a criticism of you – far from it – I think you do a great job chairing the meetings, but we are the senior team and I think it would do no harm to look at our meetings.

Director of Housing and Environmental Health   I couldn't agree more. You all know that I get frustrated at times in our meetings. I think it would be a really good idea to look at them.

Director of Finance to Director of Housing and Environmental Health   You would say that. You are all for these way-out approaches. I can't see any reason to do this so-called exercise. What is wrong with how we do things? It has been working well for years.

Chief Executive   Do any of the rest of you have anything to say?

(Silence, accompanied by head shaking)

Well, in that case, I decide that it is a good idea and the first item on our agenda for our meeting next Monday will be reviewing the team meetings. I think the Director of Personnel has yet again been very helpful.

So the first item on the agenda for the next meeting of the management team is to review the meetings of the team. Participants are invited to take the roles of the management team members and hold the meeting.

Members of the management team

There are seven members of the management team. Public knowledge about the members of the management team is given here. More details about the views held by each member will be given separately to the person taking each role. Each role can be taken by either a man or a woman.

Chief Executive
The Chief Executive has been in post for 6 years and has always been a local government officer, with a legal background. The Chief Executive is now 51 and is starting to think of taking early retirement. The current changes in local government are a bit taxing to this person, who does not welcome change and innovation. This is a person suited to a traditional bureaucracy, with a liking for a regular, ordered and systematic organisation with clear roles and accountabilities. The importance of local democracy is paramount to this person, and pride is taken in maintaining good working relationships with elected members. The Chief Executive is not a team worker by personal inclination, preferring to work alone. However, recognition is given to the importance of the directors getting together regularly, hence the continuation of the Monday management team meetings. Preference is shown for meetings that are orderly and tightly structured, with an aversion being shown to disagreement or conflict. The Chief Executive takes pride in being firm in the chairing role.

Director of Personnel
The Director of Personnel is a newcomer to Loamdale, having been in post for only 6 months, with a background in the private sector. A much

younger person than the Chief Executive, the Director of Personnel welcomes new ideas and views people and people management skills as central to effectiveness in the organisation, a view not shared by all the Directors. It is at the Director of Personnel's suggestion that a special review of the meetings takes place. As this director holds particular favour with the Chief Executive, the suggestion, although hardly welcomed, was accepted.

Director of Finance
There are no major financial headaches facing Loamdale, and the Director of Finance is therefore a happy person. The one aim of this Drector is to balance the books and not to get into any of the problems that have beset local authorities elsewhere. Over the 4 years that this person has been in post, this has been the case. Responsibility for financial concerns remains very much with the finance directorate, and it is seen as a keen guardian of the council's money. This Director sees finance as the key driver of the policies of the authority. The Director is a taciturn, sharp-talking person, who does not suffer fools gladly. The Director of Finance is the person to whom the Chief Executive usually turns to discuss matters.

Director of Legal and Administration
The Director of Legal and Administration is a mild-mannered, very shy person aged around 40. In the 10 years since joining Loamdale, progress has been steady, culminating in the position of Director, which was taken up last year. This person does not contribute a great deal in management team meetings. If there are legal matters on the agenda, the Chief Executive acts as the spokesperson.

Director of Housing and Environmental Health
The Director of Housing and Environmental Health is a warm, genial person with a very open manner and time for everybody – except the Director of Finance. The antipathy between these two is well known, although never discussed openly. A housing professional by background, the Director of Housing and Environmental Health has the ability to bring people together and creates the opportunity for new ideas to emerge – except in the management team. The frustration felt by this person with the team meetings is not successfully concealed.

The Director of Planning and Technical Services
The Director of Planning and Technical Services has a very good standing in the national field and is highly sought after for professional views outside Loamdale. A considerable amount of time is spent away from the authority on national business and playing a leading role in the professional association.

This does not always go down well with the Chief Executive, for whom Loamdale is the major focus. The Director of Planning and Technical Services is the person most likely to send his deputy to management team meetings, because of unavoidable absences from Loamdale.

Director of Leisure and Tourism
The Director of Leisure and Tourism is young and dynamic, with a strong creative streak. Getting the Director's post in Loamdale was unexpected but eagerly grasped, and the enthusiasm shown in the 2 years in the post has been much commented on. However, this Director expresses frustration at the amount of time that the management team spends on central concerns, such as personnel and financial matters, rather than dealing with more community-focused matters. Loamington's position as a major

tourist attraction is very much to the forefront of this Director's mind, and resentment is felt that the other Directors do not give this much recognition. This Director has made a couple of significant misjudgments that have caused considerable criticism in the press and some shakings of the head by fellow Directors. The Chief Executive and Director of Finance had to put in a great deal of work to rescue the situation.

the exercises

Participants are asked to divide into groups of seven, each person taking the role of a member of the management team.

The task is to take the first item on the agenda of the next regular management team meeting. This item is 'Review of the management team meetings'. Each person is asked to familiarise themselves with the background information provided and also the personal brief that will be given by the tutor.

The chief executive takes the chair of this special meeting, as with all others. This item is scheduled to take 1 hour. Participants are to seat themselves around the table in the customary way of this team, as Figure 17.1 shows.

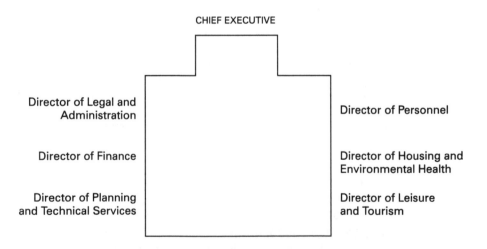

CHIEF EXECUTIVE

Director of Legal and Administration

Director of Finance

Director of Planning and Technical Services

Director of Personnel

Director of Housing and Environmental Health

Director of Leisure and Tourism

Figure 17.1

Participants are invited to use their own experience of meetings, as well as the information given in taking the roles of the management team members.

At the end of the hour, participants will be asked to note down the main points that emerged from the review, their observations on what helped and did not help the meeting to work well, and how they, in role, felt at the end of it. At this point, it is useful simply to share the feelings experienced at the end of the meeting but not to engage in discussion. It is suggested that a short break is taken to move away from the role play. Then discussion will take place for a further hour on the points that emerged from the review and the factors that helped and hindered the meeting.

FURTHER READING

Many books on team building contain useful background information to team meetings. The following are particularly helpful.

Clark, N. (1994) *Team Building*. McGraw-Hill, London.
Quick, T.L. (1992) *Successful Team Building*. Amacom, New York. See particularly Chapter 12, Holding effective meetings.

CHAPTER 18

Mentoring

Julia Davies

OBJECTIVES

The objectives of this chapter are to:

► introduce the idea of mentoring in an organisation
► appreciate the role of mentoring in helping the individual
► practise the skills of mentoring and being mentored.

INTRODUCTION

This chapter will focus on a case study of the ways in which mentoring can help managers to learn from challenges and changes at work. Mentoring can provide support in times of stress and uncertainty, and ensure that organisational learning is not lost. A variety of mentoring relationships are involved. The case study can be used in many ways: as a trigger for individual reflection, as a role play and as a vehicle for practising the skills of mentoring and the complementary skills of self-development.

The organisation described in this case study is a recently privatised company that is moving into an increasingly international market place. The office, where the case study opens, deals with customer billing and complaints. As yet, it has changed little, nor has it been influenced by the privatisation, which took place 18 months previously. All the main 'actors' have been employed by the company for a number of years and have had no formal management training or development.

The voyage of discovery

'Everything changes but everything remains the same; that could have been the mission of the organisation', thought Jane as she threaded through the commuters. A new manager was starting; she, as his assistant, would have to show him the ropes. He would not really listen; after all he was only here for the usual 2-year stay, and then it would be upward and onward. Inside the building, the big open office waited for the new manager, each desk full of piles of paper to be moved from desk to desk until the last process was complete. On a few desks were screens, for use once the new IT system was on line. Already at 8.15, a few people were sitting around. It was within the flexi-hours, and this was a quiet period before the phones began ringing; a good time to put the hours in. They talked idly about the day. 'So a new manager would arrive – well it wouldn't make any difference, only another face for a short period.' They had managed to escape making any real changes with the previous office holders. Indeed, so regular were the 2-year turnovers of manager that their induction was now a fine art. Doubtless George, the senior manager, would come down from on high and give them all a peptalk about change and challenge, and then disappear again to the upper reaches of management until the next crisis.

Paul, the new manager, was also aware of these expectations. After all, he was a product of the same culture; he too had seen managers come and go, yet did he want to be like those he had secretly or sometimes openly despised? Maybe the achievement of promotion was not enough, but why bother to be different? Paul decided that, in this job, he would make a difference, he would be a force for change. He had already picked up the talk about this division, he had visited and looked around. He knew of the reputation it had, as a group which could do the job, but saw no reason to exhaust itself. He had a plan, or thought he had: he would motivate them, challenge them, lead by example and bring in revolutionary change.

Paul's first day passed in a flash. Jane, his assistant, provided coffee and forms. People came in requesting decisions about arcane and compli-cated rules, everything to be done now. His own manager appeared once, mentioned change and then said he would be away for the next month, after which he would be retiring. Paul felt rather alone, but maybe that was the fate of managers.

After the first week, Paul was still no nearer to making any impact, under-standing what his job was or even knowing what the purpose of the divi-sion was. He had spoken to various groups of staff about the need to change – they had all agreed; there was no problem. But where to start?

During the first month, Paul studied a number of 'How to Manage' books. All gave wise and sensible advice, but, rather as with exotic cookbooks, he didn't seem to have the right ingredients or know how to start. They didn't tell him what he should say to the guy who sat in a corner doing crosswords yet whose work was always completed on time, what advice he should give to the 40-year-old whose wife had just left or how to get more work from Leslie, who was aiming to retire in a year. Overriding all was a desperate feeling of drowning and making no impact.

The possibility of finding help

A reflection here on the possible scenarios facing Paul.

In some, he will repeat his past patterns, following the lines of his predecessors in the job. He may manage to avoid drowning; he may discover something of how to cope; he may succeed by sheer willpower but with little learning or understanding. He may so use the years of experience of the division that he too leaves in 2 years for higher realms. Or he may alienate people, make serious mistakes, ignore warnings, strive for his own achievement so that he becomes overwhelmed and is seen as an inappropriate, indeed a failed, manager.

One path often suggested but needing special skills (not always recognised) is that of finding a mentor or mentors. In this voyage of discovery, that's what happened to Paul. Looking back at the end of a year, Paul could begin to see how it happened, but at the time it seemed almost random chance occurrences. If he had been told that he needed a mentor, would he have understood?

The subordinate as mentor

The first signs of help came from Jane, at the end of his first month, when Paul had to go to a meeting to present the first monthly figures for the division. Paul liked figures: at least they were clear. As Jane put them in front of him she said, tentatively, 'There is often quite a lot of politics at the meeting. I sometimes used to go with Mr T, the previous manager, to take notes.' The reality was more that Jane had actually prepared, presented and explained the figures, but only after an awful year in which the division had failed to manage the politics. Paul hesitated; pride fought against phrases from his latest management text: use others' experience, encourage junior staff, take them with you, don't be too arrogant – ask for help. Well, he didn't need help with figures, but maybe Jane would learn from working with him.

To be honest, Jane was surprised when Paul agreed to her going with him. The meeting itself was a little tricky as Paul didn't really see the traps laid for him. However, by an occasional word, comment and one intervention, the damage was kept to a minimum. Afterwards, the new senior manager, Carol, commented to Jane, 'I see you are keeping an eye on our Paul. I will have a word with him later.' 'I hope she doesn't overdo it,' thought Jane.

Afterwards, Carol arranged a meeting with Paul to discuss the division's work and the expectations of senior managers for the future. That afternoon, Paul reflected on the meeting and on Carol's request to speak to him; what did it mean? The meeting had been confusing, but Jane had seemed to understand what was going on. However, did he want to be dependent on Jane? That evening, he met a friend at the local PTA who was a manager in a similar organisation. On discussing the situation, he said, 'What you need is helpful advice from someone you work with, even if she is your subordinate!'.

The next morning, Paul asked Jane if she would talk him through yesterday's meeting. Jane wondered what she could say that was tactful and helpful but also not burn any bridges for her. The discussion was fairly general until Paul said, 'Why did you stop me in the middle of the meeting?'. This direct question helped Jane to explain the complicated history of relationships, which areas were important to stand firm on and which were irrelevant, as well as how to build up allies and ensure that favours were repaid. Paul could see that he needed help with this in the management of the division but he wasn't too sure of asking Jane.

The advisor

Paul contacted the manager he had met at the PTA, who said, 'I can see the difficulties, what you could do with is a mentor.' Paul's first question was, 'What is a mentor?'. His contact, Doug, described it to him as being someone who would be available regularly to discuss issues related to work priorities, organisational context and career choices. This sounded to Paul like the help he needed. So he went to the Human Resource Department to ask for help.

They were very encouraging but said that, although they had thought of setting up a mentoring scheme, it was not yet in operation. They did say they would contact him in a few months. Paul thought this might be too late for him: he needed guidance now. They suggested that he contact his boss and that, as Carol had already offered to meet him, he should use her for help and advice.

The boss as mentor

In the meantime, Paul went for his scheduled meeting with Carol. She asked him some general questions on his priorities and how he saw the section developing and stressed the importance of involving his staff. She also encouraged him to contact her and try out ideas with her.

In principle, Paul liked this as a way of working. However, he wasn't sure how to use Carol's advice, when to call her, what she as his boss would make of his questions. At his next meeting with Carol, he spoke to her about his wish for a mentor. 'Well that's what I thought I was doing,' she said. Paul was taken aback. Carol was younger than him, a high flier and someone who would despise him if she knew how difficult he found managing and how much help he needed. However, he couldn't refuse as that would offend her. So, swallowing his pride, he thanked her. Carol began by asking him a number of prompting questions about his priorities in his job, how he saw the purpose of what he was doing, the contribution of others. With her encouragement, he began to realise that if he were dealing with customers, he must look outside the immediate day-to-day paper shifting, that he needed to know more about customers. He needed to appreciate what the relationship was between his daily and monthly targets and the changes facing the organisation. Gradually, the mess that had threatened to overwhelm Paul began to clear, and he could now decide what the main priorities in his work were. Also, he learnt how to set objectives for himself and others, and to use their strengths.

In the office, things were only gradually improving with those who worked there. So, 9 months after he started, Paul arranged an appraisal meeting for himself with Carol. Jane was a bit shocked. She could see that Paul was a little clearer, but he sometimes just seemed to rush into things. Also, she was feeling that her own job was becoming more constricted now that Paul was managing better and all that the future held was probably the training and hidden mentoring of future new green managers.

Paul's appraisal meeting with Carol was difficult. Carol didn't say much. She seemed less interested in Paul and asked a lot of questions about how he was developing his staff and appraising them. When he tried to bring up his ideas on change, she was silent. At last he finished his prepared speech and asked for her reactions. 'How are you going to do all that you want to do by yourself?', was the query. 'I know you have a lot of energy, but even all that won't ensure change. Let alone its continuation when you are gone. I think we need to keep on meeting every few months, but first go back and start thinking of those you work with and their needs.'

Paul went back and looked around the office. 'Why bother with them?', he thought. They were a useless lot, and so many, how could he start getting them to think? Better to tell them what to do. Even when they went away on courses they came back worse, disruptive, spouting jargon, taking time off and then moving on after all the money he had spent on them, so why bother? Then he thought of the past 9 months and the help he had received, but what could he do with so many? A thought struck him: he might start with Jane; that shouldn't be too difficult. He could see she needed to improve her IT skills. Perhaps she could be involved in bringing in his ideas on a paperless office? He tapped on the glass, and Jane stopped talking to the newest recruit and came in. Paul leaned back; 'How about you going on a computer course?'. 'Why?', asked Jane. Paul was tempted to say, 'Because I say so.' Jane didn't look very happy. In fact she looked fed up, so aloud he said, 'Well, what would you like to do?'. Jane thought it wasn't the course she minded but Paul's whole approach. He wasn't getting any better; in fact, now he was more secure, he had become arrogant and offhand. Still, it didn't do to upset one's boss even if you had brought him on. She hesitated, and Paul remembered how she had helped him at the beginning; perhaps there was more to management than just telling. So he arranged a meeting to talk to Jane about her own career and development.

As the weeks went on, Paul tried to be patient and kind with his staff. Jane went on a special development course on information systems run for women. He encouraged other staff to attend events on time management, process re-engineering and corporate change programmes. At first, there was little change. However, picking up an idea from Carol, he set up special seminars and encouraged people to develop their own approach to problems and work. This was difficult, especially when he had doubts about their ability. Over time, he noticed a change that, as people became more involved, so they became less frustrated and lethargic.

Gradually, the division began to work well together. Other managers would ask his advice. Paul no longer felt that he was trying to meet all the targets by himself; he even began to enjoy work.

A formally assigned mentor

At the end of 2 years, Paul had learnt a lot about himself, different ways of operating and how things worked in his division. He was also achieving the ever-changing targets set for him, the staff turnover in his section was changing, some of the old lags had left (most of them voluntarily), and a younger, more ambitious intake was arriving. Paul had moved the section towards reducing the amount of paper shuffling, and he felt he was reasonably content with his job and understood it. All in all, he could afford to relax, if it weren't for the occasional nudges that Carol gave him. He saw less of her as she was now no longer his direct manager and she had other protégés. Paul was partly glad about this as he had never been quite happy with her as his boss and mentor.

One night, as Paul was looking through the accumulated information sent by head office, which he usually kept for 6 months and then binned, he noticed a red urgent sticker. 'All staff are reminded to recognise the importance of dealing with our international customers in a way that enhances our mission of growing our business', it said. This didn't make much sense to Paul: 'What international customers?' He then looked through the rest of the information. Most of it seemed to be about almost a different company from the one in which he worked. Next day, he rang up Carol for an appointment. It was difficult to find a time, and, when he did see her, she seemed preoccupied. She told him that the organisation was now setting up a formal mentoring scheme and that she would recommend him for the pilot, which would start in a few months. Paul went to the HRM department. Here, after tests and discussions, he was allocated a list of mentors. It felt a bit odd; who did the choosing and was it mutual, would he like his mentor?

In practice, the choice of mentor was resolved by issues of geography, diaries and Paul's own desire to have a male mentor. David turned out to be very useful in explaining the strategy of the organisation, where change was happening and why. They discussed what Paul's next career move might be, which department was looking for a new manager and then where and when he should apply and how to write his CV. In fact, the speed of mentoring was so fast that, within 6 months, Paul found himself promoted two grades and working with a team of eight area managers, all of whom had been thinking that they would get his job! Paul at first put into practice all his previous learning on involvement, motivation and sharing with a team. At first, there was some positive response. However, as soon as there was any pressure, the atmosphere became sullen and then hostile. Paul tried speaking to David, but he was not sympathetic, his view being that promotion was its own reward. So Paul decided to put a change programme into the area. He consulted the relevant section of the HRM department, who said they had no free resources but gave him a list of other contacts. These included a couple of consultants, a past employee of the company, the company's consultancy with the local college and a business school.

Help and advice from outside the organisation

Paul wasn't sure whether anyone from outside could help him, but, he approached a few of the contacts with a brief description of the problem and his own background.

> Briefly, I left school at 18, with a couple of A levels. My family weren't university types, and I got a job in my present organisation, which was, at the time, in the public sector. Along with others, it was privatised, and I have been involved in helping gradually to make changes in the various jobs I have done. I am now reporting to a board level director and I need to know how to manage a complex change management programme, with a group of people over a number of years. I am in my late 40s. As well as advice on the specific problem, I would appreciate more personal mentoring.

After considering all the responses, Paul, somewhat to his surprise, eventually chose the local business school. They talked to him and his staff. They provided him with some insightful but rather threatening information on how he was seen and on his strengths and weaknesses.

Paul worked with the two people from the business school to develop an approach to change that would begin to challenge the culture of negative resistance and tendency to blame others. Together, they developed a course to help some of his staff to begin to take responsibility for their own areas and develop new initiatives. However, all was not plain sailing. Some of the area managers whom he had at first seen as potential allies began to be less positive. He rang up his business school contact, who came over to see him, and together they talked through various perspectives and angles on the problem, including why people might superficially go along with change and who gained and who benefited from a new situation. They also discussed Paul's own feelings and why he wanted to be putting himself into structures that he found uncomfortable.

Paul began to see wider aspects of himself and the ways in which what he was doing had wider purposes than just his own career. His link with his consultant at the business school ended with the completion of the project. At first, Paul felt relieved. It had been very awkward and quite a shock sometimes to have his view of the world questioned. However, after a year or so, Paul moved to a new part of the organisation and again found himself dealing with the unknown. He was involved in a section dealing with outsourcing. He had to master a range of new regulations and contracts for this. He could see that the implications might be considerable, but what were they? How could he learn all that was needed? Time was pressing. He remembered his previous experiences and then thought, 'Why should I start with a new relationship? What about John at the business school? This time I will do the choosing and use this as an opportunity for my own development – if this were a course, the organisation would pay, so I will negotiate a learning contract for a personal mentoring scheme for myself.'

Becoming a mentor

During the past few years, Paul felt that he had learnt a great deal about himself, the organisation and the changes facing it. Not all of it had been easy, and he was still learning. Through his connection with John, he was aware of broader ideas and models. Yet he could see that the new entrants to the organisation were finding it difficult to put ideas into practice. They had difficulty in making sense of the often confusing demands on them. Many were leaving, turnover was increasing, and those who stayed were not always the best.

He wasn't sure if there was anything that he could do to help. Having found and chosen his own mentor, Paul felt an increased wish to act as a mentor to others. It seemed a pity that each new group had to relearn all the old lessons and that valuable ideas were forgotten or lost as people moved on in an organisation.

Paul had become friendly with a new entrant whom he had met at the company sports club. They had discovered that they had interests in common, and Paul offered his help to Tim to find his way about the organisation.

As he worked with Tim, Paul found himself asking even more questions. This helped him to keep on introducing new ideas. He found it a source of satisfaction to help someone else. Tim became more confident and applied for jobs in other divisions, eventually moving into international sales. Once Tim moved, Paul missed the contact and approached HR with a plan. The plan was for a more consistent and formal mentoring scheme for new employees. After some training, he was offered the role of being a mentor in such a scheme, and he accepted. This new scheme was linked to a more formal approach to management development. Paul, together with other mentors, found that his links with younger managers enabled him to share past experiences and to continue his own learning.

Conclusion

At this point in his career Paul looked back at his experience of being mentored. Some of the relationships had been quite difficult. He could see more clearly his own strengths and weaknesses. The path had not always been clear to him. Mentoring was sometimes more visible in retrospect than at the time. He had learnt that, in order to help others, it isn't always necessary for them to make the same choices as oneself. Understanding patterns and purposes was often a more subtle and complex process than it first appeared. Finally, he learnt that change, both personal and organisational, was never complete. There was always more to find out!

---

the exercises

The objectives of these exercises are:

◆ to understand some of the emotional and affective issues involved in learning and mentoring
◆ for students to relate the possibilities of mentoring to their own situation at work
◆ to develop some early skills in mentoring each other
◆ to objectively consider some of the advantages and disadvantages of mentoring.

Exercises 1, 2 and 5 can be done individually. Exercises 2 and 3 can be carried out in groups of two or three (benefit would be gained from using the third person as an observer). Exercises 1 and 2 can be undertaken as a role play.

Arriving in a new situation

Ask the students to start by taking 10 minutes to consider their own experience of arriving in a new work situation. Whom did they turn to for advice and why?

Ask the students to review Paul's experience of arriving in a new job, his feelings and the feelings of others.

Use this as a comparison with their own experience, in particular to consider what help they had and what opportunities there should be for formal/informal mentoring at the start of a new job or career.

Advice to Paul

Having read the case study, what advice would you have given Paul, at specific points in his career, on his needs and the potential role of a mentor?

How do you evaluate his experiences of mentoring and why? What criteria would you use to make these judgments?

What skills and experience might Paul bring to being a mentor? What additional help might he need?

Mentoring in context

This should ideally be undertaken by three people, one acting as an observer. The three roles are as follows:

◆ The problem presenter, A, should describe to the listener the present challenges and difficulties facing them in their work.
◆ The role of B is to clarify the type of help needed and to explore what the role of a mentor might be in this situation.
◆ The observer C should comment on the process.

The whole exercise should involve each person undertaking each role.

Time: 10 minutes for presenting the problem, 7 minutes for clarification, and for observer feedback, 3 minutes. The total time is 20 minutes each round, times three, that is, 1 hour.

The skills needed in mentoring

This exercise builds on Exercises 2 and 3 (which could be shortened).
The group can discuss a number of questions:

◆ What skills are needed in mentoring?
◆ How can a mentoring scheme be set up?
◆ What are the disadvantages and advantages of such schemes?
◆ What are the networks they already use and the importance of choice in mentoring as a process?

There is a potential opportunity here for individuals to try out the skills of mentoring each other and creating future support networks.

Career development and mentoring

This provides an opportunity for individuals to consider their own careers. Using either a conventional CV or a chart of highs and lows, ask them to identify any mentors that they have had or times when they might have benefited from a mentor, and why? Why was this?

If you had a mentor, who were they and was it explicit? What did you value in the relationship? If you did not have a mentor, were there explicit barriers in you or in other people? Was it a missed opportunity?

Do you act as a mentor? When, how and what are your own feelings? What would help you to develop this role?

FURTHER READING

Carter, S. (1994) *An Essential Guide to Mentoring*. IM Foundation, London.
Clutterbuck, D. (1992) *Everyone Needs a Mentor*. IPD, London.
Shea, G. (1992) *Mentoring, A Guide, 1016 Basics*. Kogan Page, London.

CHAPTER 19

Negotiating

Linda Marsh and Peter Belsey

OBJECTIVES

The objectives of this chapter are to:

▶ introduce the key concepts of negotiation
▶ give some experience of planning to negotiate
▶ gain insight into face-to-face negotiation skills
▶ give some experience of using those skills.

INTRODUCTION

This chapter provides you with the opportunity to experience planning and carrying out negotiations. In this case, the negotiation is between a waste management company and a potential banker. It is a group exercise, and the tutor will assign various roles in the two organisations to members of each group. You will find it helpful to have some knowledge of the basic financial issues faced by companies, but you will not require a detailed knowledge of banking and accountancy to conduct the role play successfully.

As you read this chapter, remember that the basic idea of negotiation is to reach agreement by trading something that you want for something the other party wants or wants to avoid losing. The financial information included gives you ammunition to bargain with.

This chapter is organised into four sections:

◆ a case study with a general briefing, giving an outline of the overall market situation, the waste management industry and investment banking, information that would be common to both parties in a negotiation
◆ a description of the exercise and the various roles that participants can take
◆ a brief outline of key concepts and skills that need to be considered when planning and conducting negotiations
◆ a further reading list, although not needed before carrying out the exercise.

To prepare for the negotiation, participants will need information specific to each party from the Tutor's Notes.

Introduction: General briefing

Background to the meeting

Today's meeting has come about as a result of a seminar on the environment run by Midwest Bank, which the Managing Director of Greenfields attended. During cocktails afterwards, the Chief Executive of Midwest charmed the Greenfields MD into further discussion about how Midwest could help him to develop his business with better financial arrangements. There have been two or three meetings between the two of them, and they have established a good relationship. The issues they have discussed are listed at the end of this section.

They have agreed that it is time to see whether an agreement can be reached and have brought in other people from their organisations to conclude the deal.

Market situation

Waste management

The European waste management industry is currently going through the biggest transformation in its history. Increased public concern for the environment is forcing the EU and its member states to stiffen regulations. Over the next few years, new legislation will be introduced. It will encourage companies producing substantial amounts of waste to call in professional waste management companies, thus creating much new business. Stiffer regulations will also inevitably mean an increase in costs for the environmentally acceptable disposal of waste.

Even though the implementation and interpretation of this legislation will vary by country, it means the best of all worlds for established players in the sector, such as Greenfields. There are now considerable barriers to newcomers, and the investment required to deal with new legislation is putting pressure on smaller, weaker waste management companies, many of whom are likely to quit. So, on the one hand, there will be fewer suppliers, yet on the other, the amount of business available is expected to rise sharply.

Threats to Greenfields come from:

- 'cowboy operators' who will undercut the legitimate operators such as Greenfields by breaking regulations and disposing of waste unlawfully
- major competitors in the UK and abroad who are likely to have the same ambitions for expansion
- varying interpretations of the legislation in different countries that will favour 'national operators' either because of design or because they understand the legal and market situation better.

Investment banking

The banking industry is in flux, as can be seen in the trend towards globalisation together with deregulation, liberalisation and the increasing sophistication of information technology. Major US banks are entering the market and taking market share away from the European investment and clearing banks. The main differences between the two types of bank are that investment banks:

- ◆ do not have a retail network
- ◆ are able to offer more sophisticated services in areas such as hedging and trading in foreign exchange, trading in futures and options, raising equity finance and the purchase and sale of companies
- ◆ can offer these services multinationally, often globally.

The large clearing banks are fighting back hard and developing business in markets traditionally dealt with by investment and merchant banks, sometimes by developing their own expertise in these areas and in other cases buying investment or merchant banks. European banks are also expanding into the US market, with varying degrees of success. Customers of these banks also take advice from the major accountancy and law firms. A major issue is whom they rely on for their main advice, as that source will influence what decisions are made and the closeness of their relationships with other organisations. The major accountancies are also strengthening their position by developing tighter links with law practices in the rest of the EU and potentially here in the UK.

Threats to Midwest, an investment bank, come from this market situation. A company such as Greenfields, which is well run and has a good share of its home market, is well placed to take advantage of expansion opportunities in the UK, the rest of the EU and the USA. It represents an attractive proposition to many banks and other professional advisers.

General market information
The other relevant information of which you need to be aware is detailed in the outline of negotiable issues, basic principles and numbers in Exercise 1.

Greenfields

Greenfields is a closed limited company, that is, its shares are not quoted on the Stock Exchange. Public information about Greenfields shows the following information, the past 3 years' financial results revealing a consistent record of increasing profits:

	Turnover £m	Profit after tax £m
Last year	200	23
2 years ago	134	17
3 years ago	108	13

Greenfields' balance sheet is strong and the gearing low enough to enable the company to borrow more if it wants to. Alternatively, the company could obtain capital by floating on the Stock Market. This is being actively considered by the board.

In the UK, Greenfields is involved in both domestic and commercial waste collection and sand and gravel quarrying. The latter reflects Greenfields' traditional activity, from which it grew naturally into landfill activities and then into waste collection, treatment and disposal. Greenfields moved into the US market in 1984 by acquiring a private industrial waste services company in Florida. Since then, Greenfields has acquired a number of other private companies in order to diversify into domestic waste collection and to strengthen its geographical coverage across the eastern states.

Turnover and profit are divided equally between the UK and the USA.

Midwest Bank

Midwest Bank is a medium-sized investment bank with a good reputation; it operates throughout Europe and North America. Like other banks of all sizes, it is continually on the look out for new clients with a sound financial footing.

Generally within the banking market, Midwest Bank is known to be more expensive to deal with than its competitors, but it is also generally agreed that it provides a better-quality service. Its reputation is particularly good in the areas of management information and efficient cross-border financial transactions. This is potentially important as few companies are entirely happy with the administration and information services offered by banks. In fact, one of the most common complaints is that 'My bank doesn't understand me.' Similarly, an efficient cross-border service is valuable to any company wishing to expand internationally into new geographical areas.

Issues discussed so far

The MD of Greenfields and the CE of Midwest have discussed the following issues.

◆ terms for a loan – the amount, terms and interest rate
◆ the fees for an equity issue
◆ acquisitions – advice on targets and financial aspects together with the fees for any finance required
◆ other fees for administration, advice, surveys and market reports.

On the table at present are the following numbers:

◆ New funds raised by an equity issue valued at £100m. The current position is that Greenfields wishes to place this issue through three different banks. Large equity issues are typically offered through more than one bank to spread the risk to each institution if the equity issue is not taken up, that is, the shares offered for sale are not bought. Midwest have not been offered a role as verbal promises have already been given to three other banks. The fees for the three other banks would be around £200,000 each.
◆ A finance facility of £15m for the next 5 years.This amounts to an optional loan so that Greenfields can, but does not have to, borrow up to £15m in this time. To guarantee the funds, Midwest has proposed a setting up fee of 0.25 per cent, equal to £37,500, together with an interest rate of 13.5 per cent on the funds actually used. These are above the rates typically quoted in the market over the past 12 months, which range from 0.15 to 0.20 per cent and 12.2 to 13.0 per cent respectively.
◆ Interest cover covenants (basically an alarm bell that, if sounded, would cause the loan to be repayable immediately) have been discussed but no numbers put on the table. (See 'basic principles' below for an explanation of interest cover.) This is typically at a ratio of 1.75 to 1. Greenfields currently has loans without covenants because of previous strong profit levels, so they are unlikely to want to agree to interest cover.

the exercises

exercise 1

Roles in the negotiating team

Greenfields is represented by two directors: the finance director and the business development director. Midwest Bank is represented by the relationship manager and a corporate finance specialist.

Each team can also have a 'coach'. This role is similar to that of a sports coach. They take a full part in the planning and then observe the negotiation, noting what is and is not working, to provide their team with help and advice during the negotiation and with insight into reasons for the result afterwards.

Decide which issues you wish to negotiate around and use the information in the next section to give a framework for planning numbers and trades. You do not have to negotiate on every issue listed.

Some basic principles and numbers

As well as the guidance given above, you should assume, for the purposes of this negotiation, that the following numbers typically apply to any financial transactions. Of course, some banks will charge more and some less.

◆ Assume that the bank base rate is 10 per cent.
◆ Loans and facilities are usually offered for periods of 3 years.
◆ Interest cover covenants are based on a calculation to assess a company's ability to pay the interest; this is profit divided by interest. A loan becomes repayable if the profit level falls below this. For example, if interest amounted to £50,000, a covenant of 1.75 to 1 means the profit must be at least £87,500.
◆ Equity finance versus debt finance. Equity finance – raising money by issuing shares – means that the board can vary, or even halt, payments to shareholders (dividends) depending upon the company's performance while debt finance is at agreed rates of interest, so payments must be made and cannot be varied by the board.

Typical market charges for the services likely to be discussed are as follows:

◆ Long-term loans (for 5 years or more) are typically 2 per cent above base, that is, 12 per cent interest.
◆ Short-term loans are typically 5 per cent above base, that is, 15 per cent interest.
◆ Costs to bring a company to the Stock Market (flotation) range from £500,000 for an AIM listing to £5m for a full listing. The total figure is not negotiable in this case study, but Midwest's share of it could be; that is, will Midwest have a share, and if so, what proportion? AIM is

the Alternative Investment Market – floating here is cheaper than on the full Stock Market – but there may be fewer investors willing to take equity in a company unless it has effective advisers (in this case, the banks). Companies may stay in the AIM for a number of years before upgrading to a full listing.

♦ The administration of loans is charged at 0.2 per cent of the loan facility total on top of the interest charge. In the case of a £15m loan, this would amount to an annual charge of £30,000 per year.

♦ Bespoke advice is charged at an hourly rate of £100 per hour from the relationship manager and £200 from specialists.

♦ Market surveys vary from free to £250 per report.

It is safe to assume that Midwest Bank will want to charge at least the standard rates and possibly more for some of the services discussed so far. At the same time, Greenfields will be interested in discounts on the rates, particularly if several services are used.

Additional information specific to each organisation and role is available from the Tutor's Notes. This gives additional instructions from your superiors or peers and their suggestions for how the negotiation should be conducted. It does not add more financial information.

exercise
2

Guidelines for running your planning meetings

Whichever team you are in, Greenfields or Midwest, you will find it helpful to identify the following during your planning session:

1. Agree what your objective is for this negotiation. Ensure that it is:

   S = Specific
   M = Measurable
   A = Ambitious
   R = Realistic
   T = Timebound.

   Ensure that your objective is neither too broad nor too detailed. It should specify the final goal of the agreement and, ideally, give some clue to the overall approach. Phrase it in the form, 'I want... so that I can...', for example 'I want to get a long-term agreement on funding so that I can implement my expansion plans in Europe.'

2. Brainstorm all the issues on which you might be able to negotiate. As well as the major issues such as interest rates and loan terms, are there any others that you might be able to offer or use to get movement from the other party?

   Look carefully at your major issues. Would it be sensible to break them down at all? Would this offer you more flexibility and room for manoeuvre? Prioritise your issues as high, medium or low.

3. Identify for each issue the best deal you think you could obtain and the minimum deal you would be willing to accept. Check that these ranges are consistent with your objective.

4. Think about what the other party is likely to be aiming for as an objective and what issues they might want to discuss.

Guidelines for preparing to negotiate

1. Plan a strategy for the negotiation. Remember that you need to:

   ◆ Set the right atmosphere (we suggest that you aim for win/win, as a relationship between a business and its banker is ideally long term and mutually beneficial)
   ◆ Establish that you have a strong position
   ◆ Bargain effectively; remember that negotiation involves movement by both parties towards a mutually acceptable agreement. Making concessions is not negotiation, nor is refusing to move on any issues
   ◆ Confirm and check out exactly what has been agreed before the negotiation ends.

2. Consider a trading strategy for your major issues.

   ◆ Which issues can be linked?
   ◆ If you move away from your best on one issue, what movement do you need to see in another to make it worthwhile?

3. Agree your roles. It is important that where there are two people in your team, you both have the opportunity to take part in the negotiation. You will find it helpful to divide the issues between you on the basis of your assigned 'job roles'.

FURTHER READING

Fisher, R. and Ury, W. (1981) *Getting to Yes*. Hutchinson, London.
Fisher, R., Kopelman, E. and Kupler Schneider, A. (1994) *Beyond Machiavelli: Tools for Coping with Conflict*. Harvard University Press, Cambridge, MA.
Neale, M.A. and Bazerman, M.H. (1991) *Cognition and Rationality in Negotation*. Free Press, London.
Rackham, N. and Carlisle, J. (1978) The effective negotiator, parts 1 and 2, *Journal of European Industrial Training* 2: 2–10.
Raiffa, H. (1985) *The Art and Science of Negotiation*. Belknap Press, Cambridge, MA.

CHAPTER 20

Political Skills

Heather Höpfl

OBJECTIVES

The purpose of this chapter is to:

◆ introduce the importance of an awareness of motive for understanding political behaviour in organisations.

INTRODUCTION

Most textbooks on organisations deal with the political aspects of organisational life in terms of power relationships and conflict and conflict resolution. This chapter takes a rather different starting place in that it deals with the micropolitics of interaction. Of course, in practice, these are embedded in the wider network of social relationships, as will be apparent from the case study. By giving attention to motive, the case study aims to give students the opportunity to explore a multiplicity of different standpoints that have a bearing on a situation and its interpretation. The case invites students to explore the motivations behind a range of different positions described in the case. It also asks students to reflect on their own experiences and motivations. The primary objective of the case study is to make students aware of the importance of being able to ascribe motives in order to understand the behaviour and, in this specific instance, the political behaviour of other actors in an organisational and domestic setting. Being able to read the motives of others and to predict their reactions to situations on the basis of that reading is a considerable political skill and one which affords some protection and comfort in the complexities of organisational life.

The Colleystone's Brewery Assignment

Matthew Wilson had successfully completed an Honours Degree in Business Studies with Accountancy at the University of South Yorkshire in 1994, had travelled in the USA for a year and had returned home, having had a lot of fun and met a lot of people but with little idea of what he wanted to do with his life. He met Sandra in a club in Manchester just before Christmas 1995. Sandra worked for a travel company, had studied French and Italian at university and had got her present job after working as a courier and resort representative for a large holiday company. She had hated those jobs, but her tenacity had paid off and now she had a career she enjoyed, recruiting reps and travelling to holiday resorts around the world. After going out with Sandra a few times, Matthew began to feel that his life was in a rut and that Sandra was kind but unimpressed by the fact that he was unemployed. One night, Matthew was looking through the local paper to see what bands were on that week when he saw an advert which caught his eye:

Derwent-Bridge Associates

Have you got what it takes to make a difference?

Dynamic young consultancy seeks recent graduate to strengthen an existing team of six. A background in accountancy with some knowledge of broader business issues would be an advantage. Full training given. Realistic salary.

Interested? *Call Simon on* **01777 443399**

Well, Matthew was interested, and so was Simon. They got on from the start. This was just as well since Simon said that experience was less important than chemistry and the ability to work in a team. Simon Derwent-Bridge was perhaps 10 years older than Matthew and had a confident, charming manner and a large BMW Coupé. Matthew and Simon shared an interest in rugby – both had played for their schools – and there was really little more to it. They found that they came from the same mould. Simon had worked for Grimm Brothers Consultants for a couple of years before deciding to start his own business. He had an MBA from a 'good' business school and a striking lack of self-awareness, which, ironically, seemed to be a considerable asset in his business. The way Simon explained it, the job was simple.

'What we actually do,' he confided in Matthew, 'is to spend a few days in an organisation analysing the *problem*. We've found that senior managers like to believe that there is *a problem*, and, frankly, they're happier if we tell them that it's a complex problem but one that we're familiar with. Clients like to think that there is an *answer*, so the more reassuring we are, the better they like it. This little consultancy I've set up specialises in financial problems – it's us – that's what we do and so far so good.'

Sandra was encouraging, and Matthew thought that a little experience of real-world problems would help him out of the unenviable position he was in and into the world of work. His first assignment was in a small drawing office. He found that he was doing little more than might be expected of a wages clerk, but it was all experience and he was only there for 2 weeks. There was no consulting involved in his second job either. He was sent to a small engineering works. They had a problem reconciling computer data with information they kept in a card index. The problem was easily resolved. The firm was grateful and Simon seemed happy, but Matthew wanted something to get his teeth into. He was to find it rather sooner than he might have wished.

Matthew's third assignment found him allocated to a job at a small brewery. The other members of the team joked with him about his luck and warned him not to drink away the profits. Simon warned him that this was an important customer and advised him to tread warily. Colleystone Brewery was a family-run business, and Giles Colleystone, Executive Director, was the head of the family and an old school friend of Simon's father. Competition for Giles' time – other business interests and a planned expedition to the Himalayas – had resulted in the appointment of Peter Connor as Managing Director. He had been in post for 2 years but as soon as Matthew met him he was aware that Peter Connor was very much under the thumb of the intimidating Giles. To be fair, Giles was extremely concerned about his business and his staff, probably in that order. The company was historically paternalistic, and many of the employees had been there for some years.

Matthew was given the task of investigating cash procedures; in effect, he was required to undertake a cash audit to follow the trail of procedures through a series of transactions. He was given an office to use during his stay and told he could have access to any document or information he might require. Almost immediately he started work, Matthew had the sense that all was not well. As is often the case in such circumstances, this was not so much from the data he was given to scrutinise but from the tacit, the intangible, an inkling. He had been working in the firm for about a week and a half and had found nothing irregular when one day there was a rather timid knock on the door of the office. A young woman came in, introduced herself as Barbara and asked if she could have a 'quick word'. 'I know it isn't really your problem,' she began, 'but there's quite a large discrepancy in the invoices.' Matthew gestured for her to stop. 'I'm sorry,' he said, 'but you must talk to the Financial Director about this. I'm afraid anything you've discovered has nothing to do with me. This is a problem that only Mr Spence can handle.'

The young woman hesitated but did not move. 'He won't talk to anyone,' she said. 'Everyone knows he has a closed door policy. He's very old fash-ioned. He believes that he does his job and we do ours. I've never seen the inside of his office.'

Barbara was quite new. She had been appointed as a temporary sales ledger clerk to cover for sickness and had just been given a permanent contract. She was sharp and had not only found a discrepancy in the invoices, but also asked some questions and made some investigations of her own. She now had some idea of what was going on but did not know whom she should talk to. She had spoken to Matthew in the hope that he might have found some similar discrepancies. Of course, Matthew had found nothing but, as an outsider, he had a sense of his invulnerability and, for this reason, he offered to talk to Mr Spence and provide him with the information that Barbara had collected. Matthew was not prepared for the reaction he was to receive from Spence.

Spence listened to Matthew with a look somewhere between irritation and self-righteousness. Matthew finished his explanation of where the discrepancy lay and offered some thoughts on the direction in which they might look for the source of the problem. At this point, Spence turned on the young accountant with a razor-sharp gaze as he began, 'Well, laddie, you must be feeling mighty proud of yourself. Found a mistake have we? Well, of course, you've had so much experience haven't you? What – 3 weeks outside the classroom and you can tell us all where we're going wrong can you? That damn clever are you? Well, you can get yourself out of my office, get into that nice company car they give you to play with and get the hell out of here. Go home sonny and get your nose out of things that don't concern you. Get out! Just get out!'

Worse was to come. Matthew rang back to his office and told Simon that he had some grave suspicions about the running of the firm. 'I'll not talk about it over the phone. I'll explain when I get back to the office,' he concluded. The reaction he got from Simon startled him. 'Look Matthew, I warned you to tread warily. This could be difficult for you. Don't come back here. I tell you what, ring me tomorrow and I'll see if I can smooth things over. Don't make contact with Colleystone's in the meantime and don't say anything to anybody until we have a better idea of what's going on. Don't make waves for God's sake.'

Matthew went home and talked to Sandra. He was confused and depressed. 'What have I done?', he asked Sandra. 'I'm supposed to be the good guy. Do you think they're all involved in what's going on? Is Simon involved too? Is the firm getting a cut?' Sandra began to get impatient: 'Worrying about it isn't going to help anyone,' she sighed, 'and you're beginning to get paranoid.'

Nothing happened the next day. Matthew rang his office but was told that Simon was not available and had left a message to say that he should keep clear for a few days and that he, Simon, would ring when he had any useful information. Four days passed, and Matthew had a telephone call from Spence. 'I think we should talk. I suggest we meet in the Markley Moat House on Friday afternoon at, shall we say, 3 o'clock.'

On Friday afternoon, Matthew turned up at the appointed time and waited with some trepidation for Spence to arrive. Spence was conciliatory. 'We have a problem at Colleystone's,' he conceded, 'but we are working on it. I have been aware of irregularities in the accounts for some time, but I haven't pinned down the person responsible yet. When you confronted me, I was angry because you are an outsider and, frankly, know bugger all about business. I was put out that you had uncovered a problem in so short a time.' Matthew was prepared to hear Spence out and began to sympathise with his predicament. As Financial Director, Spence continued, he was somewhat embarrassed by Matthew's revelations. Matthew had not anticipated the next development. Spence picked up his briefcase and placed it on the seat between them. He cautiously opened the case and took out an envelope. 'There's £1000 in this envelope. It's yours if you keep your mouth shut about our discussion. It's not that I have anything to hide – you must understand that. It's just that it would be better all round if you let me uncover the problem and deal with it in my own way. If you can trust me to do that, the money is yours.'

Matthew was shocked. He looked from the envelope to Spence to his feet and then gave his emphatic reply, 'No, I'm afraid I can't do that. There are many reasons why I can't be involved in this but I must tell you that first, I don't know what's happening in your company; second, I don't know who's involved in whatever is going on; and third, I'm really shocked that you think you could buy me off with the offer of money. What kind of person do you think I am?'

Spence appraised him sneeringly from head to foot and, with contempt, pronounced, 'A fool – and don't worry, sunshine, you'll learn not to mess with me.'

That evening Matthew told Sandra what had happened. 'It sounds like a Hollywood film,' she commented. 'Are you sure you're not making any of this up?' Matthew was angry. 'If I can't get any sympathy from you, you can just shut up. I've had a hell of a day and all I get from you is sarcasm.' 'Well, you must admit that all this is rather far-fetched,' Sandra offered. 'It does sound more like a novel than anything I've experienced where I work and, honestly, I've seen a lot.'

The next thing to happen was a call from Matthew's boss. 'What the hell kind of game do you think you are playing?', he demanded. 'Do you know, I've just had Vincent Spence on the phone and he tells me that you asked to meet him in Markley and then told him that unless he handed over £1000, you would tell Giles Colleystone that there are irregularities in the books. Now, I don't know what exactly you think you are involved in, but I'll have you know that my family and the Colleystone's have been friends for years and that anything that damages that relationship will be sorted out by me personally. Do you get my meaning? I do hope so.' Matthew's attempts to offer his version of the story were met with stony resistance. Matthew was convinced he had stepped into a nest of vipers. Simon Derwent-Bridge was clearly a man to be reckoned with. 'They're all as thick as thieves,' Matthew complained to Sandra when he got off the telephone. He was frightened, probably more frightened than he was prepared to admit even to himself.

'Is there no-one you can talk to at Colleystone's who isn't a member of the family? Could this Barbara say anything in your defence perhaps?' Matthew thought for a minute. 'Who'd take any notice of Barbara,' he reflected, 'she's only a sales ledger clerk. I don't expect she'd want to put her job on the line for me – and who'd listen anyway? There is Peter Connor though. He has only been there 2 years. He seems a bit afraid of the family set-up, but he also seems pretty straight. Perhaps I could talk to him. Perhaps someone might believe me.'

'Peter Connor.'

'Hello. This is Matthew Wilson, Mr Connor. I've been doing some work for your company for Derwent-Bridge Associates. I have a problem, and I wonder if you might be willing to talk to me?'.

'A problem, Matthew? What kind of problem? I haven't seen you around the place for a few days. Are you ill?'

'It's about the accounts – I can't talk about it over the phone. Can I see you? Preferably off-site.'

'It's a bit of a nuisance. Especially if you won't say what it's about. I'm in Wickham tonight for a Round Table meeting. I could see you for 10 minutes in the bar of the Green Lion at, say, 6.30 – would that do?'

However, Vincent Spence got in first. He told Connor about the alleged bribe and, worse, claimed that Matthew had created the entire story as a smoke-screen to cover up the fact that £1000 in cash had disappeared and that Matthew was the obvious suspect. When Matthew met Connor, it was brief. Connor threatened police involvement if Wilson did not back off and return the cash he had stolen immediately. Simon Derwent-Bridge washed his hands of the whole affair and told Matthew that 'You've got yourself into this mess and you can get yourself out.' Matthew was now in utter despair, and his relationship with Sandra was under enormous pressure.

At this point, circumstances took over. Matthew had been excluded by Colleystone's under threat. He had been excluded *de facto* from Derwent-Bridge Associates, and Sandra had difficulty believing his story. As the weeks passed, he found that he himself could hardly believe what had happened to him at the brewery. 'Perhaps,' he concluded, 'I was just a fool. There must have been something I could have done to help me avoid all this mess.'

---

the exercise

This exercise is intended to be used in a 3-hour workshop session. It is designed to help you to consider complex situations and to understand why the ability to ascribe motive is an important political skill. Question 1 should be answered individually. Question 2 is intended to be answered by students working in pairs. Question 3 should be answered by class discussion to draw out what has been learned from Questions 1 and 2. Question 4 is to be answered by small groups of three or four. The groups should then report back to the full group, and a list of motives should be identified and discussed by the tutor. Question 5 is to be worked on by the same groups as Question 4. Groups should then report back, and the tutor should compile a list of the motives identified and might usefully compare these with Matthew's motives identified in Question 2. Questions 6 and 7 are for class discussion.

You will find two chapters in Luthans' (1992) edition of *Organizational Behaviour* very useful as a straightforward introduction to some of the issues identified in the text. In Chapter 6, Motivation theory: needs and processes, Luthans offers a range of what he terms primary and secondary motives (Luthans, 1992, pp. 147–54). These should help you to reflect on the range of motivations that might be considered in the analysis of the case. However, you may also wish to draw on common-sense interpretations and see how these compare with those suggested by Luthans. You should also give some thought to the problem of conflicting motives and their resolution. In Chapter 15, Power and politics, Luthans examines the political context of organisational behaviour (Luthans, 1992, pp. 425–61). Pay particular attention to pages 438–44, where Luthans identifies a range of strategies for attaining power in organisations. The list presented is not exhaustive but might provide some clues to the types of behaviour identified in the case study and their political basis. Chapter 4 of Sims *et al.* (1993), Dealing and double-dealing, makes for interesting and instructive reading on organisational politics, and Fineman and Gabriel (1996), in their extraordinarily powerful and realistic accounts of various experiences of organisations, offer a particularly relevant chapter, 'Who gets the blame?' (Chapter 9) in *Experiencing Organizations*. Hirschhorn (1988) provides some insights into scapegoating.

A full account of what actually happened to Matthew is provided in the Tutor's Notes. You should be aware of the outcomes. This additional information should contribute to the range of issues raised for the conclusion of the discussion.

Session Outline:

Tutor instruction to the session: 5 mins
Reading the case   10 mins
Question 1 – individual work   10 mins
Question 2 – in pairs   15 mins
Question 3 – class discussion   15 mins
Question 4 – in groups of 3 or 4   15 mins
    – groups report back   15 mins
    – summary by tutor   5 mins
Refreshment break   15 mins
Question 5 – work in groups   10 mins
    – reporting back   10 mins
    – list of motives   5 mins
Tutor: what actually happened   10 mins
    – discussion   10 mins
Question 6 – class discussion   10 mins
Question 7 – tutor-directed discussion   10 mins

The questions

1. Outline the chronology of the events that led Matthew to his present position.

2. Identify the points in the story at which Matthew had choices to make, and for each provide a brief explanation of what seems to be the primary motivation for his behaviour.

3. Some courses of action clearly had more serious consequences than others. Which actions do you feel were most significant to the outcome of this story?

4. For these significant events, consider the alternative personal strategies that Matthew could have adopted.

5. List the main characters in the story and try to assess what motives they might have for their attitudes and behaviour.

6. Is Matthew politically naïve? If you think he is, how would you advise him to act in the future?

7. What can be learned from this case study? How might students be made aware of the political complexity of work situations?

191

ACKNOWLEDGEMENT

The author wishes to acknowledge the contribution of J. L. Dale, Management Consultant, on whose sundry experiences this case is based.

REFERENCES AND FURTHER READING

Clark, T. and Salaman, G. (1996) Telling tales: management consultancy as the art of story telling. In Grant, D. and Oswick, C. (eds) *Metaphor and Organizations*. Sage, London.

Ditton, J. (1977) *Part-time Crime: An Ethnography of Fiddling and Pilferage*. Macmillan, London.

Fineman, S. and Gabriel, Y. (1996) *Experiencing Organizations*. Sage, London.

Hirschhorn, L. (1988) *The Workplace Within*. MIT Press, Cambridge, MA.

Jay, A. (1967) *Management and Machiavelli*. Holt, New York.

Kakabadse, A. (1987) Organizational politics, *Management Decision* **25**(1).

Luthans, F. (1992) *Organizational Behaviour*, 6th edn. McGraw-Hill, New York.

Sims, D., Fineman, S. and Gabriel, Y. (1993) *Organizing and Organizations: An Introduction*. Sage, London.

Yukl, G. (1990) *Skills for Managers and Leaders*. Prentice-Hall, Englewood Cliffs, NJ.

CHAPTER 21

Presentation Skills

Dot Griffiths

OBJECTIVES

The objectives of this chapter are to:

▶ introduce the principal skills involved in making an effective presentation
▶ provide some experience in preparing and delivering a presentation
▶ provide an opportunity to recognise the importance of being able to make an effective presentation.

INTRODUCTION

This chapter describes the experience of Nita Gopal giving a presentation. It allows a comparison of Nita's presentation with others. Following the case, there are three exercises that draw on the material in the case. The final exercise involves students preparing and delivering their own presentations. Some resources may be needed for this, for example flip charts, overhead projector slides and pens.

Nita Gopal's Presentation

Nita Gopal is 28. She works for a voluntary sector organisation called PetFriend. PetFriend is a charity that provides pets (mainly cats, dogs, hamsters and budgies) to the elderly and the sick. Old people find that pets provide a structure for their lives, as well as giving them something to care for. For many sick people, contact with animals raises their spirits and may even have a therapeutic benefit. There is, for example, evidence that blood pressure drops when you stroke a cat or a dog.

PetFriend was founded in 1925 by a bequest from Miss Dorothea Ellis of Knutsford, Cheshire, who requested that 'a charity be established to rescue unwanted animals and place them with the elderly and infirm such that they find comfort and solace from that presence... and further, that these animals be fed and protected by my bequest in such cases as the elderly and infirm are unable so to do.' It wasn't clear whether Miss Ellis was more concerned about homeless animals or the elderly and ill, but, in the way of such animal-focused charities, the Dorothea Ellis Bequest, as it was originally known, attracted further bequests over the years and established a number of branches across Britain. It changed its name in the 1960s as it began to work more systematically with health and social services. The focus is now more on people welfare than on animal welfare. As such, it receives funding from a variety of sources: bequests (the animal welfare element still attracts some people's money); an annual flag day; (declining) grants from social service budgets and health authority budgets; and local 'Friends' fund raising.

London North PetFriend is based in north-west London. It works closely with social services, the health authority and local animal charities. Social services often identify elderly people who could benefit from a pet following a bereavement or the loss of their own pet. The health authority works with PetFriend on two schemes: taking animals into the local hospitals (Kensal Rise Infirmary and Cricklewood General) to visit sick children, and work with the local (privately funded) hospice, St Francis of Assisi. Local animal charities supply many of PetFriends' pets. PetFriend is a major 'outlet' for unwanted pets in North London.

Nita Gopal has worked for PetFriend for 3 years. She is a qualified social worker and counsellor who previously worked in children's homes. She found the work in children's homes too harrowing and was delighted when PetFriend advertised a vacancy for a counsellor in London North. She loves her work at PetFriend: the mix of client types, the counselling itself and the pets. She has also just been promoted to the post of Team Leader. This will involve her in a wider range of tasks, including external liaison.

Nita's problems began when the local secondary school, Cricklewood High School, decided to adopt PetFriend as its charity for the forthcoming year. Each year, the school adopts a charity and the children work on projects with the charity and raise funds for it. As the Team Leader responsible for external liaison, Nita had to manage this for PetFriend.

Nita and PetFriend were delighted when the head teacher, Mark Kerrison, contacted them to ask whether they were interested in becoming the charity for the next year. For PetFriend, it represented a chance to build a link with a key local institution and to make contact with a lot of local people through the school's pupils, their friends and their parents. Improved interaction with the local community would also serve to strengthen PetFriend's bid for support from the local authority's social services department. The London Borough of Kensal was always keen to encourage and support collaboration across departments.

Cricklewood High School has a Charity Council consisting of a group of senior pupils, the head of the Upper School and the Head Teacher. The pupils run the council and organise the link to the charity and the fund raising events. Each year, the school holds an Open Day on a Saturday, to which parents and the local community are invited. One of the events of each open day is a presentation from the charity that has been adopted for the forthcoming year, complemented by presentations from other relevant bodies. This year, PetFriend was to be joined by a local vet and a local animal shelter.

Nita was not entirely happy about having to give a presentation. The thought of standing up in front of people made her stomach sink and her palms sweat. She looked at the letter from the Head Teacher and saw 'Presentation... 2pm, Saturday, June 9th' and felt terrified. All she could think about was what would happen if she stood up, opened her mouth and nothing came out.

The Head had suggested that, if PetFriend was willing to be adopted, Nita should visit the school to meet the Charity Council and to discuss some of the ways in which the pupils of various ages could become involved in PetFriend's activities. Nita enjoyed the meeting. The pupils were bright and enthusiastic. PetFriend had decided that the children could contribute to their activities by dog walking for the elderly, providing home support (a daily rota to feed and clean pets), naming newly rescued pets, work in the PetFriend Animal Shelter (including more dog walking, grooming, feeding, and so on), and accompanying PetFriend staff and volunteers on outings with the PetFriend donkeys. These proposals were well received, and there seemed to be plenty of ideas for fund raising activities.

As the Open Day drew closer, Nita began to get more and more tense. She began to prepare her talk. Her first problem was what to say. Luckily, PetFriend Manchester had recently produced a history of the charity that Nita had found very interesting, so she decided to base her own talk on this. She read it carefully and took notes. The history was divided into three sections: The Early Years, 1925–35, The Dorothy Ellis Bequest; The Middle Years, 1935–60, Expansion; and PetFriend, 1960 onwards. Nita had found the history very entertaining; there had been some funny old souls who had left bequests in the early days, and some real characters had acted as volunteers over the years.

The head had told her that she should talk for about 20 minutes, so Nita worked on her notes and turned them into a text that was six pages long. This seemed plenty of material to fill 20 minutes. She typed it up carefully. The invitation had asked her if she was going to use any visual aids. She wondered about taking a dog to sit by her while she talked but decided that this was probably too risky, and anyway there would be dogs and other animals for the children to pet at the PetFriend display, which was being organised in the playground. The PetFriend donkeys, Monty and Jeremy, were also going to be there.

The day finally arrived. Nita didn't sleep too well the night before, but at least it would all be over by tonight. She arrived at 12.30, as the Head had invited her to the buffet lunch for distinguished visitors. As soon as she arrived at the lunch, she felt uncomfortable. Everyone else there was rather more smartly dressed than she was. She definitely regretted the trainers as she was introduced to the Chair of the Governors, the members of the Governing Body, and worse, the Chair of Social Services, officers from the local council and the warden from the Restwell residential home. The Chair of Governors gave her a sinking feeling when he said that the choice of PetFriend had been controversial but that, having selected it, 'they' were all behind it now and were looking forward to hearing about her proposals for the year ahead. Proposals...? (When she re-read the head's invitation letter afterwards, she saw that she had been asked to talk about PetFriend in the local community and how the school could contribute in the year ahead.)

Later, Nita could not recall much about the rest of the lunch. By 2 pm, she had severe butterflies in her stomach, a beating heart and very sweaty palms as she climbed on to the platform with the Head, the Governors and the other speakers. The Great Hall was full – PetFriend was popular with the children and parents, if not with the governors!

The head teacher stood up. Nita noticed that he held some small cards in his hand, which he used as a prompt as he spoke. He welcomed all the people present: the platform guests, other distinguished guests, the parents, the pupils and, of course, the speakers. He began by outlining some of the main achievements of the school over the past year. He then explained why the school adopted a charity each year and how the charity work was organised by the Charity Council, and described some of the achievements of the previous year's charity (Kid Aid). He then announced PetFriend as the adopted charity for the forthcoming year and outlined the presentations that were to follow. There would be a speaker from PetFriend, followed by a local vet and then a representative from a local animal shelter. Afterwards the speakers, visitors and pupils could visit classrooms to see displays of work, visit the teaching staff, visit the PetFriend and other animal events in the playground and generally get to know the school and its environs a little better. He concluded by thanking everyone for supporting the school and introducing Nita, who would, he said, be introducing PetFriend's work in the area, explaining the role of pets in welfare (he mentioned her background as a social worker) and outlining some of the projects to which the school would be contributing.

Nita's stomach lurched harder. All she had to talk about was old biddies who had left money to cats! But there was no avoiding it now. They were applauding and looking expectantly at her. She stood up...

The next 20 minutes were among the most unpleasant and unhappy 20 minutes Nita had ever spent. Having to talk in front of all of those people would have been quite bad enough... but having to do it while your mind was in turmoil about whether what you were saying was appropriate was even worse. It was like living through a nightmare. Her bounce and confidence had completely disappeared. She thought that everyone could see that she was shaking. To stop herself trembling, she stood with one foot crossed in front of the other and held her notes in both hands. If only they would stop looking at her.... As soon as she started, she realised that it didn't sound right reading out her notes – it was too formal and uncomfortable and gave her the awful sensation of hearing her own voice floating out from her. She tried to read the next sentence and then speak it but that didn't work. She couldn't read one thing while speaking of something else. She paused, seized by panic; she looked up and saw all those faces looking at her and wished she had the courage to run off the platform and away. She looked back at her notes. Now she had lost her place, another pause while she found it. She could hear the audience getting restless. She felt their attention burning into her. She fell into reading from her notes. She was too miserable to look up any more. What her audience heard was a history of PetFriend, read in a monotone and without impact – hardly what they had expected from the head teacher's introduction. Nita's talk was boring, and they were unimpressed. The Chair of Governors was furious. Nita, meanwhile, carried on reading her talk. Her six pages lasted 9 minutes, 52 seconds. She dried up. If it were possible for her to feel yet more terrified and panicked, she did. How could she fill the chasm of time left to her? She started to *ad lib* and fell into talking about some of the pets which had been rescued and how the school could name them. This seemed to please the juniors at the front, but by now the older ones at the back were beginning to look rebellious. She looked at the Head in terror. He responded with a question about the impact of the contact with pets on sick children. Nita's mind went absolutely blank. Impact? Impact? What did he mean by impact? Then she realised and was able to chat quite happily about the therapeutic effects of contact with animals. The Head then rescued her by thanking her for her talk and wishing PetFriend well for the year ahead. She sat down to muted applause. Frankly, she would have preferred to sink through the floor. She couldn't bear to look at anyone. All she wanted to do was to disappear.

The Head Teacher stood up again and spoke for a couple of minutes about why the school had selected PetFriend. What had attracted them was the link between animal welfare and people welfare. Children, he explained, were more easily interested in sick animals than sick people. The school hoped that PetFriend would make illness and age more approachable for the pupils. He then introduced the next speaker: John Irvine, a vet from the local veterinary practice. He had been asked to speak about work with animals. Had Nita been able to concentrate on what he was saying, she would have found John's presentation very different from her own.

He began by thanking the head and the school for inviting him. He then put on an overhead projector slide and went through the outline of his talk. Unlike the head, who had used cards to remind him what to say, the vet spoke from his slides without any notes or prompt cards. His theme was working with animals, and he planned, he said, to explain how rewarding it could be and to tell them some of his own experiences. He would also be outlining some of the careers available in animal care and some of the ways in which they could become involved in animal care as volunteers... but first he would tell them a bit about himself. He decided to become a vet because he liked animals. He made everyone laugh when he said that it was helpful to have a good sense of humour and a poor sense of smell if you wanted to be a vet. A sense of humour for the middle of the night when you were helping a cow to calf, and a poor sense of smell for a cow with an upset stomach! He talked about some of his experiences as a vet: there seemed to be a story for everyone. The pregnant cat in the traffic accident who survived and produced a healthy litter (complete with a picture of the proud mother and her family) for girls in the junior years; ethical issues about breeding animals for experiments for the senior years; a story about being the vet for the day for a film production company using the local park as a location for an advertisement involving a tiger and how he had to get a metal splinter out of the tiger's paw at the end of the day; and using an electric drill to do a filling in an elephant's tooth for the cynical male adolescents. This group also looked quite impressed when he described getting sperm from an extremely large bull! Each of his stories was accompanied by a picture or a cartoon, and he explained what he was going to talk about at each stage.

Having won the interest of his audience with his stories, he then went on to describe some of the careers available working with animals. Again, there were helpful slides as he discussed a range of careers including, of course, becoming a vet, working with animals as a veterinary nurse, being an animal keeper at a zoo, animal charities, wildlife, the Forces, stable work... the list went on and, like his stories, included something for everyone. All interests and abilities were addressed. His last section was on the opportunities for voluntary work with animals in which the children could participate. PetFriend got a mention here, as did a number of other options. Again, everyone was included. He had bothered to find out about activities outside the immediate area so he could talk about the urban farm in a neighbouring borough and the donkey sanctuary on the outskirts of London, as well as more locally based activities. He had also produced a leaflet giving contact names and addresses. He concluded his talk with a brief summary of what he had said, thanked everyone for listening and sat down to thunderous applause.

The final speaker was Rosa Minniallis from the local animal shelter, who was to talk about 'Owning a Pet'. She, too, approached the task differently from Nita. Like John, Rosa began by thanking the Head and the school for inviting her. She had, she said, three messages to deliver about owning a pet. First, having a pet could be a source of a lot of fun and a lot of learning; second, having a pet was a serious responsibility; and third, before you got a pet, there were three questions you should ask yourself: am I willing and able to make a long-term commitment to this animal?, do I have the resources to look after this animal?, and have I really thought through my choice of pet? She then worked her way through each theme. She discussed some of the pleasures of owning dogs, cats, gerbils and so on. She discussed some of the things you needed to learn about if you were going to get a more exotic pet (appeal to the adolescent youth again!). She discussed pets as a responsibility and gave some sad examples of neglected pets. To stop the atmosphere becoming too sombre, she concluded this section with a happy ending. Having shown a picture of an emaciated and bruised dog (like the vet, she had slides and pictures), she whistled and a colleague opened the door, and Rusty came bounding into the hall and onto the platform. Rusty now 'worked' as a PetFriend dog and was one of the animals taken to the infirmary for sick children. She used Rusty's story to raise again the questions she wanted them all to ask before they got a pet. Again, like the vet, she summarised her key messages in her conclusion and thanked the audience for their attention. Her presentation was very clear, but she kept turning to the screen to look at what was on it, consequently losing contact with her audience. Rusty, however, was a star. So she also sat down to an enthusiastic response.

The Head Teacher stood up again, thanked all the speakers and explained where the various displays were and the other arrangements. People then began to move out of the Great Hall. Nita couldn't look at anyone. She felt dreadful. The presentations by John and Rosa had been so much livelier, more interesting and more engaging than hers. She held back as the others left the platform; she couldn't face them. As the Chair of Governors went by, he said, 'A wasted opportunity, young woman'. Tears began to fill Nita's eyes and she sat down again. Noticing this, the Head came across and said kindly that public speaking was a skill that took lots of practice. Everyone had some bad experiences when they began, he continued. She shouldn't take it to heart, but she should give another presentation soon. He then invited her to address a school assembly on the plans for PetFriend activities in the school at the start of the next term. She mumbled something and went to leave. As she was leaving the platform, she noticed that John had left a folder on the lecturn. She took it to return to him later. As she went to pick it up, her hand slipped, and the folder fell open. It contained the following:

1. a laminated card, about the size of three credit cards, headed Presentation Skills (Figure 21.1)
2. a couple of pages of handwritten notes (Figure 21.2)

3. two slides (Figures 21.3 and 21.4).

Nita shuffled them all back Into the folder and walked slowly out of the Great Hall into the playground to the PetFriend display. As usual, it was surrounded by children wanting to pet the (very patient) donkeys and the various furry creatures. The PetFriend parrot, Charlie, was also there chattering away on his perch and being generally disdainful of all the attention.

The afternoon was an experience Nita never ever wanted to repeat. She looked carefully at the contents of the vet's folder before she gave it back to him. She decided that she had to learn to give a decent presentation, so she accepted the Head's invitation. She also wanted to feel better about the school, so a second chance to make a better impression was welcomed. This time, she began by thinking about who she was giving her presentation to and why, and what her audience might be interested in. She prepared carefully. She wrote some phrases to remind her of what to say on some prompt cards and made slides. She rehearsed.

On Wednesday, September 15th, a very nervous Nita stood up with a beating heart, churning stomach and sweaty palms at the Cricklewood High School assembly. As she stood up, she was holding a set of prompt cards. She stood with her weight on both feet, took a deep breath and placed her first slide on the projector. She knew exactly what her opening sentence would be. Ten minutes later, a euphoric Nita sat down to an enthusiastic response and to congratulations from the Head.

PRESENTATION SKILLS

Preparation

Objectives:

◆ Be clear on the purpose of the presentation and the outcomes required.

Key messages:

◆ What do you most want your audience to remember? They should be short and sharp and few in number.

Audience:

◆ What are their expectations?
◆ How much knowledge can you assume?
◆ How many will there be?
◆ Volunteers or conscripts?

Structure:

◆ Introduction: capture attention.
◆ Main part: deliver key messages.
◆ Conclusions: restate key messages.

Practice:

◆ Rehearse

cont'd

Delivery

Pace and tone:

◆ Don't rush.
◆ Vary your speed.
◆ Speak clearly and loudly, but don't shout.

Eye contact:

◆ Look at your audience.

Posture:

◆ Stand up straight with your weight on both feet.
◆ Avoid mannerisms such as jingling coins in your pocket.
◆ Relax, smile and convey interest in your subject.

Support

Notes:

◆ Don't write out your presentation and read it word for word.
◆ Prepare prompt cards or speak from your slides.

Visual aids:

◆ Direct attention away from you.
◆ Keep visual aids clear and simple.

Equipment:

◆ Check what is available.
◆ Check that it is working.

Figure 21.1   The laminated card

Talk to Cricklewood High Plan

Key messages:
work with animals is fun and varied
there are lots of careers with animals
you can work as a volunteer

Outline:
opener: question???
introduction: why I'm a vet
                      key messages

Main body:
stories for young children, adolescents, older
children

Careers:
vet, and so on

Voluntary work:
Kensal Shelter/Fur and Feathers Shelter,
and so on

Close:
key messages
thanks

Introduction: Plan

- thank head
- hello to all
- introduce self – SLIDE
- elephant toothache – SLIDE

4 minutes

Figure 21.2   The handwritten notes

John Irvine B.Vet Med MRCVS

PAWS VETERINARY PRACTICE

■ Animals are fun
■ Lots of careers
■ We need volunteers

HAVE YOU EVER WONDERED WHAT
HAPPENS TO AN ELEPHANT WITH
TOOTHACHE?

Figure 21.3 and 21.4   The slides

the exercises

The case study can be used in a number of ways:

◆ to identify the qualities of a good presentation
◆ to identify the mistakes that Nita made in her presentation and to suggest what she could have done differently
◆ as a background for students to prepare, support and deliver a short presentation of their own.

Each exercise, except the delivery of the presentation, can be undertaken either individually and/or in a small group. The presentation is prepared individually and delivered to a small group.

The qualities of a good presentation

This exercise has three parts. Ask the students to:

◆ identify the qualities of a good presentation
◆ use this list as a template to examine Nita's first presentation and performance compared with that of the Head, John Irvine and Rosa Minniallis
◆ produce a checklist that could be used to give feedback on a presentation.

Advice to Nita

Ask the students to imagine that they are a presentation skills consultant. Nita Gopal, following this experience, has asked them to help her to improve her presentation skills. The exercise has a number of steps:

1. Students first identify a list of the ways in which Nita's presentation could have been improved. Again, they can make comparisons with the other presentations.
2. Using this list, students then prepare a set of guidelines for effective presentations.
3. An optional additional step can be to role play giving Nita feedback on her presentation.

Identifying key messages

Since the key messages are such a crucial part of any presentation, this exercise focuses on their identification. Allocate students a topic and ask them to identify the four or five key messages that they would want to deliver on this topic.

Theory into practice

Ask students to prepare and to make a short presentation of their own. Ideally, they should make quite a substantial presentation of, say, 5–10 minutes in length. Their presentation should be supported by some kind of visual aid.

FURTHER READING

There are many, many guides to making presentations. Some of the particularly helpful ones include:

Fowler, A. (1996) How to provide effective feedback, *People Management*, 11 July:44–5.
Goodlad, S. (1996) *Speaking Technically*. Imperial College Press, London.
Linver, S. (1994) *Speak and Get Results*. Simon & Schuster, New York.
Peel, M. (1998) *Successful Presentation*, 2nd edn. Hodder & Stoughton, London.
Vicar, R. (1997) *How to Speak and Write Persuasively*. Kogan Page, London.

CHAPTER 22

Project Management

Graham M. Winch

OBJECTIVES

The objectives of this role play are to:

▶ relate the individual and organisational levels of decision making
▶ explore the dynamics of coalitions of firms in collaboration
▶ show how conflicting interests can be resolved
▶ introduce the concept of stakeholder analysis.

INTRODUCTION

This chapter is concerned with the processes and skills of compromise and negotiation in seeking to satisfy a range of conflicting interests held by different stakeholders – a central issue of project management.

 **Revitalising Sheffield**

By the mid-1980s, Sheffield had suffered the severe and permanent decline of its traditional industrial base, leaving large areas of the inner city derelict. Like many provincial British cities, it sought to revitalise its economy and urban fabric through investment in cultural and leisure facilities. In 1986, it saw an opportunity to do this by offering to host the Universiade XVI (16th World Student Games) in June 1991. This, it was argued, would provide the investment opportunities and lever the capital grants that would lead to the desired regeneration. However, Sheffield City Council received no support from central government for its efforts, at a time when relations between Sheffield and some other Labour-controlled cities and the Thatcher government had reached a nadir.

A number of projects were involved – the Ponds Forge swimming pool, the Don Valley Stadium and the conversion of the semi-derelict Hyde

Park flats into a games village. An additional requirement for an 'events hall' was identified in order to house gymnastics, basketball, volleyball and ice sports. As funds were not available from central government, and there were many other demands on the resources of the city, it was decided to seek a private sector partner to design, build, finance and operate the facility. It was also clear that the facility could not be commercially justified on sports uses alone. Therefore, a multiuse facility was proposed, which could also host concerts and exhibitions, to be called the Sheffield Arena.

The overall programme for the games was managed by two companies set up by Sheffield City Council. Sheffield for Health Ltd would build and run the facilities, while Universiade GB Ltd would run the actual games. Both were companies limited by guarantee, with Sheffield City Council as the first guarantor. Sheffield for Health Ltd would borrow in the open market, while Universiade GB Ltd would live off sponsorship money. During 1989, neither strategies were raising adequate funds, and both companies were running up serious debts.

By the middle of 1989, the design for the Arena was well underway, and enabling works had started on site. This role play will focus upon three key design issues that caused crisis for the management of the project at that time. In addition to the enormous time pressures generated by the immovable deadline of 1 June 1991 for the opening of the games, an event completely unconnected with the project had an enormous impact – the disaster in Sheffield's Hillsborough football stadium in April 1989, in which 95 people were killed when spectators were crushed during crowd surges in the stands. At the time of the events that form the basis of this role play, the disaster was fresh in the local memory, and the report of enquiry into it was not yet published.

Owing to difficulties with putting together the funding package, the funds were not in place to finance the project during 1989, and the architects and engineers were asked by the client to work on the project on a 'goodwill' basis in order to keep things rolling, with a promise of payment when funding finally materialised. As a client representative said to the architects and engineers, 'If you do not show faith in us at this critical period, then we will have to think twice about retaining you for our other projects which we are in the process of finalising.'

The principal constraint on all the actors was time. As the project manager said, 'You cannot say to 6000 eager runners, gymnasts, jumpers and throwers: could you all come back next month, we are a little behind programme.'

The actors

This section describes the principal actors on the project and their basic functions. Other organisations were involved in the project coalition in subcontract to these actors.

Sheffield City Council was the **promoter** of the project, fulfilling what it saw as its democratic mandate to regenerate the industrially devastated Don valley in spite of intense opposition from central government and other political opponents. It saw the Universiade as a way to achieve its objectives in this respect and to provide the people of Sheffield with a lasting resource. Their interests in this respect were represented on the project by their land and planning division. Their interests were to ensure the success of the Universiade and, through that, to stimulate the regeneration of key areas of the city. They were constrained by a lack of support from central government, shortages of capital, mounting cost overruns on other projects in the Universiade programme and the fear of a revolt by local rate payers if the Council's guarantees were called in.

Mowlem Management Ltd were appointed by Sheffield City Council as **project manager**, overseeing the progress of the project on behalf of the promoter, and to chair project review meetings. They were also working on other construction projects in the overall games programme. Their interests were to ensure the achievement of their customer's interests through advising them on the progress of the project and the steps that might be taken to avert problems. Their constraints were their customer's constraints.

Spectacor Management Group (SMG) were to be the operators of the facility. They successfully tendered to Sheffield City Council to design, build and operate the facility, and came to an arrangement whereby they would help the promoter to put together a financial package from the private sector. Based in Philadelphia, USA, they manage sports facilities on behalf of public and other authorities throughout the USA. They became the **client** for the actors in the project coalition. Their objectives were to ensure that the costs of the facility were low enough and that the quality and capacity of the facility were high enough to ensure a revenue stream that would allow the financiers to recoup their investment and SMG to run the facility at a profit. As their operations manager stated, 'Give me as many comfortable seats with good sight lines as the Arena auditorium will accommodate. Remember more seats mean more revenue, more revenue means more profit.' Their principal constraints were that they would be liable to Sheffield City Council if the facility was not ready in time for the games, and a lack of understanding of how British local governments worked.

Hellmuth Obata Kassabaum Sports Facilities Group (HOK) of Kansas City, USA, is part of one of the world's largest architecture/engineering firms. Specialists in designing sports facilities, they have worked for SMG many times. They were the **concept architects** for the facility, appointed on a fee basis. Their objectives were to satisfy a longstanding customer while retaining their reputation as the leading architects in sports facilities. Their constraints were their client's, plus a lack of knowledge of the British context and the cost of putting in resources to the project on a goodwill basis.

Lister Drew Haines Barrow (LDHB) of Weybridge were leading British architectural specialists in sports facilities. They entered into a 50/50 consortium with HOK and undertook most of the detail design for the facility as **project architects** on a fee basis. They were also working in a similar manner with HOK on the Docklands Arena project. Their objectives were similar to those of HOK, with whom they were also in consortium on the Docklands Arena, as well as to build up a reputation in sports facilities. Their main constraints were those of SMG, coupled with the fact that HOK was taking the lead on the overall design, with LDHB responsible for implementing it.

Oscar Faber & Partners of St Albans were the **engineers** for the facility, responsible to the client for engineering both the structure and the mechanical and electrical services inside the building. Their objectives were to provide a service to the client while retaining their reputation. Their constraints were that they could do little until the main architectural design issues were resolved.

Poole Stokes & Wood of London were appointed as **quantity surveyors**. They were responsible both for advising the client on the costs of the various design options and for preparing the bills of quantity that would be used as the basis of competitive tendering for the trade contractors. Any proposals for changing the design from the architects or engineers would have to meet their approval from the point of view of costs. Their objectives were to meet the client's requirements for cost information and to retain their reputation as quantity surveyors.

R.M. Douglas of Birmingham successfully tendered as **construction managers** responsible for selecting and co-ordinating the trade contractors who actually carried out the 46 separate works packages for the construction of the arena. Working on a fee basis, their objectives were to meet the client's quality, cost and time objectives. Their principal constraints were that they could do little until design issues were resolved and that the National Coal Board had found a seam of coal at the eastern end of the site and had exercised their statutory right to exploit it as an open-cast mine during 1989, not releasing that portion of the site until the end of the year.

Sheffield City Council were also responsible as **statutory authority** (SA) through their building control, fire and civil defence division. These responsibilities on the project consisted of ensuring that the Arena complied with the building regulations, the statutory codes that provided for the integrity of the structure and the safety of its users. Their objectives were to fulfill their statutory obligations; their constraint was the strong local sensitivity following the Hillsborough disaster. Indeed, many of the staff concerned with the Arena project were appearing before the inquiry into the Hillsborough disaster.

The issues

During 1989, three main issues came to a head in the design process and demanded a speedy and cost-effective resolution. These were the means of emergency escape, the tiered seating gradient and the guard rail height. The relationship between architects and engineers on the one hand and statutory authorities on the other is one of propose and dispose. The design team proposes solutions that will meet client needs, while the SA comments on these design solutions, indicating the points at which they are unsatisfactory from a regulatory point of view. Redress is available in the case of dispute through an appeal to central government in the shape of the Secretary of State for the Environment.

The specific issues were as follows:

◆ *Emergency escape*. The SA insisted upon a 2400 mm wide cross-aisle to be used for the evacuation of the arena in the event of fire. This would result in the loss of 900 seats.
◆ *Tiered seating*. The SA said that the tiers were too steep, and that the rake should be lowered to ease the climbing of the stairs. This would have spoiled sight lines for the spectators and, as the raking beams were already under construction, have had severe implications for budget and programme due to rework.

♦ *Safety rails*. The SA requested 1100 mm high safety rails in the auditorium, which complied with the prevailing regulations. However, these would have obscured the spectators' view, and 800 mm was preferred by the architects.

In sum, these instructions from the SA would have the effect of:

♦ obliging structural works, already underway because of the very tight programme, to be scrapped and redone, with obvious implications for the programme and budget
♦ reducing the number of seats with good sight lines and hence the profitability of the operation of the facility
♦ reducing the comfort of users of the building and hence its attractiveness to potential customers.

SMG and their architects, HOK, took the view that they had designed and managed large numbers of similar buildings in the USA that had operated in perfect safety for many years. These were designed and operated in accordance with standards approved by the American Standards Association. Similar buildings in Birmingham and London, designed by HOK, had been accepted by the relevant SAs. As one SMG representative argued, 'It is evident that the [SA] have no idea about what is involved. We have been appointed by Sheffield as experts in our field. Surely they must rely on expert knowledge and experience.'

The SA, on the other hand, took the view that full compliance with the British Building Regulations was required in the context of high public concern following the Hillsborough disaster. However, no regulations for this type of multipurpose arena actually existed, so the SA were obliged to adopt those for theatres, cinemas and football stadiums. This led to considerable room for interpretation and argument.

The scenario is a project review meeting in mid-1989, where all the issues are on the table. The project manager is in the chair, and all the actors are represented. Your exercise is to resolve these disputes so that the objectives of all the actors can be met and the project made a success.

the exercises

exercise
1

Role play

You should select the point of view of one of the actors and argue your case in light of your interests and constraints. In reviewing the role play, you should address the following questions:

1. Can you understand the logic of the positions of the other actors?
2. How far can you compromise without undermining the logic of your position?
3. Can you think of other ways of finding solutions to the impasse?

4. How could a stakeholder analysis be applied to SMG's position?
5. How might the lessons of the Sheffield Arena be applied to the Millennium Exhibition project or another project of which you are aware?

FURTHER READING

The two main texts on project management are:

Turner, J.R. (1993) *Handbook of Project-Based Management*. McGraw-Hill, London.
Turner, J.R. (ed.) (1995) *The Commercial Project Manager*. McGraw-Hill, London.

Two texts describing the dynamics of construction projects are:

Sabbah, K. (1989) *Skyscraper*. Macmillan, London.
Williams, S. (1989) *Hongkong Bank – The Building of Norman Foster's Masterpiece*. Jonathan Cape, London.

Stakeholder analysis is presented in:

Johnson, G. and Scholes, K. (1997) *Exploring Corporate Strategy*, 4th edn, Chapter 5. Prentice-Hall, London.

CHAPTER 23

Problem Solving

Kevin Gaston and Tudor Rickards

OBJECTIVES

The objectives of this chapter are to:

▶ introduce organisational problem solving
▶ give some experience of problem solving
▶ gain insights into problem-solving skills
▶ give some experience of using those skills.

INTRODUCTION

This chapter is concerned with the ways in which people solve problems in organisations. It is organised around a case example that is itself based on a realistic organisational challenge. In its original format, the exercise was a challenge set for an MBA team by Fran Cotton, CEO of Cotton Traders. In its current format, the original material has been simplified into a short case study, together with details of the problem-solving approach (MPIA) that the MBA team applied to the case and which helped in the generation of new ideas and actions for the client.

In the following sections, background details of the sponsor's company are given, approaches to problem solving are discussed and the MPIA ('mess', perspectives, ideas and actions) method is described.

Cotton Traders: its past and future

The company, based in the north-west of England, was founded in the 1980s by a former international sportsman. It specialises in selling casual wear and sportswear. In terms of turnover, by far the greatest percentage of its sales is by mail order and consists mostly of casual wear, for example shirts, blouses and sweaters. A minority of sales are via retail outlets and focus mainly on sports wear such as track suits, sports shirts and shorts. One particularly strong product line is the sale of rugby shirts; this line alone comprises a significant part of sales by mail order. Moreover, the company has negotiated agreements to market exclusively the rugby shirts of two of the UK home nations, another international rugby-playing country and one of the top domestic English club teams. In its marketing approach, the company exploits the well-known image of its founder.

The company markets its goods through advertisements in magazines, inserts in Sunday newspapers, distinctive catalogues, occasional promotion campaigns and sports sponsorship.

In the sports wear sector, its main competitors are international brands such as Nike, Reebok and Adidas. In the casual clothes sector, Next Direct, Racing Green, Grattan, Littlewoods and other mail order companies are the main rivals. In the mail order business, competition is strong. It is relatively easy for new companies to enter the market, there is little product differentiation and there is a high degree of buyer power that is sensitive to price, quality and convenience.

The typical customer profile is in the 35–45-year-old age range, with medium to high disposable income. Females outnumber males by a ratio of about two to one.

The markets in which this company operates are extremely competitive. There is no scope for the company to stand still – it has to grow and develop.

With this in mind, the company conceived its central objective as being the need to develop an approach to the marketing of their products that emphasises the uniqueness of the company to both existing and potential customers.

---

the exercises

The problem-solving approach

The MPIA problem-solving approach has been developed at Manchester Business School for MBA teams specialising in a management of creativity and innovation elective. In 1996, shortly after the case was tackled, the MPIA system was selected by the ESRC as the methodology for creative problem solving to be supplied within an innovation initiative for all UK business schools. It has a wide range of applications and has been tested extensively as a means of supporting business projects. Results have been reported (for example, in Rickards, 1997).

The task at hand is for the student group acting as consultants to apply problem-solving techniques to the dilemma facing the client company. The creative problem-solving approach serves to sensitise a business client to his or her assumptions. Creative insights are experienced as break-outs of preconceived assumptions.

One of the challenges of real-world organisational problem solving is the tension between the problem as perceived by those who have power and responsibility to do something about it, and as perceived by those who have been requested to study it. The former can be considered the client group and the latter as having a consultant role.

The MPIA method

The creative problem-solving process adopted is one usually referred to by the initials 'MPIA'. The letters stand for 'mess'; perspectives; ideas and actions. Each step of the process is now described in more detail.

'Mess'

It is all too easy to focus down too quickly on some aspect of a complicated situation. It is important, therefore, to begin the problem-solving process by reviewing the salient features of the 'mess' before moving to problem examination. A spider diagram can help to review the main features of the topic before deciding how to proceed. Although its use in teams to build a shared vocabulary is relatively novel, the spider diagram approach is related to other mapping techniques, such as Buzan diagrams.

To produce a spider diagram, the following steps may be followed:

1. Turn the page lengthways (that is, to a landscape orientation) as this allows more of the page to be used easily.
2. Start writing in the centre of the page, with the topic in the body of the spider.
3. Add the descriptions of 6–8 key themes, one for each 'leg' of the spider.
4. Build out subthemes forming the 'fingers and toes'.
5. Look for links and connections between themes.
6. Enhance the visual impact by using different colours for differing kinds of theme.
7. Redraw, if necessary, after reviewing – a quite different view may appear at that time.

When the client is present, the spider is drawn up to capture the situation ('mess') as reported by the client. The problem-solving resource (consultant team) seeks clarification, thereby enriching the information supplied. The spider, however, represents the mind sets and know-how from the viewpoint of the client.

Perspectives

Next, in search for new perspectives, the group reframes the complex set of issues displayed in the spider diagram to clarify a previously unclear focus, vision or mission. The group generates a comprehensive list of possible goals or perspectives. It is recommended employing a standard format of statements, each indicating a specific action and labelled a 'how to...' statement, for example 'how to target younger age groups' or 'how to make existing customers buy more'. Experience has shown that active and easily visualised 'how to' statements are the most effective. At this stage and in the following 'I' stage, break-out ideas can be encouraged through the use of other problem-solving techniques, such as lateral thinking and analogical thinking. Anyone wishing to experiment with such techniques is advised to spend some time working with experienced practitioners and in understanding the conceptual rationale as outlined in de Bono (1971), Parnes (1992) and Rickards (1997).

Once a list has been generated, one or more 'how tos' are selected, in this case by the tutor acting on behalf of the client company. The process represents one in which the client clarifies the 'problem as currently perceived' (as a 'how to' statement). The consultancy team's search for a wide range of 'how tos' provides the client with scope for reframing in terms of a 'problem as reinterpreted'. The new perspective may eventually lead the client to new ways of solving the problem and/or to ways of reframing the problem. The latter may reveal that the original problem has been indirectly dealt with or rendered less central. Within the listing of perspectives, the spider provides an *aide-mémoire*. The perspectives, however, capture the views of the consultants. These are, in principle, less conditioned by the client's closeness to the situation and are more varied.

The perspectives stage is conducted in a spirit of deferred judgment. Particularly with training, the consultant problem-solving team is able to provide imaginative yet simple 'how tos' that serve to contrast the habitual 'how tos' that the client may hold and that are strongly constrained by the professional beliefs and assumptions of the client.

Furthermore, ingenious and wishful lateral thinking is as much in place at this stage as at the ideas stage. For example, a marketing group had been agonising over a difficulty they expressed as 'how to break the constraints of the generic form'. A lateral leap came up with the simple and visual goal of 'how to find out what it would take for your granny to buy this product'.

A perspective chosen for subsequent idea generation has the characteristics of novelty and potential for new and valuable ideas. The client (tutor) selects the one or small number of 'how tos' for idea generation.

Ideas

The stage of ideas generation is a second sequence of search followed by selection. The search stage is again conducted within an atmosphere of postponed judgment (brainstorming). Groups may experiment with a sequence of individual brainstorming ('nominal group brainstorming'). Deliberate efforts to introduce 'effective novelty' via lateral thinking also help the group to escape from mundane, obvious ideas.

One useful device is to ask, 'Wouldn't it be wonderful if...?'. Examples abound how such thinking can be worked into powerful new angles. 'How to invent a new camera' is a mundane challenge. 'How to develop a disposable camera' can be seen as derived from 'Wouldn't it be wonderful if people bought a new camera with every pack of film.'

In idea selection, it is a good plan to practise a more systematic evaluation process. After eliminating the trivial ideas, the shortlist can be evaluated against criteria agreed by the consultants, based on client advice. The systematic evaluation of all short-listed ideas against criteria is known as a criterion matrix evaluation. The idea evaluation matrix can be found in the Tutor's Notes. The process helps to clarify judgments on ideas and criteria. If there is a shortage of new and potentially valuable ideas, a little time should be spent 'taming down' a few of the more bizarre ones.

A simple technique here is to treat the most bizarre or impossible facet of an idea as a metaphorical position that can be modified. For example, the idea of vanishing lamp posts was proposed as a way of reducing the dangers of car impact with lamp posts. As a metaphor, this suggests energy-absorbing lamp posts. It is easier to tame down a shocking or stupid idea than breathe life into a boring one. Once a set of ideas including some unusual promising ones is obtained, a prioritisation can follow a criterion matrix evaluation. Details of this are included in the Tutor's Notes.

Actions

The consultant team should single out one or two ideas to practise idea development. An action idea is one in which the process of enacting the idea has been visualised. A good way is for the team to build up a word picture in which the enactment is described. This forces the team to be concrete and makes proposals easier to present. A summary example is provided in the Tutor's Notes.

A further technique is to pose and then answer the following checklist questions: who, what, how, where and when. This well-worn strategy still serves the useful purpose of channelling the group's thinking towards concrete and actionable suggestions.

REFERENCES AND FURTHER READING

Bono, E. de (1971) *Lateral Thinking for Management*. McGraw-Hill, London.

Buzan, A. (1982) *Use Your Head*, 2nd edn. Ariel Books, London.

Moger, S.T. (1994) Creativity and entrepreneurs. In Dingli, S. (ed.) *Creative Thinking: A Multifaceted Approach*, pp. 111–21. Malta University Press, Valetta.

Morgan, G. (1993) *Imaginization: The Art of Creative Management*. Sage, Newbury Park, CA.

Parnes, S.J. (ed.) (1992) *Source Book for Creative Problem-Solving*. Creative Education Foundation, Buffalo, NY.

Rickards, T. (1997) *Creative Problem Solving at Work*. Gower, Farnborough.

Rickards, T. and De Cock, C. (1994) Creativity in MS/OR: training for creativity – findings in a European context. *Interfaces* November–December: 59–65.

Rickards, T. and Moger, S.T. (1995) *Creative Problem Solving*, Module 4, ESRC Innovation Initiative. ESRC Business Processes Resource, Swindon.

CHAPTER 24

Quality Management

Patrick Dawson

OBJECTIVES

This objectives of this chapter are:

▶ outline the importance of context as a factor that will influence the uptake and use of quality management programmes
▶ contrast two very different experiences of quality management within a single South Australian operating site
▶ provide readers with an opportunity to apply a number of quality management techniques in a group case analysis that aims to identify factors enabling and constraining change, from which a number of practical lessons can be generated.

INTRODUCTION

This chapter aims to provide students with an understanding of the importance of contextual factors in shaping the uptake and use of quality management programmes. Since the early 1990s, an increasing number of companies have attempted to take a broader approach to quality improvement that encompasses all aspects of internal operations, involves every employee of the company and accommodates external operating practices and customer–supplier relations. This *holistic approach* to quality management and change differentiates it from earlier attempts at quality control (through quality assurance departments) and employee involvement programmes (through the use of quality circles on the shop floor). In pursuit of this aim, a number of management tools have also been developed to help organisations to implement systems of continuous improvement, such as brainstorming, flow charts, Pareto charts and cause and effect (fishbone) diagrams. In practice, however, any holistic approach has to accommodate contextual conditions as there is no single recipe to the successful introduction of quality management programmes. Consequently, this chapter sets out to highlight the centrality of context in shaping the process and outcomes of change through discussing the practical case study example of Pirelli Cables Australia Limited.

Student preparation

The main purpose of the exercise is to enable students openly to discuss and debate issues surrounding the importance of context for understanding the uptake and use of programmes of continuous improvement. In preparing for the group exercise at the end of this company example, each student should thoroughly familiarise themselves with the case. It may prove useful to read the case quickly at the outset, skim through the questions at the end and then examine the case in more detail, taking particular note of the contextual conditions under which change occurred.

Pirelli Cables Australia Limited

Over the last few years, Pirelli has put considerable time and effort into the uptake of a quality management programme in their Australian operations. A steering committee was formed from Pirelli Cables Australia Limited (PCAL) senior executives, who were trained by Blakemore Consulting in the tools and techniques of quality management. The managing director acted as the chairman of the steering committee, and other key personnel were trained as facilitators in preparation for project team formation. One of the major strategic objectives of the quality programme was to bring about a 'culture of change' and initiate a shift in employee attitudes towards greater involvement and the development of high-trust relationships.

Pirelli operations in Australia comprised three manufacturing sites and 11 sales branches, including one in New Zealand. The Minto site, specialising in power and building wire cables, was the newest plant and was located in an outer southern suburb of Sydney. The oldest plant was at Dee Why, a northern Sydney suburb, where production operations centred on the manufacture of telephone cables. Two plants were located in South Australia at the Adelaide manufacturing site at Camden Park, this operation produced plug and cord sets for the automotive and white goods market. (Approximately 15 per cent of the plug and cord sets are exported, mostly to Asia, fitted to electrical appliances and then imported back into Australia.)

In the case study reported here, shopfloor responses to change have been drawn from interview material collected from two distinct and physically separate plants in Adelaide. In both plants, there are a number of employees who are not fluent in the English language. This raises the problem of communication both between employees – who are now expected to work together as a team rather than as individual machine operators – and within the continuous process improvement teams themselves. For the most part, there has been a general reluctance for those who speak English as a foreign language to get involved in quality management groups. Furthermore, while both sites are composed of a multicultural workforce, there are considerable differences between the personnel, equipment and production processes used at the cable manufacturing plant and at the cable processing plant.

The Cable Manufacturing Plant (CMP) consists of comparatively complex equipment for the manufacture of single and multicore flexible cables. The extrusion equipment is old and therefore requires routine maintenance, the operators are predominantly male (46 out of the 47 employees), and the equipment is operated on a three-shift basis.

In contrast, the Cable Processing Plant (CPP) is predominantly female (90 out of the 106 employees) and is based largely around labour-intensive repetitive manual processing operations. This plant processes cable manufactured by the cable plant in order to service customer requirements (for example, in the type of plug and length of cable). However, Pirelli Cables has little worldwide expertise in the area of processing (cable manufacturing predominating) and the cable processing plant is consequently largely isolated from the other Australian manufacturing operations.

The shopfloor experience of quality management in cable processing

The introduction of quality management to the CPP was met with a certain degree of scepticism by the employees. They were uncertain of the nature of the programme, concerned about the potential effects on the work process and doubtful about claims for greater employee involvement. Local management advocated that quality management would enable shopfloor personnel to get involved in operational decision making through group problem-solving meetings. The intention was to get employees with a detailed knowledge of shopfloor operations to contribute to, and be part of, employee teams that would tackle shopfloor problems in order to improve the work process and increase the efficiency of shopfloor production. In the words of a line supervisor:

> When they first introduced us to it, like in many places, you don't want change, so you don't want it and everyone was very negative. Then we went to the meetings and brainstorming sessions. It does work. I am on a quality management committee and we do the ARTOS (cutting and stripping machine). We do not get the breakdowns now that we used to have. It has helped people, because they know that they can go to management and ask for anything to do with their jobs. Almost always they get it. If it costs a lot of money, not so much so, but the management do try. (Supervisory interviews)

Operatives also indicated that, while they were initially doubtful about the purpose of quality management, they now saw quality management as a positive development:

> I was asked to go on a committee, which I wasn't too keen on at first. I couldn't see why I should go and my supervisor didn't have to, to be quite honest. I thought he was off-loading something on to me. That is the truth. (Shopfloor interviews)

Employees who had been involved in quality management activities claimed that quality management was of benefit both to shopfloor personnel and to the company as a whole. The benefits to employees were the possibility of improving working conditions and reducing some of the stress and frustration associated with rework caused by minor problems, whereas the potential advantage for the company was increased efficiency rates and reduced scrap. Quality management was also seen to have facilitated greater communication between shopfloor personnel through improving employee understanding of the processes involved in manufacturing. For example, there is now a greater willingness among operators to help each other out if there are problems in particular areas. The view that there has been a movement towards teamwork was supported by the union representative in the CPP, who, in describing the work process, noted that:

> You start off at the moulding process and then it comes to our line. Because it goes through stages, everyone has to do their bit before it comes to the end. It is a team that works on the line. If something isn't right, someone will come and say that it is a little bit too long, and ask for it to be shortened. (Shop steward)

In part, the acceptance of quality management in CPP can be explained by the success of the original quality management team, which looked at the problem of downtime with the cable cutting and stripping machines (known as the ARTOS quality project). In the view of those interviewed, the ARTOS experience was instrumental in winning over shopfloor employees to the benefits of quality management. For example, a piece of internal correspondence from the production manager to all quality management teams in December 1990 was used to highlight the success of the ARTOS quality project. The document outlined the paid efficiencies for the past 18 weeks (which averaged out at 103 per cent compared with 65 per cent previously) and then set about thanking individual team members for the various contributions, concluding with a 'Thanks to all the team; your efforts and ideas is what quality management is all about.' This support and attention from management has further served to boost the morale in CPP and, in particular, the benefits of quality management to the team members. These individuals in turn influence the views of other operators on the shopfloor:

> People communicate. Before, they didn't say what was going wrong and you would look at their sheets and ask them what happened, and they wouldn't really say what was wrong. They thought it would reflect on them if they had a problem; rather than complain or say anything, they would put up with it. Everything is a lot more open than it was before. (Shopfloor interviews)

Although teamwork remains largely a function of the group problem-solving activities associated with continuous improvement (work is still organised largely on a one operator per machine basis, and there is a set rate for each machine, which operators are expected to meet), interviewees argued that improved interpersonal communication on the shopfloor and the greater collaboration between employees in helping each other out signifies the movement away from individual-based, machine-orientated work regimes, to a work process based on more open communication and greater group effort.

In evaluating the effects of quality management on shopfloor operations, one operator commented that:

> Before quality management started, we didn't have things like the machines running through our lunch break and things like

that. Now we keep the machines running right through. They are making more plugs now... [Our supervisor] looks after us a lot too. She sticks by us. If we have problems, she will be there to help us out... It is a combination of things. Before they would let things slide. Now people have got to do things right the first time. Now we can explain and give them [management] our views on what the problems are. Now they listen and involve us and the staff on the floor know what is going on. Before they [management] didn't do that. (Shopfloor interviews)

On being asked to describe the union view on quality management, the shop steward of the National Union of Workers (NUW) indicated that there had been no union involvement and no involvement by the various shop stewards other than being members on some of the quality management teams. In short, the evaluation of quality management by supervisors, operators and union representatives was favourable and supportive of the more general move towards greater teamwork and collaboration on the shopfloor.

The shopfloor experience of quality management in cable manufacturing

The experience of quality management in the CMP contrasts in a number of significant ways with that in the CPP. First, while there was general support for the philosophy of quality management, criticisms were levelled at the way in which it was being used and 'abused' within the CMP. Second, there was a greater discrepancy between the line supervisors' views of change and the attitudes and perceptions of the machine operators. Third, sectional and interpersonal conflicts were identified as major obstacles to collaborative teamwork and the development of less adversarial systems of operation. Finally, the local management team and line supervisors were viewed as a major problem impeding the successful introduction of quality management. As one employee commented:

quality management here will never take off unless management change their attitude. They have to listen to the people on the floor. When we ask for something to be done, it has to be done. We had a problem out there [shopfloor] on 90 per cent of the machines and management didn't want to know about it. It actually took an electrician five minutes to fix all the machines, and for two years we were asking for it to be fixed. The company somehow finally got the message and it was fixed. (Shopfloor interviews)

The problems of poor management were also highlighted by operators in the areas of the setting up and running of continuous improvement teams and in the general management of the plant. While there were a number of responses indicating considerable dissatisfaction with the way in which operations and employees were being managed, all respondents showed a clear understanding of the general philosophy of quality management and provided positive evaluations of the potential value of these techniques in allowing employees to help identify ways of improving efficiencies on the shopfloor:

Quality management is a fantastic idea if it is managed properly. If we had quality management managed properly, within six months we could double our production easily. (Shopfloor interviews)

During the time of the shopfloor interviews, the industry was experiencing a major recession, and a number of employees were retrenched at the Adelaide site. Consequently, there was considerable shopfloor support for changes that could potentially improve the efficiency of operations, make the company more competitive and secure future job opportunities. In some cases, the increasing pressures associated with working under 'poor management' combined with the threat of unemployment had led to very negative attitudes to work.

There was a general feeling among shopfloor employees that action should be taken to make Pirelli Adelaide more profitable so that customers could be retained and the further retrenchment of staff would not be necessary. On this count, the operators described the frustration that they felt through working within a system that had improved the communication between management and the shopfloor but which had not changed management's willingness to act upon the recommendations made by operators. Quality management was seen to have created more work for operators and yet had failed to deliver on the promise of employee involvement in management decision making. While it was recognised that quality management had facilitated greater liaison between various occupational groups and hierarchical levels within the plant, it was claimed that management action remained the preserve of 'management'. In practice, this meant that if a quality management team suggestion was made by a manager or supervisor, there was a good chance that it would be acted upon immediately, whereas if a suggestion was made by operators, it would take a considerable time before any action was taken, and only then if continual support for the suggestion had been made by employees and the recommendation had been restated over a number of months. In short, the communication channels had been opened with quality management, but the monopoly on ideas for decision making had remained in the hands of management. This 'split' between management and the workers was also seen to be reflected in the management of the quality management teams, which were largely structured on a hierarchical basis. As one operator recalled:

> At the team meetings, I will say as much as I want to say, but I have to work here still. We had a meeting last Tuesday. They asked us to try things different ways, and we do, but the moment we ask them to do something, they say no, we can't do that. They expect us to give, but they won't do anything for us. (Shopfloor interviews)

In evaluating the effects of quality management on shopfloor operations, interviewees claimed that many of the problems experienced on the shopfloor were the result of management incompetence and their failure to ensure that trained operators were working reliable machines. They claimed that poorly trained, ill-equipped operators would produce scrap no matter how many quality management teams management initiated. From a shopfloor perspective, training was therefore identified as a major issue that was not being adequately tackled by management. The common view on the shopfloor was that employees should have comprehensive training provided for the machines that they were expected to operate. In addition, interviewees argued that the machines provided should be able to operate at the set standards. In practice, operating equipment at the prescribed pace often resulted in an increase in the level of scrap produced. On this point, one operator complained that managers themselves were sometimes the cause of scrap through insisting that a machine ran at a certain prescribed pace:

> He asks why you can't produce more on your machine. I tell him that I am producing at the best pace for quality and quantity. Then he speeds the machine up. 'The book says that this is right so that is what you should be doing.' What the book says goes according to him. If he does that to me again, his number is going on the ticket – so his name goes on the scrap. (Shopfloor interviews)

Thus, from a shopfloor viewpoint, the problem of plant inefficiencies and high levels of scrap were seen to be the consequence of bad management, poor equipment and inadequate training. As one operator indicated:

> I have been on the machine for two weeks now and I have only had one full day of instruction. I have taught myself. People on other machines who have seen me struggling have come over and helped me a bit, but I haven't been allocated any training... It takes about nine months to a year to learn the machines properly. (Shopfloor interviews)

From an operator perspective, working conditions had deteriorated, morale had plummeted, and the solution to the problem, while obvious, was overlooked by management, the blame being laid to rest on the workers. Thus one of the biggest failings of local management was seen to stem from their inability to relate to shopfloor workers:

> I try to keep on the right side of them; that is only sensible. But there doesn't seem to be any empathy between the management and the workers. They treat us like machines. (Shopfloor interviews)

In contrast, line supervisors were far more supportive of local management and argued that there was now far greater communication and integration between different areas within the site and that the local management group had successfully achieved some significant changes in the organisation and control of work, which had brought about substantial improvements in operating efficiencies. Finally, in terms of the future of quality management within the plant, there was again a difference of opinion between the line supervisors and machine operators. In evaluating the future of quality management, one supervisor argued that:

> There is a long future for quality management. It has given people the freedom to say what they feel. It has brought out the fact that the people on machines know what is going on out there. The bosses don't really know what makes them tick. (Supervisory interviews)

In contrast, a shopfloor operator claimed that there was no future for quality management in the plant:

> The way it is right now? Nowhere. We have a quality management meeting, but nothing is ever done about it. They are irrelevant. They don't mean anything to us. (Operator)

the exercises

The Pirelli study presented above could be examined in a number of different ways. In this exercise, the aim is to provide students with an opportunity to use some basic quality tools to analyse the case material. The intention is to enable individuals to work in groups and to gain some experience in the skills associated with the use of quality management techniques. Although it is not feasible to detail a comprehensive package of quality management techniques, three popular techniques have been chosen to provide some initial insight into the quality process. These comprise brainstorming, the use of Pareto charts, and the construction of cause and effect diagrams (also known as fishbone diagrams).

In tackling Question 1, 2 or 3 (see Exercise 4), each group should attempt to follow one or more of the stages outlined below in order to gain some experience in the use of continuous improvement tools. Remember that you will need to go through this process more than once in order first to identify factors that support the uptake of quality management and then to examine those which impede successful change.

Brainstorming

This is a common tool used by cross-functional quality teams in business to generate a broad sweep of ideas drawing on the views and expertise of all members of the group. Each group should select someone to keep a record of all the suggestions made within the group. For example, try to identify and list as many factors as possible that may have influenced the successful or unsuccessful uptake of quality management in the Pirelli case. At this stage, there should be no evaluations, and everyone should be encouraged to participate. The aim is not to agree on a single answer but to list a broad range of possible influencing factors, however odd they may appear to others.

Once you have your lists of influencing factors (those elements which facilitate and those which impede the change process), the next stage is to determine the significance of various groups of factors. To do this, move on to Exercise 2.

80–20 Rule

The objective of Exercise 2 is to try to determine which influencing factors among the many are responsible for the greatest effect. This technique is based on the Pareto principle, which suggests that a few of the causes often account for most of the effect (the 80–20 rule). Essentially, a Pareto chart is a bar chart in which each bar represents the relative contribution of each cause. For this, you should try to group information into categories, such as machinery, supervision and training. If there are more items that can be located under machinery than any other group (being the most frequently occurring cause), place this to the left or right (normally the left), with the rest in descending order. This analysis may suggest that one or two categories, if rectified, could go a long way to solving the problem.

Once you have categorised your data and assessed their total contribution to outcome, you may need to carry out some further analysis in order to identify the significance of the individual elements that comprise the most frequently occurring cause category. For example, you may simply wish to rank order their importance and end your analysis at this stage, or you may wish further to explore the cause and effect relationships within your chosen category by moving on to Exercise 3.

Exploring the major cause category

The aim of Exercise 3 is for the group to explore their chosen category in a little more detail. In order to do this, you may find it useful to construct a cause and effect (fishbone) diagram. At this stage, you may start to unpack the items that comprise your category, and in so doing, you should attempt to identify a hierarchy of causes, ranging from minor to major ones. For example, identify the effect/goal (for example, 'promotes successful uptake') and then branch off major causes, minor causes, subsets of minor causes and so forth (your diagram may start to look like a fishbone; Figure 24.1). Once your diagram has been completed, your group should have identified those causes which are likely to have the greatest impact in terms of helping to solve the problem or facilitate the goal.

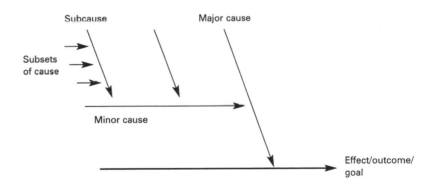

Figure 24.1   Example of a fishbone diagram

Case study questions

In examining this case and contrasting the different experiences of change between the two plants, students should work in groups of between five and eight people. Each team should either answer Question 1 or focus on the experience of a particular plant (Question 2 or 3). Once the group has tackled one of these questions, they should turn their attention to Question 4 and discuss their experience of using quality management tools in the case analysis. If time allows, each group should then spend some time in using their findings (and drawing on their own experiences, the literature and lecture notes) to construct some basic guidelines on the successful management of change. Finally, all the groups should get back together to debate the case issues and the use of quality management tools in a plenary session.

All groups
1. Compare and contrast the main factors that influenced the successful or unsuccessful uptake and use of quality management at the CMP and CPP plants?

Discuss and prepare to feedback findings. Each group should nominate a spokesperson to report back to the class as a whole.

Separate groups
2. What are the main factors that influenced the successful or unsuccessful uptake and use of quality management at the CMP?
3. What are the main factors that influenced the successful or unsuccessful uptake and use of quality management at the CPP?

Each group should attempt to answer either Question 2 or Question 3. Once again, they should be prepared to present their findings or solutions to the class as a whole. The feedback session can then be extended to involve a consideration of the similarities and differences between the cases.

Quality tools
4. How useful have you found group problem-solving techniques in tackling one or more of the questions posed above?

In answering this question, students should outline the major strengths and weaknesses of the problem-solving techniques, and list any additional benefits (if any) that would be likely to result from their use in an organisational setting.

Change management guidelines
5. What are the main lessons that can be drawn from the Pirelli example which would provide practical advice to others seeking to embark on a programme of continuous improvement?

Students should feel free to draw on their own experience, their knowledge of the literature and material covered in lectures in developing a set of guidelines for the successful management of change.

Plenary session

A plenary session should be used at the end of the exercise so that students can feedback their findings on the case and/or the use of the quality tools they have used.

CHAPTER 25

Racial Discrimination

Bola Fatimilehin

OBJECTIVES

The objectives of this chapter are to:

- ▶ give an overview of UK law relating to racial discrimination
- ▶ provide examples of situations involving racial discrimination
- ▶ begin to identify organisational and managerial costs of racial discrimination
- ▶ identify ways of preventing racial discrimination
- ▶ develop skills, personal qualities and procedures for dealing with racial discrimination.

INTRODUCTION

This chapter emphasises the need to respond effectively to situations involving racial discrimination in the workplace. It is constructed around a practical exercise aimed at getting managers, management students and all those concerned with ensuring anti-discriminatory practice to consider issues relating to racial discrimination and to practise the skills necessary for dealing with it effectively.

The chapter begins by giving an overview of UK legislation; next, it cites a number of recent industrial tribunal cases. Students are then asked to carry out some preliminary exercises, during which they will need to make notes on issues relating to racial discrimination, and the organisational policy and procedures aimed at preventing and combatting it. Once the three-part preliminary exercise is completed, students take part in a role play exercise that revolves around a case scenario. It is envisaged that students will carry out the preliminary exercises on their own and then meet with members of their student group to complete the role play exercise.

Answers to the preliminary exercise and more detailed advice on conducting and setting up role plays are contained within the Tutor's Notes.

Racial discrimination and the law

The law clearly makes it illegal for an organisation or individuals within it to discriminate against an employee or a potential employee on grounds of race. If an organisation is to avoid the costly process of being taken to an industrial tribunal, it must know how to conform to the letter and spirit of the law. Good employee relations also require that a manager/organisation is able to protect its employees from racial discrimination and harassment.

The law relating to racial discrimination in the UK is the Race Relations Act 1976. This law primarily charges employers to ensure equal opportunity for all job applicants and employees, while employees at all levels and of all racial groups have responsibilities too. Following establishment of the Act, the Commission for Racial Equality (CRE) was set up in order to help enforce it (see Section 43 of the Act). The CRE's mission is:

> working for a just society which gives everyone an equal chance to learn, work and live free from discrimination and prejudice and from there of racial harassment and violence.

The main thrust of the Act revolves around the following concepts:

◆ *Direct discrimination* consists of treating a person less favourably or differently from another in the same or similar circumstances because of his or her race, colour, ethnic or national origin. An example of this is a situation in which a job applicant is turned down simply because he is black.
◆ *Indirect discrimination* consists of applying a requirement or condition that, although applied equally to persons of all racial groups, is such that a considerably smaller proportion of a particular racial group can comply with it and it cannot be shown to be justifiable on other than racial grounds. An example of this is a situation in which Muslim women are required to wear skirts in order to work in a department store.
◆ *Victimisation* is where one person is treated less favourably than others are treated or would be treated because they have brought, been suspected of or alleged to have brought, supported others' to bring or intend to bring proceedings under the Act.
◆ *Racial harassment* is where a person receives unwanted conduct of a racial nature, or other conduct based on race, that adversely affects their dignity.

The Race Relations Act does not specifically prohibit racial harassment, but industrial tribunals have ruled that racial abuse can amount to racial discrimination if it makes the atmosphere at work intolerable and the employer has done nothing about it in spite of complaints.

Racism and its effects within an organisational context

IN 1995, the UK CRE assisted 94 complainants in bringing cases that were settled, with industrial tribunals settlements amounting to a total of £617,942. In 1996, employer settlements amounted to £658,470.

The following are examples of cases recently brought to industrial tribunals. These are useful as an aid to developing an understanding of how racial discrimination manifests itself in the work setting. They are extracts from the CRE's *Annual Report for 1995 and Racial Harassment at Work. What Employers Can Do About It* (1995), published by the CRE.

Mr Z. Milovanovic v. Hebden Dyeing & Finishing Company Ltd and Others

Mr Milovanovic, who is of Serbian origin, has lived in England for the past 41 years. He was one of 25 employees at Hebden Dyeing company and began work there in 1991. Mr Milovanovic complained of numerous incidents of persistent harassment based on his ethnic and national origin, especially after the Bosnian war began:

> We don't use the number 7 like that. You're not in f***ing Bosnia now. You're in England.

> Don't you think it would be a good idea, Zoran, to go back to Bosnia or wherever you belong and fight and die like a dog instead of our lads.

> If all the foreigners and blacks go back to their own country we would have a better environment in this country.

It all finally became too much for Mr Milovanovic. He left the dye house and telephoned to say he was giving a week's notice.

The tribunal found that Mr Milovanovic had put up with not only what he regarded as racist jokes, but also remarks that would only be addressed to someone of foreign extraction. They believed that the discrimination was continuous and accepted that Mr Milovanovic was very hurt and distressed by what had happened.

He ultimately felt so oppressed by what happened that he felt quite unable to continue in his employment, since the relationship of trust and confidence between him and the employers had been destroyed. Mr Milovanovic was awarded a total of £3,825 in compensation.

The case is an important one because it shows that, however long people from minorities may have lived in Britain, the chances are that they will suffer persecution and discrimination because of their national ethnic or racial origin, especially when there are international conflicts.

Kassimis v. Unwins Ltd

Mr Kassimis, who was born in Britain of Greek origin, was unaccountably sacked from his job as a trainee manager. There had been a racial altercation with the manager, followed by a transfer to another branch for 2–3 days and then, suddenly and simply, dismissal. Mr Kassimis's complaint of racial discrimination was simply ignored.

The company always claimed that it had decided to dismiss Mr Kassimis before the incident with the manager, and while the tribunal accepted this, it was unimpressed by the procedures followed at every turn. Mr Kassimis's complaint was successful, and he was awarded £500 for injury to feelings.

Ms Graham v. Royal Mail and Mr S Nicolson

The incident that led to Ms Graham's complaint took place when she and a colleague, Mr Nicolson, were leaving work. Ms Graham, referring to Mr Nicolson's receding hairline, shouted, 'I'll see you later, you white, bald-headed bastard.' Stung, Mr Nicolson shot back that he preferred to be a white, bald-headed bastard than a black bastard. Ms Graham took exception to his remark and, although Mr Nicolson apologised straightaway, and once again the next day, she reported the matter to her supervisor.

In line with the Royal Mail's procedures for dealing with harassment, Mr Nicolson was immediately transferred to another area and given a written warning.

The tribunal did not find any racial discrimination. Bearing in mind the fact that Mr Nicolson and Ms Graham had a fairly relaxed and informal relationship at work, which included occasional racial banter, the tribunal thought that Mr Nicolson had been provoked into making his remark, and that while Ms Graham was understandably offended, what did she expect? However, the tribunal took pains to point out that, 'in most cases of racist banter in the workplace, there can be no degree of acceptability.'

The tribunal specifically commended Royal Mail on its policy and the speed with which it had acted on it. The case is noteworthy because, even if the tribunal had found racial discrimination, it is unlikely that it would have held Royal Mail liable for its employees' discriminatory actions.

the exercises

Preliminary exercise

Students will need to complete the three exercises below on their own before moving on to, and in preparation for, the role play. All parts must be responded to in full.

What are the possible costs to organisations and managers of failing to ensure that all staff receive equal conditions of work in an environment free from humiliation and intimidation?

What steps can managers take to promote and ensure equal conditions for all employees?

Gather and read examples (two examples of each will suffice) of organisational policy and procedures listed below. Make notes on their relevance to racial discrimination and on the informal and formal procedures used for dealing with employee misconduct and grievances:

◆ equal opportunity policy
◆ grievance procedures
◆ disciplinary procedures.

Notes made in response to the above, and copies of all policies gathered should be kept as they will be required for the rest of the exercise.

Answers to the exercises above are contained within the Tutor's Notes.

Role play

The case study below has been constructed in order to give students a situation involving racial discrimination to work on. Before engaging in the role play, some preparatory work is required, as identified in Exercises 4 and 5 below. The student group is asked to identify and agree formal and informal procedures for dealing with racial discrimination, and a set of skills and personal qualities necessary for handling it. Once this has been achieved, the student group can then engage in the role play.

Identification of formal and informal procedures for dealing with racial discrimination

Using the notes devised in Exercise 3, the student group should agree a set of formal and informal procedures for dealing with racial discrimination (harassment). Students should discuss how the procedures would apply to the case scenario above. Once agreement has been reached, each student should make sure they have a written copy of the agreed procedures for use during the role play in Exercise 6.

This should take no more than 40 minutes. A set of formal and informal procedures are laid out in the Tutor's Notes.

Identification of skills and personal qualities for dealing with racial discrimination

All students will need to read the scenario thoroughly and take part in Exercise 4. Once this has happened, students should take part in discussions aimed at identifying the skills and personal qualities that the line manager and panel of managers will need in order to deal with the situation effectively. It may be useful for the whole student group to split into two groups: one group should discuss and list skills, while the other discusses and lists personal qualities. At the end of both discussions, the group should come back together and agree the skills and personal qualities required.

The discussion in groups should last no more than 20 minutes. The whole group should take no more than 25 minutes to reach agreement on the skills and personal qualities required. A list of skills should be drawn up for use during the role plays in Exercises 6 and 7.

The skills and personal qualities for dealing with racial discrimination are identified in the Tutor's Notes.

The Manager's Role

Your name is Colin James and you are a manager working within an inner city local authority. You manage a team of five, one member of which is black, the others being white.

You have recently noticed that Margaret Haynes (the black member of your team) has taken a number of days off because of illness over the past 6 months. The reasons she has given on her sickness absence form include stress, migraines and flu. This level of sickness absence is unacceptable so you decide to meet with her with the intention of discussing the matter to find out whether there is anything you can do, especially with regard to the stress. During the meeting, Margaret becomes emotional and tells you that she has been experiencing verbal racial abuse from one of her white colleagues over the past 3 months. She tells you that John Williams has been 'calling me names'. At this point, she becomes so upset that you have to terminate the meeting. Before she leaves, you tell her that you will meet with her the next day to discuss the matter further.

You are not looking forward to your meeting with Margaret! Even though she has been with the organisation for the past 9 months, you feel that you know her no better than the day she started. You have been very busy of late and have not had the time to talk to her other than about specific tasks. It is the first time you have had to directly manage a black employee.

However, the next day, you meet with Margaret to find out more. She tells you that John called her a 'black bitch', once in earshot of the office cleaner and twice when they had been working late. At this point, you inform her of her right to have the matter dealt with formally but try to coax her into letting you deal with it informally. She says that she will think about it.

You are surprised at her complaint against John and think him incapable of such an act. You have a good working relationship with him. John has been with the company for almost 10 years and has an exemplary work record. You often go for lunch with him and sometimes meet for a drink after work.

After your meeting with Margaret, you decide to find out about your organisation's stand on racial abuse and harassment; you look at the following policies and procedures:

◆   equal opportunity policy
◆   grievance procedures
◆   disciplinary procedures.

The policies clearly state that abuse and harassment constitute misconduct and are therefore disciplinary offences. They go on to say that managers, in the first instance and for a first offence, should try to resolve the matter informally before resorting to formal procedures. However, in the case of racial harassment, the equal opportunity policy states that the complainant should make the decision on whether the matter should be dealt with formally or informally.

The next day you arrive at work to find a formal letter of complaint from Margaret in your pigeon hole. It identifies John Williams as the harasser and Femi Adebayo (the Nigerian office cleaner) as a witness.

Later on that day, and with advice from the personnel department, you contact two other managers to work with you in hearing and investigating the complaint. You meet with George Graham (white manager) and Derzeen Gilbert (black manager). Together, you timetable meetings with all parties, that is Margaret Haynes, John Williams and Femi Adebayo.

George Graham works within the personnel department and does everything 'by the book'. He is often very reticent in putting his own ideas forward. Derzeen Gilbert is manager of the authority's Equal Opportunity Unit. She is very 'politically correct' and 'hot' on all matters concerning equality of opportunity. She is very articulate and not afraid to speak her mind.

You send a letter (on behalf of the panel) to Margaret Haynes, acknowledging her complaint. At the same time, a letter is sent to John Williams, informing him of the complaint against him, and a letter is sent to Femi Adebayo, informing him that he is said to have witnessed an incident in the office. All letters detail times of meetings, the need for confidentiality and that each person has the right to union representation.

The next time you see John in the corridor, he looks angry and barely acknowledges your presence. The next time you meet Margaret, she is visibly nervous as she tells you that she fears reprisal from John. You assure her there will be none. But just to be on the safe side, you write a letter to John telling him not to victimise or harass Margaret as a result of her complaint against him.

As you leave work for the day, you bump into Femi (the cleaner) at the front door. He tells you, in a quiet and timid manner, that he is very worried about the letter he has received from you. He tells you that he thinks he will 'get into trouble' and ultimately lose his job with CleanCo (the cleaning company contracted by the authority to clean its offices) if they find out that he is involved in the 'authority's business'. He also says that he doesn't want to 'get anyone into trouble'. You assure him the information he gives will be confidential to the panel, that the meeting will not take place during his work time (you are prepared to reschedule it if necessary) and that no-one within the local authority will harass him as a result of his co-operation. You also offer to write to his employer confirming the fact that he will be helping the authority to resolve an internal matter – he declines your offer. Finally, Femi says he is worried that he will not know what to say at the meeting. You suggest that he talks the matter over with his union representative, who can also come with him to the meeting. At this point, Femi tells you that he is not in any union. You then ask him if he has a friend who can come with him. Femi leaves, still looking a little worried, saying he will try to find one.

Both Margaret Haynes and John Williams attend their meetings with their union representative. Margaret's is called Marcus Shabazz, and John's is Nigel Slimmings. Femi Adebayo attends his meeting with his uncle Tunde Adebayo. They have both visited the Citizens' Advice Bureau and the local law centre before attending the meeting.

Both Marcus and Nigel are used to representing employees and have a good understanding of their role, that is, to advocate on behalf of the employee and ensure they are treated fairly. Tunde, on the other hand, has no experience of such meetings but has agreed to attend in order to make sure that his nephew 'does not end up in trouble'.

Role play – dealing with racial discrimination

The purpose of this role play is to give students an opportunity to use the formal procedures, skills and personal qualities identified in Exercises 4 and 5.

Students are asked to take on the following roles:

Margaret Haynes (black employee)
Colin James (line manager and member of panel of managers)
John Williams (white employee)
Derzeen Gilbert (panel of managers)
George Graham (panel of managers)
Femi Adebayo (office cleaner)
Marcus Shabazz (Margaret Haynes's union representative)
Nigel Slimmings (John Williams's union representative)

Tunde Adebayo (Femi Adebayo's uncle)
Observers (3–6 non-participant students)

Each member of the student group should take on the roles identified above. More details of these roles are given in the Tutor's Notes. Once roles have been assigned, students should get together, in role, as described below:

◆ *The panel of managers* should get together to decide how they will approach the meetings with Margaret Haynes, John Williams and Femi Adebayo, and how they will ensure that they use the procedures and skills identified (see Exercises 1 and 2) while taking account of the personal qualities required.

◆ *Margaret Haynes and Marcus Shabazz* will need to decide how they will approach their meeting with the panel.

◆ *John Williams and Nigel Slimmings* should decide how they will approach their meeting with the panel.

◆ *Femi Adebayo and Tunde Adebayo* should get together to decide how they will approach their meeting with the panel.

◆ *The observers* will need to get together to decide how they will observe. It may be useful for one or two students to note how skills are used effectively, for one or two students to note where there is a lack of skill or an inappropriate use of skills, and for another couple of students to note how procedures are being followed.

The discussions above should last no more than 15 minutes. The panel of managers should lead the meetings, spending no more than 15 minutes on each. However, the panel may want a break between meetings to prepare for the next. Each break should last no more than 10 minutes.

Panel assessment and follow-up

The purpose of this role play is to give students the opportunity to practise skills and procedure in deciding what action to take as a result of their investigation. This should take the form of a meeting between panel members while in role. The meeting should last no more than 15 minutes. Panel members may find it useful to refer to the notes they made in response to Exercises 1, 2 and 3. Observers and the rest of the student group should observe and note the skills and procedures used by the panel. Personal qualities displayed by the panel members should also be noted.

Debriefing

Once the role play investigation is over and a decision has been reached, the whole student group should take part in a debriefing session, the aim of this being to highlight the effects of using skills effectively and inappropriately, and the effect of following and not following procedures.

Observers should feed back their observations as detailed above; other students may also contribute their observations. The debriefing session should last no more than 60 minutes.

FURTHER READING

Commission for Racial Equality (1991) *Race Relations Code of Practice*, 2nd edn. CRE, London.

Commission for Racial Equality (1994) *Advice and Assistance from the CRE*. CRE, London.

Commission for Racial Equality (1995) *Racial Harassment at Work. What Employers Can Do About It*. CRE, London.

Commission for Racial Equality (1996) *Annual Report 1995*. CRE, London.

Jaffrey, M. and Stanley, J. (1995) *Tackling Racial Harassment: A Caseworker's Handbook*. CRE, London.

CHAPTER 26

Sexual Harassment

Mandy Wright

OBJECTIVES

The objectives of this chapter are to:

▶ introduce the concept of sexual harassment
▶ provide some experience of dealing with sexual harassment at work
▶ enable participants to practise organisational and interpersonal skills in a sensitive situation.

INTRODUCTION

This chapter is concerned with understanding sexual harassment and how to deal with it in organisations. A case study of a situation in a financial services organisation is the basis of a role playing exercise. The first phase of the exercise is described below. The other phases will be fed in during the session.

Gotham Cashback

Cashback Services is a well-known financial services company with offices in several of the major cities in the UK. It provides a wide range of financial services to individuals, including personal pensions and PEPs. The company has managed to maintain growth during the early 1990s, and capable staff have been able to progress within the organisation, albeit not as quickly as in the 1980s.

Nationally, Cashback is known to be a good employer. One of its most senior managers is a woman with a high public profile, and young women have joined it believing it to be more open to women than many other organisations. In fact, although a few women have made it into higher management, the workforce reflects the typical occupational divisions found in most organisations. Women are concentrated in the lower grades and in clerical, administration or other support service jobs. Men tend to move quickly into the specialist financial areas, or into sales and marketing, and then into management.

Corporately, the company has policies on most key human resources issues. These are set out in a staff handbook that all staff receive when they join. Policies are developed by a small central personnel department at corporate headquarters. Decisions on how to implement them are largely left to line managers out in the offices, working with personnel staff based there. Cashback Services has a recognised staff association (CSSA) with which it negotiates salary scales for the company's grading scheme, but it is left to local offices to determine bonus and other payments.

Recent moves to decentralise have given more freedom and discretion to each office. This has made it harder to ensure that corporate policies are implemented in the way intended by the corporate centre.

Gotham Cashback is a good example of how this can happen. Its management board is all male, and little real priority has been given to ensuring that corporate equal opportunities policies have been implemented.

Human resources issues generally are given relatively little attention. The MD, John Ridley, comes from an accountancy background and has little respect for the personnel manager, Geoff Stevens. The personnel section is small and has concentrated on the operational side of personnel – recruitment and 'pay and rations'. Policy is seen as the preserve of corporate HQ, and Geoff Stevens has done little so far to develop and take forward an HR strategy for Gotham Cashback. Locally, the staff association is weak, with low membership. Pay is reasonably good by local standards, and Gotham Cashback is seen as a good place to work.

One afternoon, Ann Smith, a senior clerk at Gotham Cashback contacted the personnel officer, Mary Jones, and asked if she could discuss a problem with her. Ann had worked in the pensions section for 3 years, having previously worked in lower-graded clerical posts in two other departments. She is young, attractive, good-humoured and quite level headed. She is also known to be keen to get on in the organisation.

When Ann came to see Mary, she was visibly upset. It seems that Stan Hawkins, the manager of her section, had been repeatedly asking her out over the past year. She had always said 'no' because she has a boyfriend and in any case would not want to get involved with her boss outside work. He is married with children but separated. His persistence had been annoying, but she had coped by staying out of his way as much as possible except when other colleagues were around. This meant skipping the Friday evening visits to the local pub with her colleagues in the pensions section.

One recent Friday night, however, she was meeting a friend in town so stayed in the office a bit later than usual. As she went to turn off the photocopier in a small room off the main office, Stan came in after her and started putting pressure on her to come out with him for a drink. She said she was busy, but he came right up to her and put his hands on her shoulders and said, 'Oh come on, you can't play hard to get forever!' She ducked under his arms and scooted out, grabbed her coat and left.

Over the weekend, she thought about what to do. She decided that she would say something to Stan next time he approached her, thinking perhaps he had somehow misunderstood her reactions to his overtures.

On Monday, she started off to work feeling anxious. The day went smoothly until she was on her way back from another department and found herself alone in the lift with Stan. As soon as the door shut, Stan came closer to her, put his arms on her shoulders and pushed her against the side of the lift. 'Now how about it?' It's time you agreed to come out with me. I won't take no for an answer.' Ann pushed him away and said, 'Can't you understand, Stan, I'm just not interested. Please leave me alone.' Stan laughed and said, 'I'm the boss, and I expect a better response than that. You are letting yourself in for real trouble with your attitude.' As they reached the next floor, the door opened, and Ann leapt out, feeling hot, flustered and somewhat frightened.

At home that night, Ann discussed her problem with her flatmate, Minny. Minny said, 'You'll have to go over his head and tell someone. Cashback is a good company. They'll sort it out.'

The next day, Ann went to see Mr Hartley, the head of the personal finance division and Stan's boss. After a bit of small talk, she finally blurted out that she was 'having trouble with Stan' who kept pestering her to go out with him. She told him that she'd told Stan she wasn't interested, but that hadn't stopped him. What could she do?

Mr Hartley said that he understood her feelings but that Ann should grow up a bit. She was an attractive girl, and it was only 'normal' that Stan would be attracted to her. In any case, he was sure that Stan was only being flirtatious. A girl like Ann ought to be able to cope with the 'rough and tumble' of office life if she expected to get on in the company.

Ann stumbled out of the office, feeling both angry and worried. Not only was Mr Hartley not going to help, but she had now probably given him the impression she couldn't cope, and she knew his views would be crucial to whether or not she even got a chance for promotion.

Back in the office, she found it hard to concentrate. Eventually she survived the day and went home with a terrible headache, going to bed early. The next morning, Ann found she did not want to come to work. She was nervous about seeing Stan and about what she should do. Would he keep pressuring her? Would her refusals affect her annual appraisal, which was due soon? In the end, she pulled herself together and got to work late. Before she started her work, already piling up, she dug out her staff handbook. It had a brief section that said Cashback had a policy that sexual harassment is not acceptable and that employees are expected to treat each other with respect. Ann searched through the handbook but could not find any further references to it or any guidance on what she should do next.

Ann managed to lay low and keep out of Stan's way for the next few weeks, but found she was dreading her annual appraisal 'chat' with Stan. She was becoming very irritable, and she kept making mistakes in her work. One morning, when she was feeling particularly low, she called in sick rather than face him. Ann knew she was letting her team mates down, but she felt she simply could not cope. She stayed off work for 3 more days, then finally went back in.

While she was away, a member of the section that received Ann's work ran into Stan in the canteen and complained about Ann's performance, commenting, 'Stan, I'm really disappointed in Ann's work. At first she seemed so keen, but now her work is late, and full of mistakes. I've had to have someone check it before it is sent back to the customer.'

The next week, Ann had her appraisal discussion with Stan. The previous year he had been very positive about her work and her potential career with Cashback, but she knew it would not be the same this year. In fact, the discussion was very short, and Stan was anything but over-friendly.

Stan started by saying how disappointed he was in her performance, that she had let him and the section down and that he had had complaints from other sections about her. Without asking for any explanation, or even waiting for her reaction, he told her that she was being transferred to the payroll section, starting the next day. She would keep her grade and basic pay, but Ann's heart sank. Payroll was notorious as the 'graveyard' of Gotham Cashback. No-one ever got promoted out of there into main-stream services, nor were they able to earn bonuses for their performance.

Ann was too shocked, and angry, to even speak. She gathered up her bag and notepad and left Stan's office quickly. She went to her desk and started cleaning out her drawers. What could she do? Her first inclination was to hand in her notice and go but, once she calmed down, she realised that this would be playing into Stan's hands.

Ann decided to try complaining to personnel. She approached Mary Jones because Mary had always seemed helpful and friendly. When Mary had heard the whole story, she told Ann that she would see what she could do and not to panic. She was sure it could be sorted out. Meanwhile, Ann should start in the new section.

Once Ann had left, Mary went to see Geoff Stevens about the situation. Geoff expressed surprise that Stan would act in such a way but agreed to speak to Stan after speaking to Mr Hartley first.

He managed to catch Mr Hartley the next day and explained what had happened. Mr Hartley retorted that Stan was one of his best young managers, 'a high flyer who would go places'. He was sure that the whole episode was a storm in a teacup and probably just the result of a few drinks too many at the pub after work. He assured Geoff Stevens that he would deal with it himself by having a word with Stan.

A few days later, he saw Stan in the pub after work. He took him to one side and said that he didn't want to be awkward, but he'd had a complaint from Geoff Stevens about 'this business with Ann Smith', and he was sure it was nothing, but could Stan please be careful to keep his personal life and feelings out of the office. He knew Stan was having difficulties at home, and he realised that Ann was an attractive woman, but Cashback expected staff to be discreet and professional at all times. With that, he slapped Stan on the back in a friendly manner and rejoined his other colleagues at the bar.

Three weeks later, Ann, bored with her new job and fed up with the lack of response from personnel, decided to hand in her resignation at the end of the month.

The next weekend, Ann went to a party at an old friend's house and was introduced to Angie, a young woman lawyer who worked at the local law centre in the high street. Angie asked her about her work, and Ann found herself pouring out the whole story. Angie advised her that she could sue Gotham Cashback for constructive dismissal.

On Monday morning, Ann handed in her resignation and told personnel that she was going to sue for constructive dismissal.

the exercises

Preparation

Participants should read the case study thoroughly before the session.

The non-participant observers and students representing the staff association, the law centre lawyer and corporate personnel should also read the references indicated at the end of the chapter.

The initial scenario

The exercise begins with Mary Jones, the personnel officer, contacting Geoff Stevens, her boss, to tell him what Ann Smith has done.

Students are asked to take on the following roles:

Geoff Stevens, personnel manager
Mary Jones, personnel officer
Mr Hartley, head of personal finance division
Stan Hawkins, manager of pensions section
John Ridley, managing director
Ann Smith, senior clerk
Richard Owen, corporate personnel
Angie Martin, law centre lawyer
Michaela Graham, staff association representative

In addition, two non-participant observers should be appointed.

The tasks of the participants is to try to resolve the situation without ending up at a tribunal. The non-participant observers' task is to observe what happens and provide a commentary on the effectiveness of the steps taken and of management's handling of the case at the end of the exercise.

Additional information

The personnel officer, Mary Jones, has been informed that there is a rumour – almost certainly true – that Ann Smith had a brief affair with Stan Hawkins the first year she joined the company 8 years ago. When he lost interest after a few weeks, Ann was said to have been extremely upset.

It has, furthermore, become apparent that Stan has been under a lot of stress lately and is not coping. Not only is he engaged in a battle with his wife for the custody of his children, but he has also been working long hours in the wake of the personal pensions scandal. A tribunal case would probably push him over the edge as well as guarantee that he does not get custody of his children.

Does this additional information change the conclusions reached in Exercise 1? If it does, how and why?

Organisational implications

Cashback UK, the parent company, send Richard Owen, from corporate personnel, to investigate and 'sort out' Gotham Cashback. The board of Cashback UK is unhappy with the publicity the case has received, which it feels is sullying the company's reputation as a good employer.

What new policies and procedures should Richard propose?

FURTHER READING

Commission of European Communities (1993) *How to Combat Sexual Harassment at Work – A Guide to Implementing the European Code of Practice.* Commission of European Communities, Brussels.

Institute of Personnel and Development (1997) *Statement on Harassment at Work.* Institute of Personnel and Development, London.

CHAPTER 27

Stakeholder Analysis

Karen Legge

OBJECTIVES

The objectives of this case are to:

▶ give an understanding of stakeholder analysis and to develop participants' analytical skills in this area

▶ encourage participants to identify the range and relative importance of the stakeholders involved in strategic decisions and to consider the potential compatibility or incompatibility of the respective parties' agendas

▶ encourage participants to explore the processes of negotiation and compromise in reaching an outcome satisfactory to, first, the greatest range of stakeholders, and second, the most powerful stakeholders.

INTRODUCTION

During the summer of 1997, Greenpeace UK, part of the international environmental protest organisation, and British Petroleum were locked in conflict. There was British Petroleum, a giant multinational oil company, heavily engaged in pushing forward the frontiers of oil exploration in the rough and deep waters of the North Atlantic, 90 miles west of the Shetland Islands and aptly named by the company the 'Atlantic frontier'. Two oil fields were being developed – Foinaven, which was expected to yield around 200 million barrels of oil, and, further down the line, Schiehallion, which was estimated to yield a bumper 420 million barrels. Senior executives at BP were only too well aware that the Foinaven field was already a year behind schedule, owing to the replacement of faulty well heads and that the pre-production phase of the project had cost £670m against a budgeted expenditure of £550m. In this context, further delays to the project were a serious concern.

Greenpeace and BP

All summer, Greenpeace UK had been a thorn in the flesh for BP. Arguing that, given the dangers of global warming, we have all the oil we need to burn from other fields, as long as we harness non-polluting energy from the sun and wind, and that consequently opening up new fields is madness, Greenpeace UK had engaged in a summer-long series of well-orchestrated and media-focused publicity campaigns against the development of the Atlantic frontier, with the broader agenda of raising general issues about environmental protection. It started with occupying the Rockall outcrop (well known for its daily mention in shipping weather forecasts) and graduated to activists swimming across the paths of seismic survey vessels. Then there had been the spectacle of small rubber dinghies tossing in steep seas among the cables, buoys and hydrophones just as explosive charges were due to be let off. Then Greenpeace sought a judicial review on the granting of licences by the UK government, complaining to the European Commission that the licensing granted breached EC directives. Finally, in the middle of August, Greenpeace activists scaled the slippery chains of the Stena Dee mobile drilling platform, which, at a hiring cost variously estimated at between £60,000 and £100,000 per day, was being towed to the Foinaven field, and, as one newspaper put it, 'suspended themselves from its side in a cylindrical barrel, like human limpets' (Wilkinson, *FT Weekend*, 23/24 August 1997). The occupation continued for 9 days, and the rig eventually arrived at its destination, 5 days later than planned.

On 18 August, BP took legal action against Greenpeace. A court in Edinburgh froze Greenpeace's UK bank accounts, issued a writ for £1.4m and indicted four activists for losses incurred from delays caused by Greenpeace's occupation of Stena Dee and its disruption of BP's legitimate activities. BP recognised Greenpeace's right to campaign but asked only that it ceased its unlawful sabotage. Greenpeace UK responded that BP's action could bankrupt them, as, in spite of an income of £6.8m in 1996, it had assets of only £180,000, having spent its reserves on the summer-long protest against the Atlantic frontier. While Greenpeace International's offices around the world had a total income in 1996 of £87.10m ($142m, of which $30.6m was paid into the organisation's central funds), 'None are legally liable to pay any of this and I don't think they would want to use their money to pay fines' (Steven Thomson, Greenpeace, UK, finance director, quoted in *FT*, 19 August 1997).

Two days later, a settlement was reached. BP withdrew its damages claim, as well as charges against three of the activists, in return for an undertaking from Greenpeace UK that it would stay away from Foinaven. BP had earlier tried to obtain an assurance that Greenpeace would not obstruct BP's activities in the whole of the Atlantic frontier, including the Schiehallion field, but Greenpeace refused to give this blanket undertaking. In this, they were supported by the European Federation of Green Parties, which threatened an international boycott of BP's goods and services. In suspending its £1.4 million legal action against Greenpeace UK, a spokesperson for BP stated that it was satisfied that the group would obey injunctions to keep clear of the Foinaven field. In leaving the Stena Dee, a spokesperson for Greenpeace UK said that it was ending its occupation because it feared that forecasted bad weather could endanger the safety of its activists. Mr Chris Rose, Greenpeace UK's deputy chief executive said that 'there was no question of Greenpeace giving an undertaking to cease campaigning over the Atlantic frontier and the threat new oil exploration poses to the climate' (*FT*, 21 August 1997).

Enter the stakeholders and their agendas

BP is an integrated oil company that explores for, extracts, refines and sells, oil and petrochemical products. Exploration is a major part of its business, and, as North Sea reserves run down, new technologies allow it to explore in far deeper waters than seemed possible two decades ago. (Indeed, during the course of this dispute, on 20 August 1977, BP's share price jumped 34p on upbeat broker comments on the value of its 16 per cent interest in the Dalia field off Angola.) Rarely does one oil company – as this latter comment indicates – own a complete field, but it has a stake in it. For example, while BP has a 72 per cent stake in Foinaven, its partner, Shell, has a 28 per cent stake. Money is made by getting fields on stream as quickly as possible and, in this context, being free to continue its drilling activities at Foinaven unimpeded. This mattered a lot more than a possible £1.4m damages in a long drawn out court case that would only provide Greenpeace with a publicity platform from which to berate the evils of the multinational oil companies. After all, £1.4m is chicken feed compared with the £2.6bn net profits BP made in the preceding year.

In coming to this conclusion, BP would be only too aware of the power of the media. Only 2 years earlier, Royal Dutch Shell had been humiliated by Greenpeace in its attempt to dispose of its Brent Spar storage buoy in the Atlantic Ocean bed. Shell had all the arguments on its side. It had considered 30 separate studies by independent organisations. It was overwhelmingly agreed that burial in waters 2 km deep was the best solution. It would cost only a quarter as much as onshore disposal. It would be six times safer, greatly reducing the risk of fatal accidents, and would minimise damage to the environment. The British government agreed, and no other government belonging to the Oslo Convention on the maritime environment objected.

But did the public know or care about this? 'European television viewers saw emotive footage (mostly shot by Greenpeace) of activists heroically clinging to a giant tin can full of tonnes of poisonous oil to be thrown into Europe's back yard' (Wilkinson, *FT Weekend*, 23/24 August 1996). What followed was an international boycott of Shell's products and services, and the German government's support of Greenpeace (remember that green parties are historically strong and active in Germany). It made no difference that Greenpeace subsequently admitted that it had (depending on point of view) made grossly misleading statements, or got its calculations wrong, about the amount of oil in the buoy and where it was to be dumped.

If that was not enough, BP would remember the court case only a few months earlier in 1996 when McDonald's fast-food restaurant chain, although technically winning its libel case, scored a spectacular own goal with its legal pursuit of penniless activists. Already the media were talking of Greenpeace and BP in terms of 'David and Goliath', and as one newspaper columnist put it:

> No one remembers what David and Goliath were fighting about but everyone knows who won, and whose side they were on.

Once you allow yourself to be seen as Goliath you have lost.
(Geoffrey Lean, *Independent on Sunday*, 24 August 1997)

BP could not afford to alienate the media. The last thing that the company would wish was too much analysis of its use of 'big brother' or so-called SLAPP (strategic lawsuit against public participation) tactics. This is the tactic in the US whereby lawsuits seeking millions of dollars in damages from protesters have frightened them into silence. (Hassled by animal rights demonstrators? Then try the anti-stalking law. Road protests? Look at the law on secondary picketing. In the US, 14 states have adopted 'food disparagement' acts, which bar negative comments about perishable foodstuffs and which resulted from an anti-green alliance between farmers, loggers and right-wing congressmen; see Rogaly, *FT Weekend*, 23/24 August 1996.) In no way would BP want its £1.4m lawsuit seen in this light – hence its spokesperson's comment that:

BP's principal concern is not the recovery of damages. Rather it is to ensure that its lawful operations are not interfered with and that safety is not compromised. BP has never questioned Greenpeace's right to campaign, but we do object to their employing unlawful tactics. (*The Times*, 20 August 1997)

BP, in fact, did have a positive message to give to the media. First, it followed a policy of treating the activists personally with kid gloves. For example, when they boarded the Stena Dee, the company stationed two men, not as guards, but as safety watchmen. They even asked the protesters if they would like to come on board for hot food and showers. Furthermore, leaning over backwards, BP offered to help out Greenpeace when a TV crew was stuck on board the protest ship without any means of getting ashore. After friendly negotiations with the ship's captain, BP provided a helicopter to help the newsmen get their pictures home (Wilkinson in *FT Weekend*, 23/24 August 1997). Finally, the company made it quite clear that they would not physically evict the protesters unless poor weather conditions (combined with an inability to ballast down the rig owing to the activists' presence on its legs) raised safety issues.

Second, ironically, the media themselves were quick to acknowledge that, in spite of Greenpeace UK's Atlantic frontier campaign against BP, BP itself is probably environmentalists' preferred oil company – certainly in preference to Shell (Geoffrey Lean, *Independent on Sunday*, 24 August, 1996). Why is this?

Before examining the sunny side of BP's relationship with Greenpeace UK, it is necessary to consider the latter organisation itself. For the past 10 years, Greenpeace has been largely unsuccessful in its attempts to push global warming higher up the public agenda. One problem has been the mixed messages that it has preached over the years. In the early days, Greenpeace's message was that, with rapid industrialisation, the world would run out of oil, and, unless renewable energy sources were found, there would have to be limits to growth because of fuel shortages. As this message had little resonance with a consumer-orientated public, the next campaign was directed at energy saving and curbs on cars to cut emissions of carbon dioxide from fossil fuels to save energy *and* to prevent the global warming problem – to *cut* oil production rather than to *save* energy. Opposing the expansion of an existing field, say in the North Sea, would not be dramatic enough. But the Atlantic frontier represents an escalation in oil exploration, particularly in its use of technologies that provide access to potential oil fields previously unworkable. Note, though, how Greenpeace's message has shifted from a vision of the world with *too little* oil to one with *too much*.

This shift in strategy or message has provoked the response from hostile critics (such as the Institute of Economic Affairs, the Institute of Chemical Engineers and the Aberdeen Chamber of Commerce), often with their own axes to grind, that Greenpeace is prone to calling 'Wolf' once too often and preaching unnecessarily alarmist messages (witness Brent Spar). There is the charge too that rather than talking directly with the oil companies, Greenpeace conducts a debate with the media through a series of, admittedly highly effective in terms of attention grabbing, publicity seeking stunts. Furthermore, there is some suggestion that Greenpeace loses sight of priorities and engages in whatever activities of a broad-brush environmentalist nature would appeal to an emotional public. Hence the cartoon on the bridge of Greenpeace's ship, Rainbow C, showing two activists in a dinghy looking at a 'Save Our Hedgehogs' banner that is pinned to an oil rig. One man is saying to the other, 'I sometimes wonder if we aren't losing our focus' (*FT*, 15 August 1997).

In this context, Greenpeace's opposition to BP might seem somewhat opportunist, not to say misguided. Unusually for an oil company, BP has consistently sought to raise its public profile as an environmentally conscious enterprise. In the North Sea fields, it has been in the forefront in reducing spillages and eliminating the flaring of unwanted gases. It has gone along with posting observers before firing seismic guns and sounding warning guns at low volume to protect dolphins. More importantly, in 1996, BP resigned from the Global Climate Coalition, an international energy industry lobby against attempts to control global warming. In May 1996, John Browne, Group CEO of BP, announced that the company would no longer oppose the scientific consensus that human activity was contributing to climate change and pledged that BP would 'focus on what can and should be done' (Geoffrey Lean, *Independent on Sunday*, 24 August 1997). To this end, BP announced a significant increase in its investment in solar energy research. One of BP's subsidiaries is already the world's third largest solar panel manufacturer, with 10 per cent of the $500m global annual market. Browne said that he is 'convinced that we can make solar competitive for supplying peak energy demand within 10 years'. One BP study has found that opening a single big factory for solar cells – costing half the amount so far invested in the Foinaven field – will bring down costs considerably through economies of scale (Geoffrey Lean, *Independent on Sunday*, 24 October 1997). Indeed, Chris Rose admitted that 'Our campaign is not really about BP. It just happens to be the exploration company on the spot' (Geoffrey Lean, *Independent on Sunday*, 24 August 1997).

So should BP be Greenpeace's target at all? The UK Centre for Economic and Environmental Development in Cambridge argues that coal rather than oil and natural gas should be targeted, as coal results in 30 per cent more carbon dioxide emission than oil, and 80 per cent more than natural gas. Furthermore, is Greenpeace's call to phase out the worldwide use of fossil fuels by the next 40 years practicable? Critics argue that, in spite of John Browne's hopes for the future solar energy cell industry, at present even to produce as much energy as the Foinaven field (which will constitute only about 0.5 per cent of UK's annual output), 30 million solar panels would be required, producing energy for 100 years. Furthermore, one large oil-fired electricity turbine produces the same power as about 1000 windmills with a wing span the size of the dome of St Paul's – assuming that the wind blows (*FT*, 12 August 1997). Curbing energy use by taxation and efficiency measures is one thing, but until cost-effective, fully renewable energy supplies are with us, much of industry and commerce would argue that cutting off oil supplies is the route to economic disaster. 'Remember the 1970s and the three-day week,' many darkly mutter.

Finally, there is the government. Unless governments agree to the short-term carbon dioxide reduction targets at the Kyoto UN Climate Conference in December 1997 and are prepared to implement what are likely to be unpopular increases in fuel taxes, Greenpeace's aspirations are likely to be pie-in-the-sky. Also, it must not be forgotten that, in the UK, taxation on North Sea oil revenues (and presumably on those of the Atlantic frontier) is a relatively invisible way of raising tax revenue when an electorate has, for the past 20 years, consistently shown itself to be shy of direct taxation.

On 18 August 1997, when BP took action against Greenpeace, its share price stood at 837.5p. Its closing price on 22 August 1997, when a settlement was announced, was 899p.

Epilogue

Put diplomats from 159 countries, plus lobbyists with at least as many agendas – hidden or open – into one place, and the result is bound to be hypocrisy, gamesmanship and sheer nonsense. Such was the case during the negotiations in Kyoto to reduce greenhouse gas emissions, which ended this week (12/12/97). It was not until well past the formal deadline, and gestures and language that were scarcely diplomatic, that delegates were able to cut a deal. Too bad it will never fly.... (*The Economist*, 13–19 December 1997).

the exercises

The following questions may be discussed by small groups of 5–8 people and their responses fed back to a plenary session. If all questions are attempted, 2 hours should be allowed for discussion and the plenary session.

1. Who are the major stakeholders in this confrontation between BP and Greenpeace?
2. What are the vested interests and agendas of each of the stakeholders?
3. Which stakeholders do you think have (a) the strongest and (b) the weakest case, and what criteria are you using in making this judgment?
4. Do you think the outcome achieved reflected the interests of all stakeholders? If so, in what ways? If not, why not?

5. Sketch out a scenario that involves the same stakeholders that you have identified, but where a very different outcome results. What different outcomes can you imagine, and in what sets of circumstances?

FURTHER READING

Butler, R., Davies, L., Pike, R. and Sharp, J. (1993) *Strategic Investment Decisions, Theory, Practice and Process*, Chapters 1–5. Routledge, London.

Croall, S. and Rankin, W. (1992) *Ecology for Beginners*. Icon Books, Cambridge.

Evan, W.M. and Freeman, R.E. (1988) A stakeholder theory of the modern corporation: Kantian capitalism. In Beauchamp, T. and Bowie, N. (eds) *Ethical Theory and Business*, 3rd edn, pp. 97–106. Prentice-Hall, Englewood Cliffs, NJ.

Freeman, E. (1984) *Strategic Management: A Stakeholder Approach*. Pitman, London.

Lukes, S. (1974) *Power: A Radical View*. Macmillan, Basingstoke.

CHAPTER 28

Generating Strategy

David Tranfield

OBJECTIVES

The objectives of this chapter are to:

▶ outline a case study developed with the aim of helping individuals to gain experience of generating strategy
▶ introduce the strategy-making process, including key ideas and theoretical concepts
▶ specify relevant techniques.

INTRODUCTION

This chapter is concerned with the ways in which managers in companies generate and develop strategy. The process of strategy formulation and development is a complex and difficult task, and is based on both analytical skills and careful judgements. Strategy is concerned primarily with defining the future; in both the short and the long term. The current strategy of an organisation can be seen as a gateway, bridging a past that becomes increasingly submerged and a future that is yet to be enacted. Therefore, to be able to develop effective strategies, it is necessary not only to focus on the future strategic possibilities, but also to understand strategic history, how the organisation came to be following its present course, and what strengths and weaknesses have been left as a legacy by previous strategies. Consequently, generating and implementing strategy is intrinsically bound up with the effective management of change.

These ideas will be explored in the rest of this chapter, which is organised into three sections. First there is a case study of a manufacturing company, East Midchester Products, to be used in applying the ideas below. Second, there is an introduction to the strategic generation process followed by an outline of three main techniques for use in strategy generation (scenario planning, stakeholder analysis and competency/capability audit). Finally, there is a reading list that is designed to provide background and back-up literature to help those wishing to extend their knowledge of the area.

East Midchester Products: a company in need of direction

Background

East Midchester Products (EMP), is a medium-sized company manufacturing wood products and located in the North of England. It is part of Carnival plc, the holding company, also based in the same geographical area. Carnival first became prominent during the 1980s, primarily by adopting a strategy of aggressive growth, often through acquisition, subsequent reorganisation and then reinvestment, particularly in infrastructure and facilities. By the late 1980s, Carnival was the darling of the city, having grown by a factor of three on almost every conceivable financial performance indicator. It had become notorious for recruiting and promoting a particular type of young, aggressive manager, able and willing to respond to clear financial targets with a strong 'can do' attitude. As Marc Grantham, chairman of the Carnival board remarked when commenting on his company's success:

> With youth comes a belief that one can walk on water, as well as a lack of bad experiences in business. It is my strong view that our conservative national culture has failed to allow full expression of the talent and energy that surrounds us. Our company aims to release the potential of its employees in order to win in today's globally competitive economy.

However, the successes of the 1980s were quickly overtaken in the deep recession of the early 1990s. The share price sank catastrophically from £4.53 for a £1 share in late 1988, to a mere £1.05 by 1993. The Carnival companies were all placed under the most severe constraints, many of them undergoing savage redundancy and cost-cutting programmes. The general view was that Carnival had classically 'overegged the pudding', stretching itself beyond its financial and managerial resources. It was at this time that two Carnival companies became the subject of investigation by the Inland Revenue following a suggestion of accounting malpractice in their published accounts. Having faced this crisis in the early 1990s, Carnival made a slow recovery, although it was thought by many business commentators that, when taken together, the Carnival companies generally suffered a lack of strategic leadership and direction, and many of them required an organisational rethink, coupled with a significant injection of capital if they were to succeed.

EMP and its products

EMP was a typical Carnival company. Originally Manvers Kitchens, it was acquired and relocated in 1986 into new premises on an industrial estate just 2 miles from the M18 and 10 minutes' drive from the M1 motorway. The new premises were efficient and excellent in size and general facilities. The company had prospered and grown quickly to its present size of approximately £30m turnover and 200 employees (approximately 140 being directly employed in production), with a 12-strong senior management team, including five Directors and a Managing Director.

The main products of EMP were kitchens and kitchen units made for the retail market. Most of these were based on 'standard' designs, yet tailored to give a seemingly unique product, acceptable to each of three large retail outlets. There was a small bespoke market that accounted for only 3–5 per cent of turnover per annum.

Margins were high (20–25 per cent) in this market, as opposed to the case with the provision of 'standard' units, where margins had fallen to under 5 per cent. Given these relative volumes, the successful maintenance of good relationships with the retailers, who sold through stores and warehouses to the general public, was critical to EMP. Indeed, large orders from retailers could result in the gain or loss of up to £20m of business at a stroke should any retailer decide to offer a particular 'line' of kitchen.

Overseas competition, particularly from Europe (Germany and Italy), was fierce, and two overseas companies were major competitors to EMP in the UK market. All three companies (including EMP), had about an equal market share, having adopted strategies of tying in retailers to particular kitchen design characteristics over the years. However, it was recognised that customer loyalty based on this criterion was flimsy, and it was accepted that any adoption of a new brand image by retailers could lead to an immediate and potentially catastrophic loss of orders.

Therefore EMP had three main aims that were critical to business survival: first, continually to apply downward pressure on costs; second, to increase quality; and third, to increase responsiveness by ensuring that deliveries were as close to 100 per cent on time as possible.

EMP tried to achieve the first aim by keeping staffing levels to a bare minimum. Labour costs had been reduced significantly by the implementation of two restructurings, which had resulted in downsizing (at all levels in the company) in the past 3 years, and were now at an all-time low of 18 per cent of total cost, which was about the norm for the industry. However, to the surprise of the management team, manufacturing costs in total were still 5–10 per cent higher than those of other major competitors in the industry. These figures were the source of much argument between the design and manufacturing departments, who were organised separately, had little to do with each other and regularly blamed each other for this state of affairs. About 60 per cent of the cost of manufacture was designed into most products in the form of agreed customer requirements and specifications that could only be met by strict adherence to the use of particular materials and manufacturing processes. Some of the costs of storage of finished product incurred in making to stock were defrayed by the EMP policy of paying suppliers quarterly in arrears.

EMP addressed the second aim (quality improvement) by carefully assessing its raw material inputs. However, orders usually were placed with suppliers on the basis of lowest tender from a variety of suppliers.

The third aim was addressed by EMP making predominantly to stock and ensuring that they carried a full range of wood products required to manufacture 1 month's worth of production of standard units.

EMP organisation

The main value-adding process at EMP could be characterised as shown in Figure 28.1:

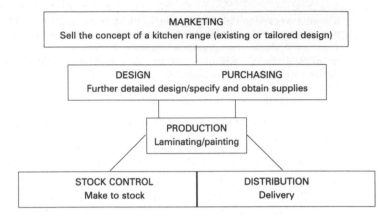

Figure 28.1   The EMP organisation

The EMP board, which meets weekly on a Monday morning is made up as follows.

The **Managing Director**, Philip Rayner, was recently appointed following the resignation of his predecessor, who left to join a firm of international consultants after serving 18 months at EMP. He is a chartered accountant by background, an unstuffy character of 44, who is seen regularly on the shopfloor and still plays in the company tennis and badminton leagues on Wednesday evenings. Previously Finance Director, he was asked to take over the company following financial irregularities in some Carnival companies (not EMP) and was a popular choice with both management and workforce. He is ambitious for the company and wants to drive it forward, toward world-class standards. His view is that a clear strategy is needed if this is to be achieved, which takes into account the improvement of the current company situation, the company's potential to identify and exploit its strengths in new markets, and the company's ability to capitalise on key change drivers and trends in a wider context.

> *Key agenda items* – how to develop a specification of overall ambition for the company; leadership issues; ensuring the commitment of others to a strategic direction; business ethics; relaunching the company and regenerative strategies.

The **Sales and Marketing Director**, Sean Dooley, is the longest-serving director and is fully versed in the ways of EMP and Carnival. At 43, he has developed a reputation of being an archetypal 'wheeler dealer'. He sees the need for flexibility and pragmatism as the two key characteristics of effective sales performance. He prides himself on having 'survived' four Managing Directors and their pet prejudices, some of which had resulted from what he saw as their 'business school education', which is his pet hate.

Key agenda items – market segmentation and differentiation; strategic shifts in the environment; establishing a marketing plan.

The **Technical and Design Director**, Les Beachill, is new to the board, having been recruited by Philip Rayner. He is 38 and worked as a creative designer before turning to engineering. Together with Alison Brad, he is the most computer-literate board member and joined the company because he thought that it had both the personnel and potential to become market leader by adopting a design-led strategy. An engineering graduate, he has initiated a pilot project using a recently purchased Computer-Aided Design (CAD) system, but he has started expressing his frustration at the lack of resources for capital investment in the latest design technology.

Key agenda items – applying and exploiting new technology; CAD; relating design to marketing upstream and manufacturing downstream; influencing EMP to become design led; developing new and flexible product ranges for exploitation in the market place.

The **Production and Manufacturing Director**, Adam Stevinson, has been with EMP for 5 years and is 45. Also trained as an engineer, he is innovative and has implemented significant cost reduction programmes in his time with the company, but is frustrated by his relationship with both marketing and design. He cannot understand why marketing has not initiated a long-term programme to identify markets for machine-laminated (glued) and painted wood products both in the UK and overseas in the construction and allied industries. He also believes that the EMP painting process is as good as can be found. This, largely to the good fortune of EMP, is due to work done by a university placement student a couple of years ago who identified a process involving complex temperature manipulation of the drying process, which produced excellent results every time. He often speculated on whether a similar process would work on other laminated surfaces in particular or other painted surfaces in general. Constant product design changes and changes in delivery schedules, he believes, place an intolerable burden on his department, which he thinks is considerably understaffed since the last reorganisation. It is now over 3 years since there was any new investment in manufacturing technology or computer-aided production management systems.

Key agenda items – computer-aided manufacturing; manufacturing as a strategic competitive weapon; time-based competition (by increasing the speed of the manufacturing process, this allows customers to be able to change their mind during the design phase without extending total time from order to delivery [lead time]); cultural change (that is, changing the shared taken-for-granted assumptions of individuals and work teams) within the manufacturing function.

The **Financial Director**, Andrew Pierrepont, replaced Philip Rayner. He sees himself as providing a specialist service and tends not to take a lead in major strategic decisions, which he thinks should be Rayner's prerogative. He sees the implementation of a new computer-based financial information system over the next 18 months as his main contribution to the company.

Key agenda items – making cases for capital investment; evaluation of capital investment decisions; performance indicators for world-class performance; the funding of change management programmes; information systems.

The **Specialist Services Director**, Alison Brad has within her remit personnel, IT and total quality. An individual of enormous energy, she is the best qualified of the board in academic terms, with a first degree in business studies and information technology and an MSc in the management of change. EMP is not unionised, but Alison Brad chairs a consultative group made up of representatives from all areas of the company, which meets monthly. EMP could be described as largely single status, which has been encouraged by both Philip Rayner and Alison Brad.

Key agenda items – modern HR strategies (performance appraisal, training, management development, reward strategies and so on); organisation structuring (teamworking, downsizing, resizing, outsourcing and so on); management of change management programme; quality strategy; office systems.

Purchasing is handled currently by Tim Naylor, a senior figure and the longest-serving manager in the company, who reports to the Production and Manufacturing Director. Philip Rayner has speculated on the appointment of a logistics director but has been unable to resolve in his own mind whether or not to do this.

Key agenda items – supply chain management (internal and external); strategic alliances and partnerships; electronic data interchange.

Current situation

Because of high workloads and the sporadic and unpredictable attendance at meetings, one of Philip Rayner's early decisions was to require all these senior managers to name a deputy who would act for them in their absence. He sees the Directors, together with this second tier, as comprising a senior management team, to be involved in all strategic discussions and decisions. In the name of improving communications and better senior management teamworking, he expects the attendance of all of this group at board meetings and strategy discussions, and does not regard the increase in numbers as problematic. Since its inception, this innovation has worked well and is supported by all of those involved.

Following the traumas of the recession of the early 1990s and having settled himself into his new position, Philip Rayner has decided that EMP is ready for its next step. He has recently received a new set of demanding financial targets from head office and realises that he must deliver a step function improvement in the performance of the business. He thinks that the time has come to stop reacting to each demand from head office and develop a coherent strategy taking into account the forces that will impact on the company long term, capitalising on existing strengths and ensuring appropriate responses to existing and potential markets. Also, he thinks that streamlining his company, together with his relatively new management team, would have some considerable potential, but he is unsure how this might best be exploited. He is aware that, over the last 5 years, capital investment in all aspects of the company has been well below what might have been expected, but he is uncertain what should be the precise priority areas with which to approach the Carnival board for funding, although he believes that the time is right to make a case to the Carnival board for a significant injection of capital into the business. He has organised a special off-site meeting of the senior management group to address these issues.

STRATEGY

Understanding strategy

Predicting future demands and then configuring the organisation to achieve optimal performance has, for many companies, proved an impossible task. A glance down the Fortune 500 list of 25 years ago in comparison to today provides compelling evidence of the inability of companies adequately to anticipate what is needed to remain in business. Yet an organisation that does not try to anticipate the future becomes 'decerebrate', reacting to events as they occur rather than proactively attempting to steer a course forward.

The importance of strategic context

Strategies are generated within the background context of changes in the wider society. The development of integrated information technologies and networks, the globalisation of the competitive environment, changes in social values and individual expectations, and changes in world politics, all constitute an unfolding backcloth, operating beyond the level of the individual organisation, yet against which companies and organisations have to develop their strategic ideas and frameworks. In generating strategy, it is, therefore, most important to have identified at least some of these key 'change drivers', understood some of the linkages between them and anticipated their potential impact on the company or organisation in question.

Views of strategy

The most dominant view of how to create competitive advantage has traditionally emphasised the importance of responding effectively to the external environment of the company or organisation. This has been labelled the 'competitive forces' perspective (Porter, 1990). Leaders are thought to be those who meet market requirements most efficiently and effectively, reading or even anticipating the future in advance of others. Teece and Pisano (1994) and Teece et al. (1992) have outlined alternative approaches to strategy formulation and generation, counterposing the 'competitive forces' view with 'resource-based' perspectives.

Whereas the 'competitive forces' view focuses attention externally, emphasising the importance of responding to markets, the resource-based view looks inside the company or organisation. It assumes that all companies and organisations, even when operating in the same markets, are very different in the ways in which they strategically configure their resources. For example, they have different financial arrangements, different facilities, different technologies and different people arranged in different structures and often with very different shared taken-for-granted assumptions (cultures). These 'resources' comprise the micro-assets of the company or organisation and enable some companies to add value more effectively than others.

For example, some organisations may have excellent teamworking arrangements, facilitating problem solving and complementing their integrated technologies. Others may have adopted just-in-time systems to reduce cost and vertically link upstream to suppliers. It is here, so the argument goes, in detailed operating arrangements, that the source of competitive advantage lies, in much the same way that sports teams, although appearing superficially similar, can be differentiated by their detailed activities and routines. In other words, advantage might be rather more appropriately thought of as being produced 'inside-out' by focusing attention additionally on 'what we are able to do to add value better than the competition' (competences and capabilities) rather than merely attending to 'outside-in' issues, that is, focusing on explicit and expected market demands.

The strategy-generating process

Figure 28.2 outlines an overview of the strategy generation process that first takes into account the broader context and then goes on to address both the 'outside-in' (market-driven, competitive forces) approach and the 'inside-out' (competences and capabilities) view. Only by including all of these ideas can the strategy-generating process address comprehensively that which needs to be taken into account.

The process represented in Figure 28.2 is best understood by first of all focusing on the outputs, that is, beginning by understanding what it is that we are trying to produce and then working backwards up through the various activities that have to be undertaken.

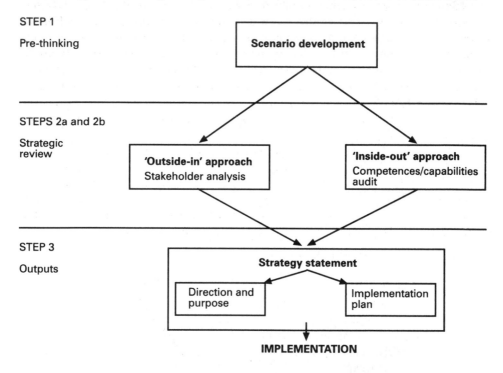

Figure 28.2   Model of the strategy-generation process

Two key outputs

Effective strategy generation by senior management results in the production of two key outputs: first, a statement of strategic purpose and direction (a mission statement), and second, a plan for the organisation of resources (a business plan). The production of these two outputs in a strategy statement leads naturally into the development of a plan for implementation. Developing the implementation plan, and later, dealing with the actual implementation, both provide further feedback loops into the whole process of strategy making. They are not dealt with explicitly within this chapter except through the identification and consideration of the competences and potential capabilities of the company or organisation. Suffice it to say that implementation dictates the extent to which strategy is both delivered and developed within the company or organisation through its policies, procedures and everyday working practices.

Strategic review – 'outside-in'

In order to be able to achieve these outputs, management teams have to conduct a thorough strategic review. This has two aspects, referred to above. First, it involves taking an 'outside-in' view, examining both the external forces and environmental stakeholders impacting on the organisation (a stakeholder is any individual, group or institution that has an influence on or is influenced by the organisation in question).

Because organisations can be thought of as systems that are open to all kinds of environmental influence and pressure, they all have many actual and potential stakeholders. In fact, the number of stakeholders theoretically has no bounds, for any institution, group or individual can be thought of as a potential stakeholder insofar as all of these make up the total environment of the organisation. However, to simplify matters, and to focus attention on the more influential stakeholder groups, it is usual to concentrate in the first instance on those stakeholders who have very significant influence over the company or organisation, such as shareholders, competitors, customers and suppliers. Other important but rather less influential customers may be considered later.

Naturally, key stakeholders differ from company to company and from sector to sector. Key stakeholder constituencies for the private sector may be very different from the public or voluntary sectors. This 'outside-in' method of analysis emphasises the importance of the need for the organisation to produce an effective response to its environment, for example to its customers, suppliers and competitors, if it is to generate effective strategies that respond appropriately to external conditions. Figure 28.3, illustrates this.

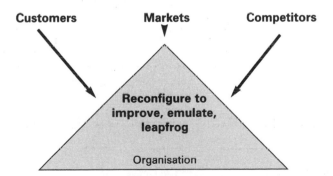

Figure 28.3   Strategy making 'outside-in' – meeting market demands

... and 'inside-out'

However, merely to base the strategic review on external factors and the demands they make of the company or organisation places managers, psychologically at least, in a reactive position, constantly buffeted by ever-changing customer requirements, or attempting 'catch-up' to the performance features identified in supposedly world-class competitors. Consequently, the second vital aspect of a strategic review is concerned with the identification of the organisation's strengths and potential, that is, taking the 'inside-out' view.

The specific mix of skills, abilities and routines at which the company or organisation already excels and which enable it to add value in excess of the competition comprises its portfolio of competences. The extent to which these are located in key areas defines whether or not they are 'core' to the business, that is, whether or not they comprise a 'core' competence. Identifying competences and their potential for further development into future capabilities is the key task in undertaking strategic review from an 'inside-out' perspective.

Every organisation is necessarily different in the way in which it configures and uses its technology, facilities and people. Its particular configuration of 'organisational assets' can be seen as a key source of corporate competence, which contributes to remaining in business and making profits. Of course, the opposite is also true, as a particular arrangement may become outmoded and irrelevant, based on routines, skills, attitudes and so on that once produced effective responses but no longer do so. Unless these adapt or are changed, they can easily become corporate rigidities working to sustain historical patterns or structures and inhibiting the regenerative process. Similarly, strategic review seeks to unearth these negative aspects with the aim of updating or removing them entirely.

Finally, it follows from this logic that every organisation has a unique configuration that is dynamic and can be changed or developed over time. It is argued that this combination of uniqueness and dynamism makes imitation or mimicry by others a futile affair.

Furthermore, it follows from this line of argument that every organisation has within itself a potential goldmine of unique resource, a real value-adding ability that cannot be matched – if only managements are able to identify precisely what it is and find ways of exploiting it! If the management team do find ways by which these key competences and potential capabilities can be harnessed and exploited in the marketplace, the company or organisation can steal a march on the competition by expressing these competences/capabilities in new products or processes. Figure 28.4 illustrates the argument.

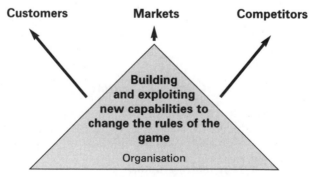

Figure 28.4   Strategy making 'inside-out' – making markets

For example, the Sony 'Walkman' would never have been invented had the company merely listened to its customers or benchmarked its competition (both of which are central to an 'outside-in' approach). Sony's success lay in identifying that it had a core competence in assembling electronics in small spaces. By focusing on its strengths and hence adopting an 'inside-out' method of undertaking strategic review, Sony was able to adopt a much more proactive stance, creating (or enacting) a market by capitalising on its unique set of skills, abilities and routines.

Understanding context – developing scenarios

In reality, strategy generation results from management creatively entwining both the 'outside-in' and 'inside-out' aspects of strategic review into a realistic, achievable and sustainable direction for the future. However, a further activity has to have been undertaken before the strategic review can begin.

As we have seen, strategic review concentrates on auditing existing external demands and market expectations, defining current strengths and taking stock of existing and potential resource allocation patterns. However, there is a need to identify and explore broader features that are driving changes in possible future contexts in which managers will find themselves having to operate their strategies. This activity clarifies and specifies the scenarios against which strategic review takes place. Therefore, in continuing to work backwards in Figure 28.2, the first step in the strategy-generating process comprises the more open-ended, ambiguous and creative task of scenario identification and planning.

Briefly, this can be understood as 'thinking prior to strategy', having as its main purpose the identification of the range of possible futures facing the company or organisation, in one of which the organisation will eventually find itself. For example, the Shell oil company was able to anticipate and cope with drastic falls in the oil price by previously having anticipated such an event by thinking of scenarios in which factors combined to produce this potentially catastrophic situation for the company. Scenarios usually consider a range of 'change drivers' occurring randomly in a variety of sources (social, economic, political, technological, and environmental), which come together to produce a particular effect.

Identifying relevant 'change drivers' and combining them into useful scenarios is a highly creative task. Developing scenarios is not concerned with the difficult business of making a prediction and then contingency planning just in case that prediction either does or does not come true. It is concerned with speculating in creative fashion on what possible futures might develop in which the company or organisation would have to survive and thrive over at least a 5–10 year timeframe. It follows from this that scenarios (experience has usually shown that it is appropriate to develop only two or at the most three) can be seen as preceding planning decisions altogether, because to develop adequate scenarios requires the suspension of firm decisions about the future. Indeed, scenarios only have potency to the extent that management actively retains them as plausible possibilities that need to be taken into account when generating strategy. The test of a good scenario, therefore, is its continuing plausibility or believability. If managers can believe that any scenario represents a world with which they might have to cope, this will continue to affect their thinking throughout the whole strategy generation process, including strategic review and the production of outputs.

Techniques for generating strategy

All of the arguments above worked through the process backwards from the finish (the outputs) to the start (scenario planning) in order to help to provide an understanding of each step of the process outlined in Figure 28.2 above. Naturally, in practice, the detailed steps are followed in the proper order, and use the detailed techniques as outlined below.

the exercises

Step 1: Scenario development

The aim of scenario planning is to develop two or maybe three long-term representations of the future made up of a wide range of key factors or 'change drivers' drawn from a broad set of headings. The list below contains possible examples of areas containing change drivers:

- ◆ social system factors
- ◆ technological factors
- ◆ economic factors
- ◆ environmental factors
- ◆ political factors.

The final scenarios need not be, and some would say should not be, diametrically opposed. For example, if it is thought that a change driver in a particular category is highly predictable and will occur come what may, it may be appropriate to include it in all scenarios. In order to be system- atic and to uncover as broad a range of change drivers as possible for inclusion in the scenarios, it is usual to use the STEEP categories shown in the list above. The identification of change drivers requires specification of the factor itself together with its predicted trajectory, that is, its path or trend. Therefore, in each of the STEEP categories, participants will generate a list of change drivers together with ideas on their current and potential impact.

Participants then should identify no more than two or three scenarios from this data set of 'change drivers'. Some drivers may appear in only one scenario, but others on which there is a definite consensus may appear in all scenarios. It should be noted that themes characterising chosen scenarios will probably not be opposites. The shared change drivers will ensure that this is the case.

Using sticky notes can be helpful in generating the lists of change drivers, and from the lists of categories, scenarios can be constructed that group particular items together to create a credible future situation. When consensus is achieved, scenarios may be named, either with a name characterising their key feature or perhaps with an abstract name such as 'red' or 'alpha'. Figure 28.5 shows how scenarios cut across lists of change drivers.

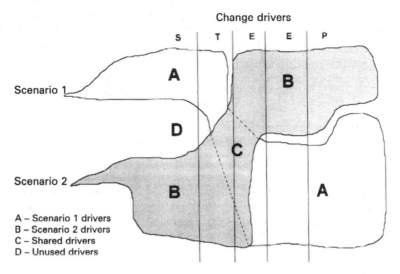

Figure 28.5   Developing scenarios from STEEP change drivers

Having named each scenario, the group now needs to answer the question 'What features would characterise an organisation that would survive and thrive in ALL of these futures?'. General categories for thinking about the way in which the organisation might be engineered to answer this question successfully are:

◆   Mission/direction
◆   Structure
◆   Technology and systems
◆   Culture
◆   Environmental linkages (partnerships and so on)
◆   Values
◆   Behavioural standards.

This list outlines a set of broad organisational characteristics that need to be addressed in defining the shape and form required to survive and thrive in each of the scenarios that have been developed. The list of dimensions is given to provoke thought and discussion on internal design dimensions such as organisation structure, technology and systems, and organisation culture (which can be understood as the shared, taken-for-granted assumptions of individuals and groups in the organisation). Key corporate values are a further consideration, for while it may be vital for some values to be shared across the organisation, others may be specifically located in separate organisational groupings such as the top or middle management teams, or separately within multifunctional work groups.

Finally, consideration must be given to the specification of a set of behaviour standards to be achieved for different groups within the company if the organisation is to survive and thrive. This is important in that dimensionalising the organisation at this level gives real guidance on specific behaviours that are required for any individual to become a 'competent member' whatever their job tasks.

Examples of statements of behaviour standards might include, 'We never walk past a problem', 'We always respond positively to customer comments', 'We always insist on 100 per cent quality no matter what it takes', 'We all have two responsibilities – doing our current job and improving it' and so on. These comprise the meaningful aspirations of those who hold them. Simple quantitative measures can sometimes be placed on them. Overall, their role is to enable strategy to be personalised and made meaningful to everyone throughout the company. However, their specification is often missed in strategy generation, which can result in a lack of strategic alignment between 'big' strategy (mission, vision, values and so on) and what actually happens day by day. This can be a source of frustration for all concerned. If properly specified, however, they can provide the touchstone of how individual performance can both contribute to immediate company success and encourage creativity, diversity and continuous improvement.

This section has focused on how to develop an understanding of the context in which the organisation finds itself, followed by a consideration of a set of broad organisational characteristics that will be required for survival and growth. Having identified the context in which strategy formulation takes place, it is now necessary to turn to the detail of the strategic review, that is, to define its content. While this process contains two specific forms of analysis, the work done so far in developing viable scenarios should not be put aside, but should be adopted as a vital input which pervades the whole of the strategic review that follows.

Step 2: Strategic review

Strategic review is composed of the two complementary forms of analysis outlined earlier. These are considered in Steps 2a and 2b below.

Step 2a – 'Outside-in' analysis – undertaking an external stakeholder analysis
External stakeholders comprise constituencies that surround the organisation. They have varying contact with, interest in and power to influence and in turn be influenced by the organisation in question. They may have been stakeholders for some considerable time or have only become so recently. Stakeholders are not just shareholders. Stakeholders comprise a much wider group and might include customers, suppliers, competitors, central and local government, the local community, pressure groups or

political parties, or indeed anyone who is involved in a reciprocal influence process with the company or organisation in question.

When undertaking a stakeholder analysis, the first step is to identify the key stakeholder constituencies (Figure 28.6). This is a matter of judgment. There is no right answer but only the answer that makes sense to the team undertaking the analysis.

Figure 28.6 Stakeholder analysis – examples of stakeholder constituencies

Second, each stakeholder constituency will have its own distinct characteristics, which need to be identified by the team. The two most important characteristics concern the amount of influence the particular stakeholder constituency is able to exert upon the organisation, and the extent to which the behaviour of the stakeholder is thought to be predictable or subject to change. Key stakeholders for any organisation are those thought to have considerable influence over the organisation, as the strategy generated must reflect their importance. It is also important to identify the expectations that any stakeholder group (particularly the key stakeholders) is believed to hold of the organisation, in order that these can be taken into account when generating strategy. This can be done using Figure 28.7 to summarise stakeholder orientations.

Stakeholder	Influence: High/low	Dynamism: High/low	Expectations held

Figure 28.7 Stakeholder analysis

The final step to conclude this 'outside-in' analysis of the company situation requires the production of two summaries developed from the stakeholder analysis. These comprise two lists, one headed 'main opportunities' and the other the 'main threats' facing the organisation.

Step 2b: 'Inside-out' analysis – undertaking a core competences/capabilities audit
Having gained a view of what the environment is demanding, it is now important to turn attention inside the organisation and systematically identify its strengths in the form of core competences or potential capabilities that can be exploited to give competitive edge in the marketplace.

Core competences/capabilities may be focused upon specific technologies and their associated formal systems, for example flexible manufacturing systems, but are just as likely to include or be centred on organisational routines, for example excellence in teamworking or supply chain management. In undertaking such an audit of the organisation, managers should follow the questions outlined in the list below. Note that in undertaking this analysis, core competences or capabilities are identified in juxtaposition to 'incompetences' or weaknesses. It is useful to develop an assessment of both and to produce, as output from this part of strategic review, listings of the main strengths and weaknesses of the organisation.

◆ List what the organisation is really good at by considering the following:

1. As an organisation we know best how to...

2. Of what we do exceptionally well, what is it that adds more value than that added by our competitors?
3. What might be the outline of a strategy for exploiting these strengths in new markets or in creative ways?

◆ List the main organisational weaknesses by answering the following:

1. What is it that is not in place yet that, if it were, would fundamentally change things?
2. Within the organisation, where is there the most potential to add value?
3. What might be the outline of a strategy for rectifying these weaknesses?

Part of your analysis might include the extent to which the organisation is able to reflect, learn and implement change, such as when developing either new products or new processes. By way of explanation, these features are often referred to as the 'dynamic capabilities' of the organisation, and the extent to which they are in place is often seen as the key feature dictating the ability of the organisation to continuously improve over time.

Step 3: Integrating Steps 2a and 2b into statements of purpose and direction, and making resource allocation plans.
The final step in the strategic generation process involves the creative integration of the data from Steps 1, 2a and 2b above, first into a statement of strategic direction and purpose, and second into a plan that allocates the resources of the organisation to ensure that the purposes are achieved. To undertake this, participants need to work through the tasks listed below, agree a mission statement as suggested and outline a specification for the resourcing requirements for inclusion in the business plan. In undertaking this latter task, because the nature of the exercise does not introduce detailed costings and revenues, participants should restrict the discussion to ascertaining the relevant heads of expenditure (capital and revenue heads) and the relative weightings they would wish to apply to them.
Therefore work through the following:

◆ Characterise your organisation's position relative to world-class performers.
◆ Make explicit the benchmarks of comparison.
◆ Add to this your analysis of strengths, weaknesses, opportunities and threats, and identify a realistic and achievable ambition for the organisation over the next time period (beginning with 'We aim to become...').

◆ Specify some initial performance indicators that might measure progress toward this ambition.

◆ Consider the general categories for organisation design listed earlier, and specify outline resource requirements for each.

In answering the first question, you should use either your own descriptions or adjectives to ascertain dimensions of difference. In the second, you should contrast your organisation with what you consider world-class performers to be, on scales that you construct. In-company management teams may wish to enhance their perceptions on any scales they outline with actual data from the organisation in question or from world-class performers. This may extend the exercise, but it is usually well worth the effort. In answering question three, the team should work on a shared flip chart or in computer supported co-operative mode, building on ideas and refraining from being too critical of the ideas of others. The fourth question requires the development of both indicators of success and level of performance, whereas the last requires an outline specification of resources against each of the organisation design categories listed earlier. The successful completion of this activity gives a detailed specification for the writing of a business plan, completing the strategy generation process.

ACKNOWLEDGEMENT

This fictitious case study is based on an integration of material distilled from consulting and research work undertaken in manufacturing management, financial services and a large public services utility. Part of the contributing casework resulted from EPSRC grant GR/J21316 – A thematic approach to the regeneration of manufacturing (D. R. Tranfield and J. S. Smith).

REFERENCES AND FURTHER READING LIST

Bowen, H.K. Hollaway, C. Leonard-Barton, D. and Clark, K. (1994) *The Perpetual Enterprise Machine*. Oxford University Press, Oxford.

Collins, J.C. and Porras, J.I. (1994) *Built to Last: Successful Habits of Visionary Companies*. Harper Business, New York.

Freeman, R.E. (1984) *Strategic Management: A Stakeholder Approach*. Pitman, London.

Gilgeous, V. (1997) *Operations and the Management of Change*. Pitman, London.

Goldratt, E. and Cox, G. (1984) *The Goal*. Creative Output Books,

Harmon R.L. (1992) *Reinventing the Factory, II: Managing the World Class Factory*. Free Press,

Johnson, G. and Scholes, H.K. (1997) *Exploring Corporate Strategy*, 4th edn. Prentice Hall, Englewood Cliffs, NJ.

Kay, J. (1993) *Foundations of Corporate Success*. Oxford: the University Press.

Kordis, P.L. and Lynch, D. (1990) *Strategy of the Dolphin*. Arrow, New York.

Lynch, R. (1997) *Corporate Strategy*. Pitman, London.

Ohmae, K. (1983) *The Mind of the Strategist*. McGraw-Hill, New York.

Porter, M.E. (1990) *Competitive Strategy: Techniques for Analysing Industries and Competitors*. Free Press, New York.

Peters, T. (1988) *Thriving on Chaos*. Macmillan, London.

Stacey, R. (1990) *Dynamc Strategic Management for the 1990s: Balancing Opportunism and Business Planning*. Kogan Page, London.

Stacey, R. (1993) *Strategic Management and Organisation Dynamics*. Pitman, London.

Teece, D.J. and Pisano, G. (1994) The dynamic capabilities of firms, *Industrial and Corporate Change* **3**(3).

Teece, D.J., Pisano, G. and Shuen, A. (1992) Dynamic Capabilities and Strategic Management. Unpublished working paper, University of California at Berkeley.

Whittington, R. (1993) *What Is Strategy – Does It Matter*? Routledge, London.

Wilkins, A. (1989) *Developing Corporate Character: How To Change an Organisation Without Destroying it*. Jossey Bass, San Francisco.

Womack, J., Jones, D. and Roos, D. (1990) *The Machine That Changed the World*. Rawson Associates, New York.

CHAPTER 29

Stress Management

Rob Briner

OBJECTIVES

The objectives of this chapter are to:

► critically appraise the idea of 'stress' and provide an alternative approach
► describe how stress situations may be assessed
► outline ways of changing relevant thoughts, feelings and behaviours
► provide experience of assessing and changing stress situations.

INTRODUCTION

Stress is currently viewed as a major problem for both individuals and organisations. For individuals, the negative feelings associated with stress can be unpleasant and distressing. So too can the fear that prolonged or intense stress may cause illness. Organisations, on the other hand, may be worried about stress because it is believed to be a cause of reduced performance and increased absence, and they may fear litigation from employees. At the same time, employers may also be genuinely concerned about the welfare of their employees and want to take steps to reduce stress and to improve the quality of working life.

In this chapter, a particular approach to managing stress is described, taking as its starting point the importance of clarifying what the term 'stress' actually means. This is important because the term 'stress' is now used to refer to so many different kinds of feeling, experience and situation that the term is often more confusing than anything else. It is, therefore, suggested in this chapter that one of the best ways of managing 'stress' is to avoid using the term altogether and instead to focus on specific thoughts, feelings and behaviours.

Structure of the chapter

The first section of the chapter considers some of the different experiences that are often labelled 'stress'. In order to assess any situation effectively, we first need to have ways of delineating it – this first section sets out some ways of describing stress situations. The second section outlines how stress situations can be assessed using the descriptions provided in the first section in terms of the thoughts, feelings and behaviours that are occurring. This section also contains two exercises that provide you with the opportunity to describe and assess a number of stress situations.

Next, some of the skills that may be required to manage such situations once they have been assessed are described. This section outlines some ways of changing thoughts, feelings, behaviours and the situation, and in each case an exercise is provided to illustrate some of these techniques. The importance of seeing 'stress situations' as part of a long-term ongoing process is also discussed in this section, and a longer exercise containing a case study is provided to demonstrate the ways in which thoughts, feelings and behaviours change over time and to show that, in understanding any single situation, it is helpful to see it as part of an ongoing process.

While individual skills are clearly very important in managing stress situations, such skills also have limitations. Equally important are the features of the work environment that may be the root cause of the problems that people experience at work. Managers are often in a position to influence and improve the work conditions of those they manage. Hence, in addition to stress self-management, managers can also develop skills that can help them to manage other people's stress problems. The last section of the chapter discusses the role of managers in helping others to manage their stress situations and the skills that may be required. The case study from the previous section is used in a further exercise to show how managers can make a difference to the stress situations experienced by those they manage and their colleagues.

What is stress?

Stress is a word used to describe a range of rather different things. We feel worried because an important deadline is approaching and we have barely started the tasks we need to finish. We become frustrated because the organisation is so bureaucratic that it is hard to get anything done. A lack of effective planning and thinking ahead leaves us feeling constantly tired as we work very hard just to catch up on all the things we have not done. We suddenly become anxious as we realise that a possible crisis is looming unless we act very quickly, and this spurs us into action. A failure to get a much-desired promotion results in depression and demotivation. The work we are given to do is repetitive and very unchallenging, and we feel bored. A boss who treats us unfairly and makes unreasonable demands makes us feel angry. A difficult relationship problem outside work makes everything at work just seem 'too much' and almost impossible to deal with.

All these very different situations, each with its rather different combination of thoughts, feelings and behaviours, can be labelled as 'stressful'. Stress is not, therefore, any one thing in particular but rather a heading or an umbrella term under which people place different things. This is an important point because, as we shall go on to discuss, in order to manage anything, we need to be as clear as possible about what it is we are actually trying to manage.

The problem with the term 'stress' is not new. Stress researchers, and to some extent practitioners, have questioned its usefulness since the term first came into popular use in the mid-1950s (see, for example, Appley and Trumbull, 1986). While in general terms it is, of course, true that events and situations can be thought of as 'stressors', which in turn produced emotional reactions of 'strain', it is also true that the picture is considerably more complicated. Sometimes the same 'stressors' produce quite different or even no reactions depending on how we are feeling at the time. At other times, we may be experiencing negative feelings for no apparent reason and cannot identify any particular 'stressor'. Sometimes the kinds of events that produce negative feelings are beyond our control, yet in other cases (as later examples will show) our own behaviour may be largely to blame for whatever negative events or situations we experience. In other words, the problem with 'stress' is one not only of definition, but also of explanation. Not all the negative feelings we have can be described as 'strain', and not all the cases of those feelings can be explained simply by identifying 'stressors'.

Although orthodox approaches to stress management (see, for example, Cooper *et al.*, 1988; Fontana, 1989) address issues of definition, they still assume that there is a single and particular thing that it is useful to label 'stress'. As a consequence, such approaches produce long lists of so-called stressors or sources of stress and equally long lists of the supposed consequences of such stressors. The approach taken here, as mentioned above, is one which argues that stress is an unhelpful term and concept that hinders rather than furthers understanding (see also Pollock, 1988).

In the past decade, there has been an increasing interest within management research in emotions at work (see, for example, Fineman, 1993; Newton *et al.*, 1994). This is, in part, a reaction to the limitations of the stress concept. What about emotions such as envy or anger or sadness? These are commonly experienced at work, yet the idea of 'stress' does little to help us understand the causes or consequences of such emotions.

A further limitation of the idea of 'stress' is that it focuses only on negative experiences. As the later examples will show, we cannot easily understand people's negative feelings if we do not also understand how they relate to other positive feelings that they also experience. For example, any long-term complex and difficult task that, when completed, may make us feel satisfied and proud is also likely to have produced a range of negative feelings along the way.

There are, therefore, at least two answers to the question 'What is stress?' The first is that it does not refer to any single thing but rather, if the term has to be used, is best thought of as an umbrella term or a heading for a range of different kinds of thoughts, feelings, behaviours and situations that people may choose to label 'stress'. The second answer is that stress is not a very helpful term because it is confusing and does not, therefore, help us analyse, understand or manage situations. How then can we best analyse those situations we may choose to describe as stressful?

Assessing stress situations

If, as discussed above, stress does not refer to anything in particular, when we talk about managing stress we are, therefore, not talking about managing one particular kind of situation or one sort of thought, feeling or behaviour. Instead, we are referring to managing any situation that seems to be causing some kind of 'negative' reaction.

If we wish to understand and manage the particular situation that is producing such negative reactions, the starting point should be to undertake an assessment of what is happening. Three key questions should be asked in order to assess stress situations:

◆ What kinds of thought or perception are occurring?
◆ What kinds of feeling are being experienced?
◆ What behaviours can be observed?

In addition, one can ask:

◆ In what ways have these thoughts, feelings and behaviours changed over time, and what might happen next?

In order to answer these questions, we need to have a range of terms capable of describing more accurately how we are thinking, feeling or behaving. Table 29.1 below gives some examples of such terms.

Table 29.1   Examples of thoughts, feelings and behaviours

Examples of thoughts	Examples of feelings	Examples of behaviours
Work demands	**Moods**	**Task behaviours**
Quantity of work	Worried	Time on task
Difficulty	Tired	Effectiveness (meeting
Urgency	Miserable	work goals)
Cost of failing to	Calm	Efficiency (effort:
complete task	Excited	outcome ratio)
Level of effort	Bored	Effort
	Gloomy	
Perceptions of task	Content	**Other aspects of**
Control	Alert	**performance**
Support		Taking on extra tasks
Clarity of demands	**Emotions**	Concern for quality
	Anger	Helping others
Perceptions of job and	Fear	
organisation	Pride	
Commitment to job	Hate	
Intentions to quit	Guilt	
Commitment to	Embarrassment	
profession	Joy	
	Self-judgments	
	Confident	
	Incapable	
	Useless	
	Skilled	
	Effective	

In any situation, we will be experiencing thoughts, feelings and behaviours but not necessarily any of those listed in Table 29.1. Remember that these are just examples rather than comprehensive lists. In order to illustrate how this table can be used, I will apply it to my current situation of trying to finish the second draft of this chapter (a situation perhaps all too familiar to anyone finishing assignments, essays or projects). In terms of my current thoughts (column 1, Table 29.1), I am thinking that I have a lot to do at work at the moment. This chapter is not necessarily a big job, but I am thinking about all the other things I am supposed to be doing. I do not perceive it as a particularly difficult task, but it is now rather urgent. I think I have reasonable control over this task and that I am reasonably clear about what I am doing (although this is a recent perception). I am not thinking about leaving my job and perceive that I am reasonably committed.

In terms of feelings (column 2, Table 29.1), I am quite alert, not at all bored and just a little worried about being able to finish it in time. I feel a little gloomy, but that could be because it is a wet, wintry Sunday afternoon. It could also be because I am feeling slightly angry with myself as I should have completed the chapter some time ago and am also feeling a little useless and ineffective. I anticipate that I will be embarrassed and guilty if I do not finish it on time.

My behaviours (column 3, Table 29.1), in relation to this task have changed very recently. Now I am spending considerable time on this task (and not being distracted), working reasonably efficiently, and my effort level is moderate to high. I am concerned about the quality of what I am doing, and, just at the moment, it is unlikely that I will help anyone else if they ask me or take on extra tasks.

Some of you may relate quite well to the thoughts, feelings and behaviours I have described in this particular situation. Others may not, and in general experience rather different things when finishing a task such as this. However, important points to note are that there are often quite a number of different things happening together in any situation that can be described and that they relate to what happened in the past and what is anticipated about the future.

Ben

Ben is the manager of a large team of salespeople. The performance of his team is not particularly good and he is consistently failing to meet targets. He recently had a meeting with his manager, who told him that the targets were perfectly reasonable and that there must be some problem with the team or his ability to manage others effectively.

Anita

Anita is the head of an information technology department in a large company. The turnover of her staff is high, and this is having a detrimental effect on the work of the department, such that many projects are now behind schedule.

Kerry

Kerry manages a finance department. She reports directly to two bosses. The first keeps telling her that her main priority is to streamline and speed up the accounts processing system, while her second boss tells her that she should be transferring all the financial data on to a new type of data-base that allows cost projections to be made. Kerry is attempting to do both things at once and not getting very far with either.

the exercises

Assessing three stress situations

Working in small groups, read each of the three case studies above. In turn, three different people in the group should role play each of the people. The task of the rest of the group is to ask the person role playing about their thoughts, feelings and behaviours in that situation.

Alternatively, each person in the group may wish to consider the kinds of thoughts, feelings and behaviours that you might experience if you were in that kind of situation.

Refer to the four questions listed above and Table 29.1 to help you complete this exercise.

Assessing your own stress situation

Working on your own, think of two situations you have experienced recently that you would describe as 'stressful'. Now attempt to write down the particular thoughts, feelings and behaviours that were occurring for you in those situations. Then think about what happened next. How did the situation change?

Managing 'stress situations'

After assessing thoughts, feelings and behaviours within a stress situation, the issue then arises of how the situation can be managed. How one manages a stress situation depends on the nature of the particular situation one is considering. There is no single way of managing stress situations, nor is there a general solution to problems of stress. Instead, following an assessment of the stress situation, it becomes possible to undertaken an analysis of what is causing the specific negative experiences present in that situation and what aspects of the situation or the person's thoughts, feelings and behaviours can be changed.

Changing thoughts

The way we think about and perceive a situation or ourselves can play a large part in determining how we then feel and behave. If such thoughts are reasonably accurate, we may not wish to change them. Instead, it is more important to test the accuracy of our thoughts as the very process of asking 'Am I right about this?', 'Is this really true?' or 'Is there another way of looking at this situation?' plays a key role in changing our thoughts. This is also easier to do once we have, as described in the previous section, assessed what those thoughts are.

Not all the thoughts and perceptions we have in stress situations necessarily lead to negative feelings. It may also be important to identify those which seem to lead to negative feelings and change those.

In some cases, we may simply not have enough information. In addition, therefore, to changing thoughts by testing their accuracy, seeking out new information about the situation may lead to completely new thoughts and perceptions.

Dave

Dave thinks he is not performing very well. He thinks he has 'too much' work to do, all of which is urgent, and has no control or choice over his work tasks. He thinks that if he does not finish everything in time, it will be a disaster. He believes he does not have the skills to do the job properly and that no support is available to him in the organisation.

Testing the accuracy of thoughts and perceptions

Above is a short description of some of the thoughts of a typical manager. First working on your own and then comparing your views with others in a small group, think about what you would do if you were Dave to test the accuracy of your thoughts and perceptions? What additional information would you need, and how would you get it?

Changing feelings

One important aspect of managing the feelings associated with stress is to bear in mind that negative feelings are not necessarily 'bad'. Work, like life in general, contains both good and bad feelings. It may be the balance of positive to negative feelings that is more important than the negative feelings themselves. In addition to reducing negative feelings in stress situations, it may, therefore, be equally important to try to increase positive feelings in other situations at work.

Again, as discussed in the previous section, an accurate assessment of feelings is the starting point for then trying to change those feelings. There are two broad ways in which feelings can be changed. One is directly to change the feeling itself, the other is to try to change the situation that may be causing that feeling. Feelings can also be changed by changing thoughts, as already discussed, and can also be changed by changing behaviours, as will be considered below.

By now, it should be clear that thoughts, feelings and behaviours are interrelated and strongly influence each other. While it can be difficult to distinguish clearly between them in some cases, it is still useful as a starting point to attempt to do so. Looking at and trying to understand the ways in which they influence each other also helps us to manage situations.

Table 29.2 below (adapted from Parkinson *et al.*, 1996) shows some ways in which feelings can be changed by changing thoughts or by changing behaviours. When completing Exercise 4 below, it may be useful to look at this table.

Table 29.2 Examples of strategies for changing feelings

Thought-based strategies	Behaviour-based strategies
Thinking of pleasant things	Doing something enjoyable
Anticipating future pleasant things	Engaging in distracting activity
Looking on the bright side	Exercising
Trying to understand feelings	Attempting to solve the problem or
Accepting the feeling	remove the cause of the negative
Thinking that the feeling will soon	feeling
go away	Telling other people how you are feeling
Trying to think of other things	Letting off steam

Strategies for changing feelings

Working on your own, think about two stress situations you have experienced and write down the feelings you had (or use those from Exercise 2 above if you have already completed it). What did you do to change how you felt? Were the things you did a direct attempt to change how you felt? Did you try to change the situation that was causing you to experience those feelings? How effective were the steps you took to change your feelings? Refer to Table 29.2 for examples of strategies you might have used.

Changing behaviours

Not everything we do in stress situations will necessarily lead to negative feelings. However, some of them almost certainly do, and, following a systematic assessment of those behav-

275

iours, it should be easier to identify those which seem to be causing negative feelings and those which should, therefore, be changed. The most important kinds of behaviour to change are those which do not actually help us to achieve what it is we are trying to do at work. In nearly all situations, we are trying to do something, that is, we have certain goals or things we are trying to do. In most stress situations, the negative feelings arise because something about the situation, ourselves or another person is making the goals more difficult or even impossible to achieve. It is also important to note that stress situations can also arise because the person has goals that actually *are* impossible to achieve.

Table 29.3 shows just a few examples of some of the behaviours that may in the medium and longer term be self-defeating or self-handicapping.

Table 29.3   Examples of self-defeating behaviours

Failing to plan

Taking on too many tasks

Not prioritising

Choosing easy tasks over difficult ones

Avoiding tasks one isn't very good at

Procrastination

Leaving things to the last minute

Avoiding conflict

Not being able to say 'no' to requests

Setting unrealistically high targets

Not thinking about what you want

Identifying self-defeating behaviours

Working on your own, think of a recent situation that you would describe as 'stressful' and write down the kinds of behaviour in which you engaged before and during that situation (or use one of the stress situations you described earlier in Exercise 2). Now also consider what it is you were trying to do in that situation. What were your goals? What were you trying to achieve? Were these goals actually achievable? In what ways was your behaviour contributing to not attaining those goals? In what ways was your behaviour contributing to attaining those goals? Which of those self-defeating behaviours could you have changed and which not? How would you have gone about changing them? See Table 29.3 above for examples of self-defeating behaviours.

This exercise is quite difficult to do, as, if one were easily able to identify self-defeating behaviours, the chances are that one would not engage in them. It may make it easier if you ask someone else whom you know, trust and can work with to suggest to you which, if any, of your behaviours in that situation was self-defeating. It may help if, as a pair, you agree to look at each other's situations and try to identify these self-defeating behaviours for each other.

Changing the situation

'Managing stress' is often seen in terms of the individual managing themselves rather than trying to change the work situation. However, as we have already discussed, managing oneself by attempting to change thoughts, feelings and behaviours may also often involve changing the situation. In the case of thoughts, we may, in testing their accuracy, go and ask our manager for some feedback about our performance. This is, in a sense, changing the situation from one with limited feedback to one with more. Changing feelings by successfully solving the problem causing the negative feelings, such as a conflict with a colleague, will also change the situation in that there will be less conflict at work. Likewise, changing our behaviours can have a large effect on the situation.

Dealing with situations we may label as 'stressful' is as much, if not more, about changing or managing the situation as about simply managing our own thoughts, feelings and behaviours in isolation from the situation. However, one of the central skills involved in doing this, as mentioned above, is being able to distinguish between those situations which can be changed in the way you would like to change them and those which cannot. However, in most cases this is unlikely to be an 'either/or' choice but rather one that involves both these questions:

◆ What can I change about the *situation* to reduce my negative feelings?
◆ What can I change about *myself* to reduce my negative feelings?

'Stress situations' as part of an ongoing, long-term process

Another important skill in managing stress situations is to understand whether and how they relate to other past and future situations at work. In other words, it is important to explore negative feelings as part of an ongoing, long-term process of both positive and negative thoughts, feelings and behaviours rather than as a simple reaction to something we do not like. An example of such a process is provided in the case study below.

Shabir

Shabir is the manager of a large branch of the Hallamshire Building Society. He has a pretty heavy workload and has not been in the position for very long so is still, to some extent, 'learning the ropes', although he has tried to ensure that he is liked and trusted by the staff. He is asked by his regional manager, Liz, if he and his branch are prepared to take part in a pilot study that involves installing a new computer system, Transax, for dealing with customer transactions. Shabir is very keen to please so he thinks he must take on this challenge and agrees instantly.

Liz is delighted that Shabir has agreed as she has already failed to persuade several other branch managers to take part in the pilot scheme.

Shabir feels that he is already doing very well given how little time he has been a branch manager. A few days later, a huge batch of documentation arrives about the new system, how it will be installed, how the branch must prepare for the installation of new hardware and software, the additional training that all staff will have to undergo, deadlines and so on. Shabir immediately starts to panic. He already has a heavy workload and he has only just about got to grips with what the job involves with the 'old' systems they already have in place. A few days later, Liz phones him and asks how it is going and what he thinks of Transax. Shabir has not read much of the documentation as he has not had time, but he assures Liz that everything is fine and it does not look like too much trouble to him. He again starts to panic but cannot let Liz know how he is feeling. He arranges a meeting for all the staff, who start to realise what this will involve and the seemingly impossible deadlines. Shabir gets cross and tells them that everyone just has to get on and do it. He refuses to discuss it any further with them.

Eventually, Transax is up and running – but 5 weeks after the agreed deadline. There have been problems with the unions and with Shabir's relationships with his staff. Shabir has been working 7 days a week for the past 10 weeks to make sure that Transax will work even if it is behind schedule. He is very pleased that it is finished at last as he has worked incredibly hard on it, is absolutely exhausted and, even if there still are some staff problems, is sure that he can eventually sort them out. Rather oddly, Liz has not contacted him for a week or so, whereas before she would not get off his back. He telephones her to tell her the good news. She says very little about it but asks him why he has not completed the Transax Pilot Study Evaluation questionnaire as the IT Director is hassling her for it. Shabir agrees to complete it and puts the telephone down. He is furious. He has slogged his guts out and got the thing working and Liz does not even sound pleased or show any gratitude. After all he has done! He starts to feel very differently about the Hallamshire Building Society. Maybe this is not the place for him after all, if that is the way they are going to treat him.

Understanding thoughts, feelings and behaviours as processes

Working in groups, try to track Shabir's thoughts, feelings and behaviours over time (see Tables 29.1 and 29.2 above for guidance). Where these are not stated explicitly in the case, imagine what they might have been. Make a chronological list of these. Can you make sense of what happened to Shabir? What should he have done differently? How could he have managed his thoughts, feelings and behaviours more effectively? What kinds of self-defeating behaviour was Shabir engaging in? (see Table 29.3 for guidance). If Shabir had behaved differently, what other outcomes might have occurred?

Managing other people's stress situations

As mentioned in the introduction, managers are often in a unique position to help other people to deal with their stress situations. One skill a manager can develop is to apply the same kind of assessment of the thoughts, feelings and behaviours described above to those whom they manage. They can then also think of ways in which they may be able to help and support those people to change in ways that will reduce the negative feelings they experience.

What can managers do to help others manage stress situations?

Look again at the case study referred to in Exercise 6. Liz is Shabir's manager. What could and should Liz have done differently to help Shabir with the stress situations that developed?

REFERENCES

Appley, M.H. and Trumbull, R. (1986) Development of the stress concept. In Appley, M.H. and Trumbull R. (eds) *Dynamics of Stress: Physiological, Psychological and Social Perspectives*. Plenum Press, New York.

Cooper, C.L., Cooper, R.D. and Eaker, L.H. (1988) *Living with Stress*. Penguin, Harmondsworth.

Fineman, S. (1993) *Emotion in Organizations*. Sage, London.

Fontana, D. (1989) *Managing Stress*. British Psychological Society, Leicester.

Newton, T., Handy, J. and Fineman, S. (1994) *Managing 'Stress': Emotion and Power at Work*. Sage, London.

Parkinson, B., Totterdell, P., Briner, R.B. and Reynolds, S. (1996) *Changing Moods: The Psychology of Mood and Mood Regulation*. Longman, London.

Pollock, K. (1988) On the nature of social stress: production of a modern mythology, *Social Science and Medicine* **26**: 381–92.

CHAPTER 30

Team Development

Sue Walsh

OBJECTIVES

The objectives of this chapter are to:

▶ reflect upon the relationship between content and process in a team development initiative
▶ provide experience of thinking about and using interpersonal processes as part of a team development
▶ begin to develop process consultation skills.

INTRODUCTION

This chapter is concerned with the development of 'process' and 'content' skills in the context of a team building initiative within the NHS. Although there is a literature on the value of teamworking within both the private (Jackson, 1996) and public (Øvretveit, 1992) sectors, it is widely acknowledged that the creation and maintenance of effective teams is not easy. This is in part due to the *ad hoc* way in which many teams are formed: managers putting together individuals with different skills, professional backgrounds, levels of power and influence, and expecting them to get on and work together. Thus there is a quite extensive literature on the problems and vicissitudes of working in teams (see West, 1996). Examples of such problems range from social hierarchy effects, in which certain individuals or professions dominate the group process, to dysfunctional interpersonal processes (such as competition, envy and poor communication), which may undermine team effectiveness.

The focus of the chapter will be to develop content and process skills that tackle such issues. 'Process refers to *how* things are done rather than what is done. If I am crossing the street, that is what I am doing, but the *process* is how I am crossing; walking, running, dodging cars, asking someone to help me across' (Schein, 1987, p. 39). However, it is too simplistic to focus on process factors to the exclusion of content factors. Process difficulties often emerge out of poor organisational structures. Thus, the *how* of the way in which things are done (the process) is connected to the *what* and *why* (the content).

The teaching exercise is built around a case study in which the context, characters and roles are outlined. At significant points in the intervention, the student is asked to identify, formulate and respond to the issues that emerge. The challenge for the user of this material is to identify those factors which impinge upon, limit or enhance the change process. More detailed theoretical information is provided in the Tutor's Manual.

The structure of the chapter is as follows. The background to the case is outlined; this is followed by a description of the team members you will be working with. At different stages of the intervention (the beginning, middle and end), you will be asked to identify the process factors (herein defined as feelings and relationships) and content factors (herein defined as organisational structure and function) that have emerged and how you might respond to them.

The background

You have been called in to implement a programme of organisational change, the focus of which is to develop multidisciplinary teamworking within a mental health service that is part of an NHS Trust. You are an external organisational consultant who has previously worked primarily with the private sector, but you are keen, for both financial and personal development reasons, to apply your skills in a new arena. You want to do this piece of work well because there is a good possibility that you will be offered more consultancy work in this organisation.

More specifically, you are responsible for the implementation of one specific type of service delivery – the community mental health team (CMHT). The CMHT is one model of service delivery within the health service that aims to bring together different mental health professionals to better meet the diversity of client need (see Øvreveit, 1992). There is a widely held belief within the Trust that such multidisciplinary teams provide a structure for bringing together different professional skills and that team-based organisational structures are perceived as an effective model of service delivery. The different professions that typically input into current services are those of psychiatry, nursing, clinical psychology, occupational therapy and social work.

The different professions currently work very much on their own, although they come together for 'token' referral meetings. The function of these meetings is the allocation of GP patient referrals for assessment and intervention. These meetings are usually dominated by the most powerful individual, the psychiatrist, or by the profession that has most members in the team (the nurses). Little effective information exchange about the needs of patients takes place, and there are long waiting lists.

You quickly notice during the course of your preliminary visits that the current service is piecemeal and fragmented. Different individuals with different professional roles and responsibilities work together on an *ad hoc* basis. Collaboration and skill mix is more often influenced by professional allegiance or which individuals like one another (or dislike one another least) than by what is best for the client and/or the employing organisation. The current situation is widely recognised as inefficient, and there is much overlap, replication and frustration. Your initial contract is to focus upon one team in the service that will act as a pilot. If this is a success, the model will be implemented across the Trust.

The team

The first team that you meet in your intervention is made up of a psychiatrist, a clinical psychologist, three senior nurses, two junior nurses, two support workers, an occupational therapist and two administrative staff. The nurses, support workers and secretaries are the only individuals who are employed full time in the team; everyone else belongs to other teams and/or occupies other job roles. The team is overwhelmed with referrals from GPs and other agencies.

There is no one overall administrative system to support the clinicians. Individuals pick up the work as they visit GP surgeries, day hospitals and so on; there is no central point of access to the team. There is no joint discussion of patient needs, and everyone works in their own way. The team meets once a week to allocate work, and the ethos in the team is that no-one says 'no' to incoming work no matter how overloaded they are. Everyone in the team holds their own individual waiting list and rushes round the city from dawn to dusk trying to carry out as many home visits as possible in order to keep the lid on their waiting list. The record keeping systems are highly individualised. There is no team leader, although the psychiatrist (the professional with the most formal power in the team) informally occupies this role.

It quickly becomes clear to you that the members appear to be either disinterested or resentful that the Trust is spending money on team development instead of buying additional resources to deal with the waiting list. The nurses are antagonistic to any possible changes to their role. They have worked in a particular way for a number of years now and have little motivation to change. Others (the clinical psychologist and the psychiatrist) are interested in the team development process and would do it themselves but they are just too busy (in fact almost too busy to attend many of the team meetings). There are significant power differences in the team. The psychiatrist is the most powerful, whereas the support workers are dependent upon the nurses for the clinical supervision and workload monitoring, thus they are not keen to appear to dissent.

When you eventually get all the staff together (which takes some time as they are all too busy to meet), they sit round saying very little, staring at the floor.

Your contract with the staff is to run for a series of six team building sessions that will explore multidisciplinary ways of working. Team building begins in earnest, but it remains a struggle to get times for everyone to meet.

the exercises

exercise 1

Identify the feelings present at this point in the intervention and describe why they might be present. What is the pattern of relationships present between you and the team and between team members. How might you respond?

What are the current operational problems (how the group gets things done) that require resolution?

The middle of the intervention

This is your third team development session. You have successfully dealt with the team's earlier response to you, and your intervention has proceeded smoothly.

However, in this session, although everyone appears to be working away on the exercise that you have set them (they are designing their administrative and record keeping systems), the atmosphere feels dull and flat. You also feel bored, and it took you a real effort to arrive on time. Even though one of the goals of the team building intervention is to develop operational procedures, there seems to be an overly pedantic focus on procedural issues, a focus on the minutiae. You find yourself looking out of the window a lot. It is a bright and crisp day, and you wish you were at home doing your garden.

You have become aware that the psychiatrist and two of the nurses are doing all the talking. This has been noticeable throughout the previous sessions but you have not done anything actively to manage this.

An apparently ordinary discussion about liaison with fund holding GPs suddenly turns 'nasty'. It begins with one of the team members, the psychiatrist, getting very angry about all the changes the team has suffered in the nature and structure of their jobs, and how she could no longer offer the service to clients that she once did. The support workers (who are usually silent) also acknowledge how isolated and overwhelmed they feel. Everyone else nods.

You try to sympathise with the team, commenting on how you can understand the difficulties of working within the health service. This intervention appears to make things worse. The psychiatrist talks about the loss of beds, the extra responsibility, that management had absolutely no idea about the needs of patients. Furthermore, the salaries of people who were not clinicians could be used in purchasing extra clinical time.

The clinical psychologist turns to you and ask you whether you think that this team building is not just a waste of all their times. You immediately feel guilty because up until the outburst you had not really been paying close attention to them.

Identify the feelings present at this point in the intervention and describe why they might be present. What is the pattern of relationships present between you and the team and between team members. How might you respond?

What are the current operational problems (how the group gets things done) that require resolution?

The ending

This is session six, your final session. Overall, the team and yourself have struggled with the development process, have stuck with it and have created a formalised work protocol. Together, you have designed the administrative system, a centralised record keeping process, identified the need for team leadership and created a business meeting that deals with issues such as the interface with the Trust management system, monitoring workloads, the development of team strategy and so on.

Even though you say so yourself, the intervention has gone well. It is the last session, which is a review of achievements and future goal setting. In the course of working with the team, you have developed a great deal of affection for them.

At this, your last meeting, one of the nurses and the clinical psychologist arrive late, and the group are slow to settle. During the course of the session, a number of the participants have to go and make urgent telephone calls about patients. You are also bombarded by anxious questions, and you start to feel anxious yourself. The questions focus on those issues that are outstanding. Your initial self-satisfaction about the work starts to fade.

Identify the feelings present at this point in the intervention and describe why they might be present. What is the pattern of relationships present between you and the team, and between team members. How might you respond?

What are the current operational problems (how the group gets things done) that require resolution?

REFERENCES AND FURTHER READING

Amando, G. (1995) Why psychoanalytic knowledge helps us to understand organisations, *Human Relations* **48**(4): 351–7.

Jackson, S.E. (1996) The consequences of diversity in multidisciplinary work teams. In West, M.A. (ed.) *Handbook of Work Group Psychology*. Wiley, Chichester.

Jacques, E. (1995a) Why the psychoanalytic approach to understanding organisations is dysfunctional, *Human Relations* **48**(4): 343–9.

Jacques, E. (1995b) Reply to Gilles Amando, *Human Relations* **48**(4): 359–65.

Øvretveit, J. (1992) *Co-ordinating Community Care*. Open University Press, Buckingham.

Schein, E.H. (1987) *Process Consultation: Lessons for Managers and Consultants*, Volume II. Addison Wesley, Reading, MA.

Time Management

Dot Griffiths

OBJECTIVES

The objectives of this chapter are to:

▶ introduce the principal skills of time management
▶ provide some experience in the use of these skills
▶ provide an opportunity to recognise the significance of time management skills for personal and interpersonal effectiveness.

INTRODUCTION

This chapter records a day in the life of a young manager who manages his time poorly. Following this description, four exercises using the material are outlined. No preparation is needed beyond reading the case study.

The Life and Times of Mike Kirov

Mike Kirov is 35. He began his career by taking a chemistry degree and then worked as a researcher for a major pharmaceutical company for 5 years. Following this, he moved into marketing and worked on product promotion for 7 years. Then he took a year out to study for an MBA. After his MBA, he took a job as the Assistant Marketing Manager of a small software company, Polly Projects. His manager recently had a heart attack and retired, so Mike has become the Acting Manager. He is hoping to get the manager post, but there are some concerns about his capacity to deliver...

This is a typical day in Mike's life. It's Monday, May 24.

8.30 Arrives at office. Collects cup of coffee and chats to colleagues.

8.45 Unpacks briefcase. This contains:

– journals on office circulation

– a report on a competitor benchmaking analysis
– a file labelled 'Games Feasibility Study'.

He hasn't managed to do any work on any of these items over the weekend. Mike almost never works at home over the weekend, but he always believes that he might, so he always carries a full case home. Actually, he can't remember the last time he worked at a weekend.

8.50 Looks at his diary. The page for Monday is as follows:

8.00
8.30
9.00 Weekly meeting of Department Heads
9.30 Ditto
10.00 Ditto
11.00
11.30 Jenny Marks: appraisal
12.00 Ditto
12.30 Presentation over lunch from Promoco
1.00 Ditto
1.30 Ditto
2.00 Meeting with Jim Conduit, Chief Executive
2.30
3.00
3.30
4.00
4.30
5.00 Meeting with Mark Brandon
5.30
6.00

8.55 Locates and then looks at the agenda for the weekly meeting as it is his turn to chair it. Realises that he has forgotten (for the second time) to produce the data from the Indian farmers' survey for the Yield project.

9.00 Arrives at the weekly meeting and passes time for a few minutes about weekend activities until most people have turned up.

9.10 Meeting commences. The agenda items are as follows:

– Apologies for absence
– Minutes of the previous meeting and matters arising
– Rosa project
– Traveller project
– Yield project
– Arrangements for staff summer barbeque
– Progress on appraisal interviews
– Review of proposals submitted by consultants for team training plus report of Training Manager's meeting with the local Business Link
– AOB

Mike decides on the following order:

1. Apologies for absence
2. Minutes and matters arising (he manages to say nothing about having forgotten to produce the Yield figures by skipping over

the item while other meeting participants were engaged in an aside about another issue)

3. Arrangements for the staff summer barbeque (as it is to be held in 3 weeks' time, some decisions are urgent)
4. Team training proposals (a decision needs to be made soon as the consultants who have submitted proposals were told by Mike that they would get a response within 2 weeks)
5. Appraisals
6. Traveller project
7. Games Feasibility Study
8. Yield project
9. AOB

The meeting overruns but has to stop at 11.15. So much time was spent on the discussion of the summer barbeque and the choice of consultant for the team training that the meeting only reached item six. Mike is not displeased at this. He was embarrassed to find that he was the only one present who still had appraisal interviews to conduct. Nor did he want the further embarrassment of having to admit that he had forgotten to produce the Yield data again and that he still had no progress to report on the Games Feasibility Study. He makes a big note to himself to sort out the Yield data and finish the appraisals. He just groans at the thought of the Games Feasibility Study.

11.20 Goes to the loo.

11.25 Back to his office. Just manages to glance at Jenny's appraisal form before she arrives. Ignores queries from his secretary and telephone messages.

11.30 Jenny's appraisal. Mike does not handle it very well because he has not really thought about it much in advance. He rather assumes that he knows about Jenny's work because she was his colleague. He flounders giving her feedback because he is thinking as he goes along and he cannot help her at all on her development questions because he is unable to find the catalogue of courses. He makes a note to find it and pass it to Jenny. They do not have time to finish the discussion because of Mike's lunch date so agree to meet again next week. (Jenny is rather annoyed about this and feels that Mike has treated the whole event as a nuisance and a duty rather than a useful and helpful discussion.)

12.30 Mike's secretary tries to catch him as he rushes off to the Promoco Presentation. She is trying to get him to give her answers to some of the most urgent queries she had left on his desk. He says he will deal with them later.

12.50 Arrives 20 minutes late for the Promoco presentation.

Waiting for him to arrive before beginning are five people from Promoco, two of Mike's assistants, Lin-Che and Charles, the Yield Project Manager, Thelma, and her assistant, Krishan.

The reason Mike was so late (the journey from his office to the room where the presentation was being made being 2 minutes at most) was that he bumped into Sue Marty. As they were passing, she asked him if he knew where the display panel clips were and if he knew what sort of display Charles was planning for the

Birmingham Exhibition. Mike went off to Marketing Resources to find the display panel clips. It took him much longer than he had anticipated to find them, by which time he was deep in a discussion, planning the Birmingham display.

Mike apologises profusely for his late arrival at the meeting and wonders if his life will ever get less hectic.

The presentation is interesting. Promoco has been asked to make some proposals for launching the Yield project in India and Bangladesh. They have produced a very thorough response to the brief that Mike had previously devised together with Lin-Che. The Yield project is a piece of software that farmers, agricultural extension workers and others can use to model pest attacks and hence inform pest control strategies. Promoco have quite a lot of experience of launching services into the subcontinent's agricultural market. The area of marketing that Mike most enjoys is that of the detailed planning of marketing campaigns (hence his interest in talking with Sue about the Birmingham Exhibition, even though it is now Charles' responsibility). He thoroughly enjoys the discussion following the presentation and makes lots of interventions. The consequence of his interventions is that Lin-Che has to agree to produce a revised brief for Promoco. 'Why couldn't he have offered these suggestions when we discussed the brief a few weeks ago,' she thinks grumpily as he leaves the meeting. Thelma is even angrier: 'Why waste mine and Krishan's time coming to a presentation to discuss the launch when he then sends the consultants back with a revised brief! What must they think of our company: a bunch of badly organised idiots with more money than sense.'

2.20 Thanks to Mike's interventions and his late arrival, the Promoco discussion runs late too, so Mike is late in seeing Jim Conduit. Jim is not pleased, and his displeasure is made worse when he hears that details of the Yield launch in India have not been finalised because Mike has had some more ideas and sent the consultants off to do more work. And when he finds out that Mike has still produced nothing on the Games Feasibility Study, he is livid. 'This man has so much to offer,' he muses, 'but he never gets his priorities sorted out and he won't get any further until he does.' When he questions Mike about why he has not yet begun the Feasibility Study, which was, after all, Mike's suggestion, his heart sinks as Mike explains how busy he has been sorting out packaging designs for the Traveller project, preparing a presentation on international marketing to be given at the local sixth-form college and organising a work experience placement for a couple of the programmer's sons.

2.40 Mike arrives back at his office. He is met by June, his secretary, who says that the printers keep calling about the Traveller packaging. They now say it is very urgent that they speak to him... and when will Mike get around to his mail. He hasn't touched it since last Wednesday.

2.45 Mike feels tired by the hectic day he feels he has had. The excitement he felt after the Promoco meeting subsidised rather rapidly during the meeting with James. James, in fact, had given him rather a rough ride. He feels he simply cannot face his desk, the telephone calls or the mail for the moment, so he decides to get a coffee and have a walk. He wants to be diverted by something more interesting so he goes for a walk across the Business Park to the showrooms of Thyme Design to have a look at their shop display systems. If he ever gets around to the Games Feasibility Study, he is going to need a lot of information on shop display options.

3.00 He still feels he cannot face his office.

3.30 He arrives back at Polly Products. His secretary looks reproachfully at him while cautiously mentioning that the printers have rung again, twice, and tentatively asking if anyone else can help them. He snaps, 'No', goes to the coffee machine and chats to Rob Michaels about Rob's recent trip to the Frankfurt Games Exhibition. Then he turns to his office.

3.50 He tells June to telephone the printers to tell them that he has gone home with a migraine but hopes to be in tomorrow and that he will contact them then. He looks at his desk and feels depressed. Many piles of paper stare at him, and a lot of yellow sticky notes glare urgently. Sighing, he collects them together so that he has some space to work and begins to go through his post. Actually, it is not as bad as he feared. Most of it is not urgent, and he can deal with it later. He calls June in and dictates a few letters that deal with the most urgent issues. Feeling more cheerful, he then logs into his e-mail and prints out all the messages. As he is doing this, Charles comes in.

4.15 Sue has spoken to Charles about Mike's conversation with her about Birmingham. He points out that, at their last discussion, he and Mike had agreed something slightly different. What does Mike now want to do? They call Sue in and agree the final design for the Birmingham Exhibition.

4.45 A trip to the coffee machine fills in the 15 minutes before the meeting with Mark Brandon. Mark is the Sales Manager, and the meeting was fixed some time ago to discuss the Games Feasibility Study.

5.00 Mark arrives. He has produced all the material that Mike had vaguely asked for and is very enthusiastic about the idea. Mike, almost regretting that he had ever proposed it, finishes the meeting as quickly as he can.

5.30 He looks at his desk and decides he must do some sorting out. Perhaps June could help with some of the filing if he could decide how he wanted it organised. He found his predecessor's system rather hard to follow.

5.35 He pulls his overflowing pending tray towards him. In it he finds:

- the last six monthly digests from the Institute of Marketing
- the last three issues of *International Marketing Management*
- the last five issues of Polly Products' in-house news
- the, by now out of date, programme of seminars on international marketing being given at the local business school
- the in-company training brochure he was looking for during Jenny's appraisal

- details of two courses he had thought he might like to attend. The application date for one has passed but there is still (just) time to apply for the second
- scattered throughout the pile, a number of *FT* cuttings relevant to the Games Feasibility Study
- a week's worth of e-mail messages that were not urgent when he received them
- 15 internal memos that were not urgent when he received them
- the printer's proofs of the packaging for the Traveller project. They are exactly to Mike's specification but the problem is that he has decided he does not like it. This will be the third time he has changed the spec
- a subscription renewal form (final reminder) for *International Marketing Management*
- the last four monthly reports from the Market Research Agency on the Yield project. These should have been collated and summarised for the morning meeting
- an invitation to speak at the local Chamber of Commerce. The date has now passed
- an invitation to Angela's (the receptionist) farewell do before she goes off on maternity leave. It says RSVP by a week ago
- the Marketing Report on the Traveller launch in Spain, dated 23 April. It indicates some problems that need to be addressed fairly rapidly. The Traveller Project is a piece of software that facilitates tourist travel forecasts from their mode and point of arrival in a country
- Market trend forecasts for Singapore, Malaysia and the Netherlands, all of which need digestion and reflection. There are plans to launch the Traveller software in each of them
- a pile of tatty sticky notes with some old messages on them
- the internal telephone directory
- the application form for the Cape Town exhibition. It is quite expensive, and he had meant to ask Jim about it
- his personal Access bill from 2 months ago ('Which explains why I had to pay interest,' he mused as he found it)
- catalogues from all the main actors (and hence potential competitors) in the games market
- a half-started draft of a letter contesting an invoice from a market research agency.

6.15 He throws some of the out-of-date stuff away, promises himself that he will face up to the Yield data analysis and the printers' wrath tomorrow and resolves to start thinking about the Games Feasibility Study before the end of the week. It is now 3 months since he was given the go-ahead.

He pulls out some of the most urgent items and starts trying to rewrite the specification for the printers. Then he stops and starts filling in the application form for the course. A feeling of panic begins to overwhelm him about how much there is to do. He decides to try to sort out the Cape Town exhibition. Finally, he gives up. It's too late, he's too tired and it's all too awful.

6.45 Leaves for home. In his briefcase, he places the same items that he removed from it at 8.30 am. He has not looked at the e-mail messages he printed out earlier, nor has he returned to his post. If he had he would have found:

- letters that have been awaiting signature since he dictated them when he last did his post, last Wednesday. June has mentioned them to him several times and placed them in his 'For Signature' folder in the middle of his desk
- 15 flyers of various descriptions for marketing publications and seminars
- a letter from the local business school asking about projects and placement opportunities
- 20 items of ongoing correspondence in relation to surveys, promotions and so on
- an invitation to Jim Conduit's for dinner the coming Saturday (all the department heads have been invited)
- three letters asking for replies to previous ones.

As he drives home, Mike muses on the day. 'Where did it go? Why do I never manage to create enough space to get started on the Games Feasibility Study? I know it's important but I can't ever get a day to think about it without interruptions of some kind.'

Monday, May 31

The printers have been given the revised specification.

The Yield data has been sorted out in time for the morning meeting. Once he got down to it, it was neither as time consuming nor as difficult as he had feared.

Jenny arrives for the follow-up of her appraisal. Mike forgot she was coming because he had rushed off to the Promoco presentation without noting it in his diary or mentioning it to June.

There has been no progress on the Games Feasibility Study.

The Games Feasibility Study

Most of Polly Products are commercial, like the Yield project. However, Mike believes that some of the software could easily be adapted into a game format and marketed as such. He proposed a feasibility study. Jim was very keen. The games market – while it is very competitive – is also very attractive. He readily agreed to commit whatever resources Mike wanted to the feasibility study. The Games Feasibility Project could be the most important development in Polly Products for some time.

---

the exercises

The case can be used in a number of ways:

◆ to analyse Mike Kirov's problems with time management
◆ to make recommendations for improving his time management skills
◆ for students to practise and to reflect on their own time management skills.

Each exercise, with the obvious exception of the role play, can be done:

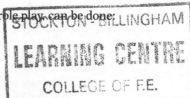

STOCKTON - BILLINGHAM

LEARNING CENTRE

COLLEGE OF F.E.

◆ individually
◆ in small groups
◆ individually followed by small group discussion.

Mike's problems of time management

Ask the students to review Mike's day and to identify all of the ways in which he has managed his time poorly. Explain why and how each is an example of poor time management.

Advice to Mike

1. Students are to take on the role of Jim Conduit and decide what advice about time management Jim should give to Mike.
2. Students can work in twos, threes or fours and role play Jim giving feedback to Mike. Each student should take a turn to play Jim and Mike. Where there are trios and fours, the other students can act as observers and give feedback.

Mike's in-tray

Ask students to review Mike's in-tray and decide what they would do with each item or group of items, such that all that remain are items depending upon the actions of others, as well as Mike, to address.

Personal time management effectiveness

This exercise should not be undertaken unless Exercise 1 has been completed.

Ask the students to reflect on the major principles of time management and to identify those in which they have strengths and weaknesses. Then ask them to devise an action plan to address some of their weaknesses.

FURTHER READING

There are many skill-based texts on time management. They all contain more or less the same messages. Some that are particularly helpful are:

Allan, J. (1990) *Personal Management Skills*, Kogan Page, London.
Fowler, A. (1996) How to provide effective feedback, *People Management*, 11 July:44–5.
Garratt, S. (1985) *Manage Your Time*, Fontana/Collins, London.
Johns, T. (1993) *Perfect Time Management*, Century Business, London.
Whetton, D. and Cameron, K.S. (1991) *Developing Management Skills*, 2nd edn. Harper Collins, New York.